elcome to the 10th edition of Itchy. W
u're an Itchy virgin or an old flame,
re to help you make the most of goi
Manchester. We hope you enjoy you
much as we have over the last 10 ye

-HOUSE TEAM

itor: Mike Toller
cal editor: Joly Braime
atures editor: Alexi Duggins
itorial and production assistants:
are Cullen, Alix Fox
itorial assistants: Jon Lynes, Anton Tweedale
itorial assistance: Iliana Dracou, Sam Shields,
chmed Esser, Cory Burdette, Lily Gorlin,
ozanne Gelbinovich, Maisie McCabe,
lie Dyer, Jackie Fishman
esigners: Paul Jones, Sara Gramner
esign assistance: Katelyn Boller
cture research: Tiago Genoveze,
hilip Kelly, Neha Bhargava, Katelyn Boller
roduction consultant: Iain Leslie
ational ad sales: Sue Ostler, Zee Ahmad
ocal ad sales: Gemma Coldwell
istribution: Efua Hagan
inancial controller: Sharon Watkins
anaging director: Ian Merricks
ublisher: Itchy Group

BN: 978-1-905705-35-1

MANCHESTER TEAM

City editor: Liane Baddeley

Contributors: Hannah Smith, Lauren Potts, Alex Hall, James Crowne, Joanne Hooper, Clare Wiley, John Kelly, Helen Fletcher, Lauren Norris, Richard Keane, Bridget Mills-Powell, Simon Binns, Melanie Aram, Hugh Wilson, Richard Freedman, Jane Ramsay, Nicola Powell, Wendy Moore, Anna Addison, Laura Schneider, Lindsey Evans, Michael Durrant, Noel Mellor, Laura McQueen, Emily Heward, Oliver Kempski, Victoria Conway, Clare Wiltshire, Sarah Warren, Sara Wallaya, Dame Amy
Photography: Joe Millson, Selma Yalazi Dawani, Tiago Genoveze, Tim Ireland, Juliet Hookey, Rebecca Lee, Chris Grossmeier, Mario Alberto
Cover and feature illustrations: www.si-clark.co.uk

Itchy

Itchy Group, 78 Liverpool Road, London, N1 0QD
Tel: 020 7288 9810 **Fax:** 020 7288 9815
E-mail: editor@itchymedia.co.uk
Web: www.itchycity.co.uk

Itchy

Contents

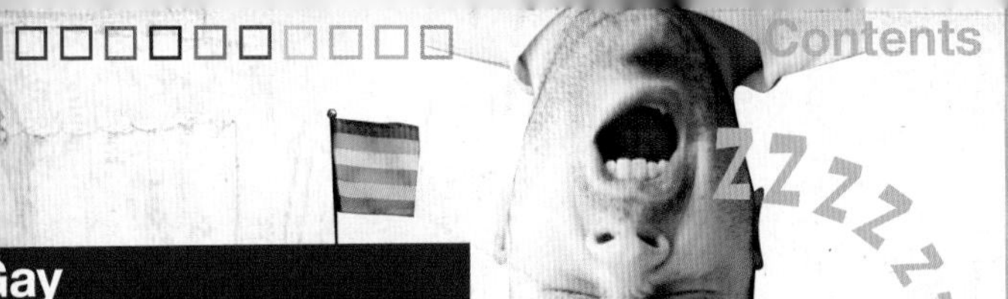

BACKSTAGE

Welcome to Manchester

GO MAD FOR IT IN MANCHESTER

Happy birthday to us, happy birthday to us, happy birthday dear u-us, happy birthday to us. We can hardly believe it's been 10 years since we first opened our pages to the sights and sounds of good ol' Madchester, this Mecca amongst metropolises. But don't worry, we're not quite ready for the knacker's yard just yet (and when we do get sent down, we're taking you with us). We're still brimming with excitement at all things Manchester. Whether we're floating round Fallowfield, dawdling aroun(Didsbury or camping it up on Cana Street we always find somewhere t(have a spanking good time. With nightlife that turns other cities gree with envy, Manchester is the beating pulsing, cosmopolitan heart of the North and it doesn't know how tc take no for an answer. So, let's all holc hands and take a deep breath as we plunge headlong into all the delights that Manchester, the capital of the North, has to offer.

Changes in Manchester over the last ten years

WOW, 10 YEARS OF ITCHY. WHEN WE STARTED OFF HERE *THERE'S SOMETHING ABOUT MARY* WAS ON AT THE CINEMA AND BRITNEY HAD JUST HIT THE POP SCENE… BUT WHAT WAS HAPPENING IN MANCHESTER? A LOT OF BUILDING WORK, MAINLY. THERE WERE CRANES COVERING EVERY SINGLE INCH OF THE SKYLINE. THE BOMB HAD HAPPENED TWO YEARS BEFORE AND THE COMMONWEALTH GAMES WERE FOUR YEARS AHEAD. SO, QUITE A BIT OF PRESSURE TO GET IT ALL LOOKING SMART, THEN.

To everyone's surprise, the 2002 Commonwealth Games went really well. People from other countries realised that Manchester existed, rather than being some kind of lost city somewhere oop-north. And thanks to its new worldwide status, the city became a home for other high-profile events, like the biennial International Festival.

There have been bonuses for residents too, with regeneration making parts of the city less minging. We're thinking particularly of the Arndale Centre and Piccadilly. So you might not like the world's biggest Next, or giant concrete walls, but it's better than grubby toilet-style tiles and the city with the world's highest concentration of muggings.

In 2006, a real, live skyscraper appeared in the shape of the Beetham Tower, with several more given the go-ahead. Yeah, we know there were towers already but let's face it, anyone from New York would just think they were big houses.

Have there been any changes for the worse? Well, chains. Some we don't mind, and even one of each would just about be tolerable. But the city centre and Didsbury Village compete to outdo each other for the title of 'Most Clone-filled'. Their shininess attracts scallies and corporate morons like magpies.

And the clubs. Don't get us wrong; there are still plenty of good ones – but not with anything like the world status they used to have. The decline happened some time just before the craze for new-style r 'n' b and garage, in the early 2000s.

How about the next decade? Well, there'll be about a million more apartments, on top of the already-huge glut. But we'd rather see buildings regenerated than left to decay.

Itchy thinks Manchester is firmly on the up. If the independent and alternative sectors continue to balance out the clones and WAGs, we'll be sorted.

Local Lingo

JOE = TAXI. SCRAN = FOOD. THA'S BOB ON = THAT IS CORRECT/GOOD. DO ONE/DONE ONE = GO AWAY/DISAPPEARED. SUBSTITUTING 'THR' WITH 'FR' – I.E. ONE, TWO, FREE; OR SUBSTITUTING DOUBLE 'T'S WITH DOUBLE 'K'S – I.E. LIKKLE BOKKLE. SCROATS = YOUNG SCALLYWAGS. BAG O' SHITE = RUBBISH. RED SAUCE = KETCHUP. A SWEAR DOWN = I'M TELLING GOD'S TRUTH. LEVVER YOH = LEATHER YOU = BEAT YOU UP.

Top five places to have your photo taken

Outside the Rover's Return on the *Corrie* set. Bemuse the mad fans who gather regularly at the Granada TV gates by requesting photos with them and ignoring the stars of the show when they come out.

Manchester Wheel in Exchange Square in the Millennium Quarter. Either up it or in front of it, if you're a big wimp.

Rusholme. It's like Blackpool illuminations all year round, but without the roller coasters.

By the thoroughly horrendous-looking Piccadilly Plaza, before they finish its makeover.

Supermarket photo booth, holding a can of Boddingtons or Special Brew to make it more Mancunian. V-sign optional.

Quirky facts

There's a network of massive tunnels and bunkers deep under Manchester. Built in the 1950s, the aim was to maintain communication in the event of an atomic bomb flattening the city.

Manchester's Victorian structure was built over older bits – even whole Georgian houses and streets; and various rivers. The city's 15th-century Hanging Bridge has been excavated and can be seen in the cathedral's underground visitor centre.

Friedrich Engels lived here and he based his book The Condition of the Working Class in England on his observations of Manchester in the 1840s. His work was deeply influential on the writings of Karl Marx.

Manchester is the birthplace of many firsts: the computer; the the canal; vegetarianism; professional football leagues; industrialisation. Oh, and Mr Rolls met Mr Royce in the Midland Hotel. No, not like that.

The Hilton Deansgate Beetham Tower (48 stories, 169m), will soon be joined by two other skyscrapers: the Albany Crown Tower (54 stories, 160m) and Piccadilly Tower (58 stories, 188m). Several other designs are in progress.

Eat

Eat

Welcome to Eat

Manchester's restaurant scene has always had its fair share of diamonds in the rough, but in recent years it's begun to sparkle a bit more. We can recommend plenty of places for top-notch nosh, but let's start with the time that food is arguably appreciated most: when you're hungover. We recommend either branch of **Trof – in Fallowfield (2A Landcross Road, 0161 224 0467) or in the Northern Quarter (5–8 Thomas Street, 0161 832 1870)** – for fantastically hearty breakfasts and brunch food in relaxed surroundings. Alternatively, you could wait a few extra hours and have a Sunday roast at **The Metropolitan** in refined **West Didsbury (2 Lapwing Lane, 0161 374 9559)**. If you're not a fan of flesh, you can hop over the road to Manchester's poshest veggie restaurant, **Greens (43 Lapwing Lane, 0161 434 4259)**, with food so good, even the most hardened carnivores won't moan.

Top five cheap eats

This + That, Northern Quarter – Rice-n-three outlets in the Northern Quarter are legendary.

Gabbott's Farm, City Centre – This is to chicken wings and pork ribs what Greggs is to pasties.

Room, City Centre – Bordering on posh, but mains are £7 before 7pm.

East z East, City Centre – Shabby prices in a chic setting.

Chinese buffets, Chinatown – Manchester's most famous all-you-can-eat. A well-earned reputation.

Top five places for a posh meal

Jem + I, Didsbury Village – Michelin award-winner, but without wallet-bashing prices.

The Lime Tree, West Didsbury – The description 'staple' was invented for this place. As in diet, not the paper fastener. Idiot.

Choice, Castlefield – Never a bad, err, choice.

Juniper, Altringham – There goes another Michelin star.

The River Room – Make up any excuse for coming here.

How to get your meal for *Free*

'THE BEST THINGS IN LIFE ARE FREE', SANG JANET JACKSON AND LUTHER VANDROSS. AND WHO ARE WE TO ARGUE WITH SOMEONE WHO HAS THE WORD 'DROSS' IN THEIR SURNAME? HERE, THEN, ARE ITCHY'S TIPS FOR GETTING YOUR MEAL FOR FREE WHEN DINING OUT

Take offence – What do they mean they're a steak restaurant? You're a vegetarian, goddammit, and the very presence of a piece of meat on your plate constitutes a grave slur against your lifestyle. Though a free meal might stop you calling your animal rights activist mates.

Spot a 'rodent' – Bag yourself some form of wind-up animal toy, and unleash it across the floor of your restaurant. As soon as you release, leap up screaming 'Mouse! Mouse!' in the most hysterical voice you can manage. Have an accomplice waiting to retrieve the toy in the confusion, and they'll have to let you off paying to make it up to you.

Make up a stupid food allergy Food allergies are all the rage nowadays; you can get away with pretending you're allergic to pretty much anything. Make up an allergy to something suitably ludicrous, then nip to the toilets, inflate a balloon, stuff it down the neck of your top, and draw on your face with red felt tip. Hey presto: instant swollen throat and rash. They're bound to give you a freebie after doing all that to poor old you.

Fake narcolepsy – Every time the waiter attempts to present you with the bill, pretend to drop off. No way can they charge you if they can't rouse you. Sooner or later they'll give up and carry you out onto the street, where you can sneak away with a belly as full as your wallet.

Illustration by Si Clarke

ACADEMIC DISTRICT CAFÉS

Eighth Day

111 Oxford Road, Academic District
(0161) 273 1850

For the health-conscious – or simply those of us scraping the bottom of the financial barrel – below the Eighth Day wholefood shop lurks one of the best budget eateries in Manchester. It seems that cutting out the added crap has been reflected in the prices. Serving up a hearty selection of vegetarian, vegan and organic grub; and a variety of delicious smoothies. Apart from anything else, your mum would definitely sleep better at night knowing you were here instead of guzzling kebabs for breakfast, lunch and tea.

Mon–Fri, 8.30am–7.30pm;
Sat, 9.30am–7.30pm

Umami

147–153 Oxford Road, Academic District
(0161) 273 2300

On the face of it, this place seems like a Wagamama rip-off. And in some ways it is: wooden table and bench set-up, noodle bar menu, even the same chopsticks. But once you're settled in, the little differences start jumping out. Instead of one cup of green tea for a quid, you get free refills. Instead of staff mentally willing you to pay and get out, you get a more relaxed approach. The friendly independence of this place lets it stand out, and with great deals like the express lunch menu for £4.95, who can complain?

Mon–Sat, 12pm–11pm; Sun, 12pm–10pm
Fokkien fried rice, £6.95
£11.95

ACADEMIC DISTRICT RESTAURANTS

Moso Moso

403–419 Oxford Road, Academic District
(0161) 273 3373

This is the place to go if you're a student who needs some major feeding up. The set dinners are gigantic, but it's great for real-worlders too. In fact, once you've discovered Moso Moso and are feeling in dire need of a budget Chinese or Thai meal, there's little point in going elsewhere. The only criticism is that you get too much food for your money. If that even counts as a criticism.

Mon–Sat, 12.30pm–2.30am;
Sun,12pm–12am
Combination banquet, £16.50 per person
£12.50

CASTLEFIELD RESTAURANTS

Akbars

73 Liverpool Road, Castlefield

(0161) 834 7222

You may wonder if you've accidentally swallowed an illegal substance in pre-meal drinks when Akbars' naans appear, as they are about the size of India itself. Nay, the entire subcontinent. Just to give you an idea, one will comfortably serve three people – unless one of them is due to appear on a 'Why are you so fat and greedy?' Jeremy Kyle special at nearby Granada Studios. It also helps that it's located in Castlefield for a post-meal canalside stroll. Nicer than dodging fumes and fights in Rusholme.

Mon–Sun, 5.30pm–11.30pm

Seafood balti, £11.95

Choice Bar & Restaurant

Castle Quay, Castlefield

(0161) 833 3400

If you spent any of your childhood as a boy scout or girl guide, you have a distinct advantage when visiting Choice. And no, we don't mean that you'll be expected to cook your own meal in a billy can over a little fire made from sticks you've collected in the woods. Proving that good things are often hard to find, this restaurant is almost entirely hidden behind the Key 103 building in Castlefield. Once inside, understated poshness abounds, with high-end (but honest) food, excellent service and magnificent riverside views of the Medlock.

Mon–Sat, 11am–11pm; Sun, 12pm–11pm

Glazed belly of pork, £16.50

£14

Albert's Shed

20 Castle Street, Castlefield

(0161) 839 9818

The building's previous owner, Albert, stored his tools here – and agreed to move out only if the restaurant was named after him. Albert's Shed has made ripples among the swanky canalside bars of Castlefield with its slap-up Mediterranean cuisine and a great selection of pizzas. Al fresco dining is very popular: for larger groups they do a cheaper set menu, and the chic interior means there's not a rusty bike or dirty boot in sight.

Mon–Fri, 12pm–2.30pm & 5.30pm–10pm (Fri, 10.30pm); Sat, 12pm–11pm; Sun, 12pm–9.30pm

Pesto beef pizza, £7.95

£12.95

Sapporo Teppanyaki

91–93 Liverpool Road, Castlefield

(0161) 831 9888

The experience at Sapporo is based firmly on awe-inspiration. And also perhaps some nervousness, as the show chefs employ a lot of fire and utensil-juggling, which in our experience always goes wrong. And when we say utensils, we mean BIG SHARP KNIVES. There's sushi too, which isn't cheap, but, when you're dealing with raw seafood, consider the prices reassuringly expensive. Nothing spoils the memory of an evening more than spending the rest of the weekend hugging porcelain.

Mon–Sat, 12pm–11pm; Sun, 12pm–10.30pm

Ninja combination, £26 per head

£12.95

CHORLTON CAFÉS

Jam Street Café

209 Upper Chorlton Road, Chorlton

(0161) 881 9944

First, let's get something straight. We like the Jam Street Café. There's loads to like. Atmosphere, location, staff (on the whole). Unfortunately, its famous breakfast was a big disappointment. It may have featured in *The Observer's* best breakfasts of 2006. It may include local, organic, Fairtrade and GM-free food. But should it really take an hour to serve a fry-up? Cold – and not particularly well-prepared. Added to that, the staff plainly didn't give a shite. We wonder whether there might be some complacency afoot...

Sun–Thu, 10am–12am; Fri–Sat, 10am–1am

Chicken and chorizo stew, £8.50

CHORLTON RESTAURANTS

Azad Manzil

495 Barlow Moor Road, Chorlton

(0161) 881 1021

Azad Manzil serves Phal on its specials list – the only dish commonly known to be spicier than Vindaloo. This is a warning, as Itchy doesn't want anyone crying to us after trying to be clever by thoroughly searing their insides. But if someone feels the need for this proof of daring, you certainly won't lose out by joining them on a visit to Azad Manzil. The menu is dazzling, varied and tastes gooood.

Fri–Sat, 5.30pm–2am;
Sun–Thu, 5.30pm–12am

Nepal king prawn, £7.95

£7.70

Mink

48 Beech Road, Chorlton

(0161) 862 9934

Arriving at this über-modern, stylish venue, the first thing you're likely to see is a hubbub of equally stylish people enjoying an affinity for the pavement tables. Inside, the sexy black and almond décor features luxuriously-papered walls and vibrant artwork. What else to do but sip tea and cranberry juice, checking the vibe? Surprisingly, the food is honest and varied, ranging from goat's cheese to roast lamb and Yorkshire puds. Even leaving is special, with leftovers packaged in a foil swan.

Mon–Sat, 12pm–11pm;
Sun, 12pm–10.30pm

Sunday roast, £8.95

£10.95

Leo's

356 Barlow Moor Road, Chorlton

(0161) 861 9092

Leo's is rather a hidden gem in Chorlton, but consistently superb reviews are meaning that it's getting difficult to secure a table at short notice. It's a tiny place – and this relates to Itchy's only complaint. If anyone stands up to chat with a neighbouring table (which, in a place filled with regulars, they tend to do) you feel overshadowed and a bit awkward. So, not the best place for a date, unless you request a table away from the centre. But the food is superb and the service very friendly.

Mon–Thu, 5pm–10.30pm; Fri–Sat, 5pm–11pm; Sun, 12pm–4pm & 5pm–10pm

Steak Roma, £14.25

£12.95

CITY CENTRE RESTAURANTS

Brasserie Blanc

55 King Street, City Centre
(0161) 832 1000

Formerly Le Petit Blanc (and still part of Raymond's empire), Brasserie Blanc leaves a grande impression on the tastebuds. You can taste the quality in the air, which buzzes with pure enjoyment. The food is more satisfying than watching Paris Hilton get thrown back in jail, and, like a hand-selected cherry to top it all off, the staff actually give a damn if you have a good time. Not that they need worry.

Mon–Fri, 12pm–2.45pm & 5.30pm–10.30pm; Sat, 12pm–11pm; Sun, 12pm–10pm

Raymond's ultimate hot smoked Loch Duart salmon fishcake, £14

£12.95

Chaophraya

Chapel Walks, Off Cross Street, City Centre
(0161) 832 8342

Stress is a terrible thing... But fear no more, as Manchester has welcomed in a veritable oasis of calm and karma. 'Chow-pie-a' is also an upmarket experience, with dinky water features and delicate incense. Providing a quickie bar lunch or ballsier à la carte, the food is a luxurious, Western take on traditional Thai. And once you've sated your appetite for Eastern cuisine, you can jump in the restaurant's Tuk-Tuk and go racing down the M56.

Mon–Sun, 12pm–10.30pm, call in advance to book the restaurant's own Tuk Tuk to take you to and from the restaurant

Pad Thai (traditional), £8

£11.75

Croma

1–3 Clarence Street, City Centre
(0161) 237 9799
www.croma.biz

The über stylish Croma is a slice of tasteful dining at an affordable price. Specialising in pizzas, Croma excels at doing the simple things well and has an excellent cocktail menu to boot. The décor is chic and modern, with plenty of elegant touches and plenty of chrome, of course. But despite all of the posh trimmings Croma is actually as easy on the wallet as it is on the eye. Look out for Croma Chorlton and Croma Prestwich too.

Mon–Sat, 12pm–11pm; Sun, 12pm–10.30pm

Pizza americana, £6.20

£10.95

East

52–54 Faulkner Street, Chinatown
(0161) 236 1188

As ever in Chinatown, Itchy guarantees you will be asked every five minutes by a different member of staff whether you want anything, or whether you're ready to move on; and your wine will be repeatedly topped up. But be patient and let it go over your head. Eager to turn tables though they may seem, the staff are genuinely nice – and, most importantly, the food is worth it. The hugely varied menu and circular tables make it a great venue for eating with friends.

Mon–Thu, 12pm–11pm; Fri–Sat, 12pm–3am; Sun, 12pm–10pm

Assorted seafood with crystal vermicelli casserole Szechuan style, £9

£10.90

EastZEast

Princess Street (beneath Ibis Hotel), City Centre
(0871) 811 4950

If curry houses were WAGs, Rusholme's curry mile would be Colleen: it scrubs up nicely and holds a special place in our hearts; but ultimately, there'll always be that chavvy quality lurking beneath the bling. EastzEast, on the other hand, is for those who like their curry Posh. Reminiscent of Mrs Beckham, this place has transformed curry into a classy affair – complete with an indoor water feature, soothing lighting and a friendly chap in a turban on the door. The finesse justifies the extra couple of quid on the bill.

Sun–Thu, 5pm–12am; Fri–Sat, 5pm–1am
Balti garlic chilli chicken, £7.95
£12

Kro Piccadilly

1 Piccadilly Gardens, City Centre
(0161) 244 5765

Sister venue to the brilliant Kro Bar, you'd hope for a decent eating experience. Hmmm. Fair enough, it was a weekday evening, but the staff surely can't have been as surprised as they seemed that we might actually want to use the restaurant. Then the main menu couldn't be used without moving to another section. Slow service was down to there being only one guy in the kitchen, apparently. Gordon Ramsay's next 'Nightmares' mission, we reckon...

Mon–Thu, 8am–12am; Fri–Sat, 8am–2am; Sun, 8am–11pm; food, Mon–Sun, 8.30am–9.30pm
Scandinavian platter, £8.50
£11

Livebait

22 Lloyd Street, Albert Square, City Centre
(0161) 817 4110

'There's no getting around it. If you're going to eat at Livebait, you have to REALLY like fish. And on a brave level – inclusive of wormy and sinewy shellfish. Even if you go for the more straightforward fish and chips, it's more-than likely one of your companions or a neighbouring table will have opted for the famous platter. The presentation is impressive; but, unfortunately, the atmosphere, service and food quality can be a bit patchy, to say the least. Still, if you have a big platter, make sure you share it. No need to be shellfish.

Mon–Fri, 12pm–3pm & 5.30pm–10.30pm; Sat, 12pm–11pm
Shellfish plate, 10.95

Pacific

58 George Street, Chinatown
(0161) 228 6668

Everyone raves about Pacific, meaning it'll always be a bit of a struggle for it to match up to expectations. So we might as well point out the bad bits now, then you'll probably be delighted. The dual China/ Thailand concept is still quite a talking point, but, décor-wise, parts of it are a bit more North Sea than Pacific. The prices are also perhaps a little high, yet the lunch buffet is great value. And most importantly, food-wise, it absolutely does deliver.

Thai, Mon–Sat, 12pm–3pm (buffet) & 6pm–12am; Sun, 12pm–4pm (buffet); Chinese, Mon–Sun, 12pm–12am
Stuffed scallops with minced prawn in salt & chilli pepper, £11.50

CROMA
CROMA

Piccolino

8 Clarence Street, City Centre

(0161) 835 9860

The food quality is unfailingly brilliant and the drinks are great too – although not particularly cheap. But what really gets visitors talking about this particular (and original) branch of Piccolino is its service and atmosphere. The restaurant area is buzzing, especially near the bar, though some might find loud business groups a bit overwhelming while eating. But despite this, it's still one of Manchester's most popular eateries – and deservedly so.

Mon–Sat, coffee, 11am–12pm; restaurant, 12pm–11pm; Sun, coffee, 11am–12pm; restaurant, 12pm–10.30pm

Tortelloni ai funghi, £10.50

£13.50

Room

81 King Street, City Centre

(0161) 839 2005

Break the piggy bank, hire that limo service and pretend you are a WAG for the night. But try not to start a handbag fight in the toilets. With its statues, turrets and chandeliers, everything is nice to look at, from the fare to the bouncers. Just make sure you book well in advance, because this is a place where Manchester's trendy crowds like to be seen. While the cocktail bar alone is worth the visit, the food is to die for. And, although a bit pricey, you can get a good deal if you go before 7pm.

Mon–Wed, 10am–11pm; Thu–Sat, 10am–2am

Fish casserole, £15

£14

Stock

4 Norfolk Street, City Centre

(0161) 839 6644

They don't say it's 'probably the best Italian restaurant in Manchester' for nothing. It's certainly the grandest. Set in Manchester's Old Stock Exchange, the domed ceiling and marble features create a hell of an atmosphere. On top of that, the wine is superb, the service very good, and we can't go on enough about the fish. It may be on the pricey side, but seriously, try the lobster here. You'll thank us.

Mon–Sat, 12pm–10pm

Bistecca di cervo, £18.95

£16.95

Tampopo

16 Albert Square, City Centre

(0161) 819 1966

Does Manchester city centre really need THREE of these? It's nice. It's alright. But, despite the spicy menu options, Tampopo is a bit, well, bland. The long plain tables and chairs may be traditionally East Asian, but the rest of the décor hasn't been given enough attention to avoid the feel of chain hell. On the bright side, the prices are reasonable and the service quite quick.

Mon–Sat, 12pm–11pm; Sun, 12pm–10pm

Yaki Udon – chunky udon noodles with shredded leek and red pepper, fried in a soy and rice wine sauce, £7.95

DEANSGATE RESTAURANTS

Dimitris

Campfield Arcade, Tonman Street, Deansgate

(0161) 839 3319

After the fear and stress of shopping, how better to recover than with a relaxing meal? At Dimitris you can even risk being extra-healthy by getting some fresh air, as it's shielded from the traffic and irritating tourists littering Deansgate. Located in a cool, vine-laden arcade on the edge of Castlefield, for a while you can almost believe you're in the Mediterranean, complete with excellent fresh meze and attractively shabby décor. But no random trampy cats to make you feel bad.

Mon–Sun, 11am–12am

Kalamata meat platter, £13.95

£11.95

Evuna

277–279 Deansgate, Deansgate

(0161) 819 2752

If eating at a certain tapas chain has polluted your view of the cuisine with images of greasy fried cheese and the like, try this as your next attempt at educational culture. The food, service and décor are all authentically Spanish – and, thankfully, not cheapest-possible-holiday-in-Benidorm-type authentic. Main dishes of chicken, fish and beef can be mixed and matched with smaller more traditional tapas dishes. As if that isn't enough, they also have a huge wine collection, for budding someliers out there.

Mon–Sat, 11am–11pm

Paella frutos del mar (seafood), £13.95

£15

El Rincon de Rafa

Longworth Street (off St John's St), Deansgate

(0161) 839 8819

By the time you find this place – and have waited for a table – you'll be so drunk or hungry that the food on offer might be irrelevant. In fact, you'll probably feel that you've travelled directly to Spain when you walk down the stairs to this basement jewel and look around you. It's some of the most genuine Spanish food and drink (and yes, slightly tacky décor) in the city centre – and there are plenty of Spaniards there every night to prove it. Most importantly, the food is pretty damn good.

Mon–Sat, 12pm–11.30pm; Sun, 12pm–11pm

Tiger prawns, £4.95

£10.95

Gaucho Grill

2a St Mary's Street, Deansgate

(0161) 833 4333

Maybe it's the red meat. The blood. The cowhide. The frantic scraping of steak knives echoing in the grand arena. Itchy has it on good authority that this place is famed for domestics. Fat chips in flight, tears of rage and storming retreats to the toilets. So beware that fateful second bottle of wine and contentious discussion about ex-partners. Luckily, this passion also engulfs the faithfully Argentinean food. Marvellously honest, rustic plates, and the best T-bone in town, bar none.

Mon–Thu, 12pm–10.30pm; Fri–Sat, 12pm–11pm; Sun, 12pm–10.30pm

Bife de lomo (fillet), £20

£15.50

Gourmet Burger Kitchen

Leftbank, Spinningfields, Deansgate

(0161) 832 2719

Forget all other burgers. Freezer-to-fryer varieties in the pub, the strange ones at Maccy Ds... They all pale in comparison next to GBK's towering sandwiches. The Kiwi option is so big it needs two wooden skewers to hold it together. All beef burgers are made from Aberdeen Angus steak mince – and served medium as standard, which is nice to see in itself. There are options for children and veggies – and even those slightly strange types who might prefer chicken, or perhaps even venison burgers over lovely beef ones. Fools.

Mon–Fri, 12pm–11pm; Sat, 11am–11pm; Sun, 11am–10pm

Kiwiburger, £7.50

Luso

63 Bridge Street, Deansgate

(0161) 839 5550

Unfortunately, a shoestring budget won't go far here, but that's the only drawback. Imagine: it's the weekend, you've just been paid, feeling a little flush, you're in the mood for wining and dining. You are looking for somewhere with sophistication and a menu that gets your taste buds all excited. Tucked away on Bridge Street, Portuguese haven Luso offers all of this and more.

Mon–Sat, 12pm–10.30pm; Sun, 12pm–10pm

Frango Portuguesa (chicken breast stuffed with garlic & oregano, chilli-roasted potatoes, smoked bacon and Madeira jus), £14.95

£12.95

Linen

235 Great Northern Warehouse, Deansgate

(0161) 828 0300

Linen is an enjoyably sumptuous dining experience, not least due to the fun aspect of feeling like you've had some of Alice In Wonderland's shrinking potion. The tables and glassware are ridiculously huge – and this sense of grandeur extends to the menu, which delivers on presentation and flavour. The jury is still out on whether it's quite worth the extortionate price tag, especially considering you're in a casino so are already being heavily milked for your money – but, on the flip side, that partnership makes for a very satisfactory night out. Unless you have addiction issues, obviously.

Tue–Sat, 6pm–11pm

Negresco

310 Deansgate

(0161) 839 7794

The former home of the fairly ordinary, slightly depressing Pig and Porcupine pub is now anything but. Well, still depressing, but in a proactive fashion – complete with solid black décor, macabre imagery, chequered floor and animal trophies. The food is suitably Franco-Italian and pretty good, but hasn't found its balance quite yet. The pizzas are gigantic, while the mains are small – and it's a bit on the stodgy side. Itchy particularly recommends cocktails in the bar.

Sun–Wed, 11am–12am; Thu, 11am–1am; Fri–Sat, 11am–2am

Bolognaise Roberto, £8.95

£12.95

DIDSBURY CAFÉS

Saints & Scholars

694 Wilmslow Road, Didsbury Village

(0161) 448 2457

In the world of pricey chains, commercial pubs and self-important yuppies that is Didsbury Village, Saints and Scholars sticks out like a sore thumb. This small restaurant has a characterful atmosphere – and 'random' doesn't quite capture the paraphernalia attached to every wall surface. Nevertheless, being surrounded by cowboy hats and old tricycles while munching on your cajun chicken fajitas is actually quite pleasant.

Mon–Thu & Sun, 9am–10pm; Fri–Sat, 9am–10.30pm

Chicken fajitas, £9.95

£9.95

Bistro West 156

156 Burton Road, West Didsbury

(0161) 445 1921

If Itchy were being cynical, we'd say it was dead as a doornail and the service was slow, but to be fair, we visited on a weekday lunchtime. Bistro West 156 has excellent food, and a menu with plenty of posh words on it. You can laugh all you want at the fact that you're the only one there – and their insistence on playing Simply Red – but when the food arrives, you'll be lauging with joy. Just as long as they turn off the Simply Red and let you enjoy your meal without puking into your plate.

Mon–Sat, 10am–10pm

Smoked ham and mozzarella croques, £5.95

£11.95

DIDSBURY RESTAURANTS

Casa Tapas

704 Wilmslow Road, Didsbury Village

(0161) 448 2515

Prides itself on its visitors having to wait for tables. Hardly surprising, as being on Dids Village high street means haughtiness comes with the territory. A rich man's La Tasca, there are a couple of things that would improve the experience – not least lowering the piped Latin jazz a few decibels. But the bustling atmosphere is enjoyable, and the food is tasty. Stuffed peppers and gratin-style dishes are done particularly well, with vegetarians spoilt for choice.

Mon–Sat, 6pm–11 pm; Sun, 5.30pm–10.30pm

Pincho Moruno, £3.05

£11.50

Felicini

747–751 Wilmslow Road, Didsbury Village

(0161) 445 2055

Felicini is the kind of place pretentious people go to convince themselves they know what authentic Italian food should be like. Unfortunately, the large menu and postmodern orange furniture hardly disguises the fact that Felicini is a chain restaurant with a fancy name. Avoiding the caesar salad is wise, as the dressing tastes suspiciously like butter. On the bright side, there's a good range of pasta and pizza – and the ridiculously oversized desserts are worth the morning-after regret.

Mon–Fri, 11am–11pm; Sat, 12pm–11pm; Sun, 12pm–10.30pm

Pan-fried gnocci, £8.95

£13.50

The Great Kathmandu

140 Burton Road, West Didsbury

(0161) 434 6413

It may have a shiny new sign, but the interior of the legendary Kathmandu is something very different. It's cramped, shabby and a bit musty – sort of like a Nepalese-themed middle-England antiques shop, run by an old lady with failing eyesight – but this frankly horrendous décor is actually part of the charm. Rumour has it that this is one of Manchester's original curry restaurants, and we always trust rumours. The menu prices are only very slightly higher than the Mile – and when this is ratioed against the awesome quality, the Kathmandu is unrivalled in Manchester.

Mon–Sun, 12pm–2.30pm & 6pm–12am;

Kathmandu chicken makhanwala, £6.95

Gusto

756 Wilmslow Road, Didsbury Village

(0870) 401 2107

Didsbury has many restaurants, but not many can also boast a singer to serenade you through your meal. On arrival, once you've managed to wade your way through the crowd of scallies who tend to congregate outside the next-door corner shop, you're greeted by an array of attractive serving staff. It's really quite an impressive juxtaposition. In fact, maybe they put the chavs there on purpose in the knowledge that they'd benefit greatly by the contrast.

Mon–Sun, 11am–11pm

Chicken and sausage with saffron risotto, £11.95

£15.50

Greens

43 Lapwing Lane, West Didsbury

(0161) 434 4259

Thinking of treating your new veggie bird to a Quorn burger and Argos necklace? Instead, impress with a visit to this celebrity chef venture in leafy West Didsbury. Greater Manchester native Simon Rimmer started Greens in the early 1990s. Despite being a carnivore, he wanted to discover as much about vegetarian food as possible – and the fruits of his labours are certainly on proud display here. They include veggie black pudding – which, without gristly pig blood, has to be a winner.

Mon–Sun, 5.30pm-10.30pm; lunch, Tue–Fri, 12pm–2pm; Sun, 12.30pm–3.30pm

Gnocchi with red wine ragu, crispy artichokes and pea and mint pesto, £10.95

Jem + I

1c School Lane, Didsbury Village

(0161) 445 3996

Strange name, but not exactly a mystery, as the place is run by an extremely well-reputed chef called Jem – and also happens to be a jewel in South Manchester's crown (sorry). Perfection is clearly the goal here, most notably with the food. It isn't exactly famous for its service, which is a shame, but you can forgive anything when what you're eating is good. In fact it's so good, Itchy imagines that's why it was awarded a Michelin Bib Gourmand. At a guess.

Mon, 5.30pm–10pm; Tue–Thu, 12pm–3pm & 5.30pm–10pm; Fri–Sat, 12pm–3pm & 5.30pm–10.30pm; Sun, 12pm–3pm & 6pm–10pm

Beer batter cod and chips, £11.25

£10.75

The Lime Tree

8 Lapwing Lane, West Didsbury
(0161) 445 1217

It's hardly surprising that West Didsbury is often considered the epicentre of South Manc smugness, considering the sheer number of superb, award-winning restaurants on the doorstep. And the legendary Lime Tree is right on top of that pile. Everything on the modern-British menu is cooked perfectly, the wine list is excellent – with many by the glass – and the place doesn't even feel snooty. Plus there's an equally marvellous early doors menu for those who really can't justify dinner prices.

Tue–Fri & Sun, 12pm–2.30pm & 5.45pm–10.15pm; Sat & Mon, 5.45pm–10.15pm

Pan fried duck breast and confit leg, £13.95

£12.95

MILLENNIUM QUARTER RESTAURANTS

Harvey Nichols

Exchange Square, Millennium Quarter
(0161) 828 8888

In need of refreshment after flexing that credit card? The second floor glossy bar, glam brasserie or groovy restaurant have something for everyone, whether you're after coffee, champers or a sumptuous meal.

Restaurant, Mon, 12pm–6pm; Tue–Sat, 12pm–10.30pm; Sun, 12pm–5pm; brasserie, Mon, 10am–6pm; Tue–Fri, 10am–10.30pm; Sat, 9am–10.30pm; Sun 11.30am–5pm; bar, Mon, 12pm–6pm; Tue–Sat, 10am–11pm; Sun, 10am–6pm

Seared tuna nicoise salad, £14

£13.50

Thai E-Sarn

210 Burton Road, West Didsbury
(0161) 445 5200

The food isn't the star at Thai E-Sarn – Wendy is. She's the host and the main attraction of this legendary Thai restaurant-cum-karaoke bar, inexplicably popular with hen parties and local minor celebs alike. All we'll say is this: part Elvis, part Shirley Bassey, all woman... But between us and the doorpost, we have some suspicions about alien or supernatural ingredients too. You really have to experience it for yourself. Though maybe eat before you go. We meant it when we said the food isn't the star.

Mon–Sun, 12pm–2.30pm & 6pm–11.30pm

Main courses, £6.95

£12

Yo! Sushi @ Selfridges

1 Exchange Square, Millennium Quarter
(0161) 838 0614

Welcome to 21st century eating. Tucked in a corner of exclusive Selfridges, there's a conveyor belt which is actually a sushi restaurant. The game is to snatch whichever travelling, colour-coded plates you like the look of from under your fellow diner's nose. Under no circumstances should you push the button for serving attention – in this place, ignorance is bliss. But it's also a delicious experience, where the fish is definitely fresh. For extra entertainment, why not take the 'rentals, give them some wine and watch them fret over chopsticks?

Mon–Sat, 12pm–8pm; Sun, 12pm–5pm

Individual plates, from £1.50–£5

£12

NORTHERN QUARTER CAFÉS

The Koffee Pot

21 Hilton Street, Northern Quarter

(0161) 228 1484

The Koffee Pot has kept its head, while all around it others are losing theirs – turning into overpriced faux Italian café bars. When your soul is aching on a Sunday morning, head here for a proper fry-up with tea, and suddenly all is right with the world again. The staff are heartbreakingly lovely and even the walls are interesting, titillating pickled brains. But what makes this place really special is the Teatime Sessions, with evening gigs from local bands.

Mon–Fri, 7.30am-4pm; Sat–Sun, 9am–3pm. Teatime sessions every Friday, from 6pm

Full English breakfast, £4

Earth Café

16-20 Turner Street, Northern Quarter

(0161) 834 1996

Earth is a delightfully cheap vegetarian café and juice bar, which guarantees the highest quality homemade food, juices and smoothies. Vegans can eat everything on the award-winning menu and the place is entirely run by Buddhists, so you can enjoy some spirituality with your spinach. Earth makes the most of seasonal local produce so you'll have a clean conscience when you're sinking a savoury snack and a Fairtrade coffee. In fact, this place is so ethical and healthy you'll feel no qualms about devouring a McDonald's bacon double cheeseburger on your way home.

Tue–Fri, 10am–7pm; Sat, 10am–5pm

Spinach dhal, £2.20

NORTHERN QUARTER RESTAURANTS

Market Restaurant

104 High Street, Northern Quarter

(0161) 834 3743

Firmly established for over 25 years, the Market Restaurant has been around since before the Northern Quarter was cool – and has seen off a whole host of inferior restaurants in the city in the meantime. It can only be described as dotty, but with some of the finest locally-sourced food you'll eat in any restaurant. Coupled with the feeling of being in your favourite nana's front room.

Wed–Fri, 12pm–2pm & 6pm–11.30pm; Sat, 7pm–11.30

Roasted lamb fillet, £16.95

£13.95

Oklahoma

74–76 High Street, Northern Quarter

(0161) 834 1136

Yee-haa, they know their food here. A grea choice of smoothies and milkshakes is also on offer. In fact, the Northern Quarte would be incomplete without this multi coloured haven of kitsch. Yes, there are places offering a vintage-accessories-and café combination, but this place truly does fulfil all your quirky purchasing needs, from original jewellery to lampshades; and retro toys to novelty cards. The range of foreign and art-house films to rent, as well as ar gallery and vinyl collection, will surprise you. And there's nowt hippy about that

Mon–Sat, 8am–7pm; Sun 11am–5pm

RUSHOLME RESTAURANTS

Al Bilal

87–91 Wilmslow Road, Rusholme

(0161) 257 0006

There's absolutely no question, Al Bilal is and always has been Itchy's favourite curry house on the Rusholme mile. Two floors of the finest cuisine from a place that's been established for over ten years. For those watching the waistline, Al Bilal's low-fat grill 'is guaranteed not to get you fat', and for the more hearty diner, there's the Tandoori chicken mixed grill and a range of masalas – and the staff never fail to make you feel welcome.

Sun–Thu, 12pm–12am; Fri–Sat, 12pm–3am

Chicken jalfrezi, £5.90

£12.50

Darbar

65–67 Wilmslow Road, Rusholme

(0161) 224 4392

Darbar is open every night until 4am, except Sunday, when it settles for a more conservative 2am – probably a welcome break for the staff, who must have iron-willed patience. But Darbar is best for its superbly authentic food and good value. It's actually one of the most revered curry houses on the Mile. Instead of the all-too-common dullness that you suspect may have come from a Patak's jar, the familiar dishes are a standout, sitting well alongside less common ones such as Karahi Gosht and Paey (lambs' trotters in broth). Sounds delicious.

Mon–Sat, 3pm–4am; Sun, 2pm–2am

Chicken balti, £6.50

Lal Haweli

68–72 Wilmslow Road, Rusholme

(0161) 248 9700

Lal Haweli is a blaring, proud, bright star of the curry mile. It's bang in the middle of the strip, has a frontage that shouts louder than its neighbours, is absolutely massive – and charges no corkage on your bought-elsewhere bottles. It has big round tables for parties, so none of the neck strain you get in places where they sit everyone on conversation-dwindle-inducing oblongs, in order to cram more of you in. Best of all, there's no sneaky charge on the opening poppadums; and even a special low-fat menu to tempt in dieters. Curry perfection.

Mon–Thu, 12pm–1.30am; Fri, 12pm–2am; Sat, 12pm–3am; Sun, 12pm–12am

Chicken cilli, £6.90

Falafel

26 Wilmslow Road, Rusholme

(0161) 256 1372

It'd be easy to assume it's just another kebab outlet with grease-stained walls, but Falafel's haven of chickpeas stands out as one of the healthier takeaways on the neon rainbow of the curry mile. Its extensive Middle-Eastern menu far exceeds its unimaginative name. From freshly-made motabel (aubergine-based hummus) to fatayers (a sort-of arabic calzone), olives – and that classic eastern dish, pizza – everything boasts a home-cooked flavour and is washed down with some frantic Arabic beats to give you indigestion. Friendly, clean and cheaper than the chippy.

Mon–Sun, 10am–12.30am

Dish of the day (varies), £3.50

Sanam Sweet House

145–151 Wilmslow Road, Rusholme

(0161) 224 8824

Let's get this out of the way first: the bar is alcohol-free. But fear not, because the food is varied and delicious enough to distract you, with balti, karahi and makani combinations among the spices alive in the air. If the oral delights are not enough there are also the seats – bouncy, maroon and actually a little reminiscent of 1970s Bollywood – and fluorescent-patterned window panes alongside a South Asian heart theme. From the staff to the tandoor, everything is warm and even a little luxurious. Nearly enough to forget you're in Rusholme.

Mon–Sun, 12pm–12am

Lamb karai, £5.60

SOUTHERN QUARTER RESTAURANTS

Bouzouki by Night

38 Princess Street, Southern Quarter

(0161) 236 9282

If this place were a person, Trinny and Susannah would have it sectioned. Cartoon pelicans and Club Tropicana-style pink banners on its frontage are just the start. This aside, it does itself proud with superbly traditional Greek fare and an atmosphere to match. Dancing with the waiters to the house band is practically mandatory. But that's not all, as Bouzouki bills itself as: 'the perfect place for all special occasions like birthdays, work parties, anniversaries and even divorces!!'.

Meze (Greek Banquet), £19.90

£12.90

OTHER

Eat

1 St Ann Street, Central

(0161) 832 7872

When you're hungry in the cold Manchester weather, the last thing you want is a barely-defrosted rocket-and-lemon-mayo thing masquerading as a sandwich. Eat provides a welcome alternative to the coffee-chain outlets with its small-yet-hearty meals. The service is admittedly not fantastic (if you're paying the VAT to eat in, it'd be nice to have a plate instead of a cardboard tray, or a real mug), but maybe they'll improve that with time. We live in hope.

Times vary

Chicken pot pie, £2.80

Cocotoos

57 Whitworth Street West, Southern Quarter

(0161) 237 5458

The interior of Cocotoos is a textbook example of how to spruce up an old railway arch: make like Michelangelo and model it on the Sistine Chapel. We will admit the experience of drinking there is slightly surreal, especially considering that instead of alcohol next door's arch serves up MOTs and car repairs – but, if you ignore the occasional Phil Mitchell lookalike wandering past outside, you can almost imagine that Manchester really is like renaissance Florence. Alright, so it's possibly a bit of a stretch.

Mon–Sat, 12pm–2.15pm & 5.30pm–11.15pm

£16.95

Fuzion Noodle Bar

264 Wilmslow Road, Fallowfield

(0161) 248 6688

Hmmm, a bit pretentious for Itchy's liking. Individuals embracing their 'cultured' side by eating noodles on long, awkward tables. Fortunately, the venue's title comes into play, as these bad points are fused with flavoursome, organic food. Sigh. Itchy has tried to appreciate the cosmopolitan vibe, but we just aren't buying it. Can you tell? Sod it, perhaps compromise with a Fuzion take-out, then you can enjoy the fanastic produce with a decent bottle of wine and the comfort of your own place.

Mon, 5pm–12am; Tue–Sat, 12pm–12am; Sun, 12pm–11pm

Char sui and main, £5.50

£11

Eat

The Greenhouse

331 Great Western Street, Moss Side

(0161) 224 0730

The Greenhouse is a rundown shack on the edge of Moss Side, which makes it sound about as appealing as playing tennis with a bees' nest while naked and basted with honey. But come on, where's your adventurous spirit? The place proudly proclaims itself 'meat free since '83' – which makes it the longest-running server of farty-pants food in the whole city. So strap on your two-gun rig, wear a stetson and a duster, take the trek through the badlands and discover danger dining at its best.

Mon–Sat, 6.30pm–11.30pm; Sun, 6.30pm–10.30pm

Main courses, £8.65

Himalayas

945 Stockport Road, Levenshulme

(0161) 248 8882

The Himalayas is the kind of curry house which attracts middle-aged couples on the brink of divorce. Its marvellously distasteful wallpaper and eerie ambience make it a great spot to let your other half know exactly what you find most irritating about them. Should your relationship survive intact, a trip back to town on the 192 will probably finish it off. If you're after somewhere different to go with friends, this place is ideal. The food is cheap and a bit different, and you can have no end of fun earwigging on the crisis talks around you.

Mon–Sun, 7pm-12am

Lamb curry, £5.20

£8

Hellfire Club

Queens Road, Harpurhey

(0161) 277 9346

'The UK's only horror-themed restaurant' is apparently located in a haunted building - and is next to a graveyard. This certainly, ahem, hammers home the point. There are no half measures at the Hellfire Club with the international menu boasting delights such as 'Eyes Without a Face'. Add to this bloodstained goblets to drink from, rough wooden thrones, inverted crucifixes, skulls, fake corpses and black-caped owner-manager Peter, and you have a truly horrific experience. As intended. Seriously, there's even a hearse.

Tue–Sat, 5pm–11pm; Sun, 1pm–8pm

Braised lamb shank with mustard mash and red wine sauce, £9.95

Isinglass English Dining Room

46 Flixton Road, Urmston

(0161) 749 8400

Look up from your heaving plate and you might be startled to remember that Isinglass is not in some fashionable Northern Quarter back street or trendy Chorlton terrace. It's in Urmston, opposite a couple of truly horrendous bars and next door to a bog-standard curry house. Don't let that put you off. The ever-changing menu of locally-sourced, hearty and unpretentious food has won awards and acclaim, making Isinglass well worth the trip.

Tue–Sat, 11.30am–3pm & 6pm–10pm; Sun, 12pm–4.30pm & 6pm–10pm

Venison toad-in-the-hole, £13.90

£12.50

Drink

Welcome to Drink

Seeing as we're in what's probably the drinking capital of Britain, you won't struggle for choice. Why not start as you mean to go on, with Happy Hour? If you're in a pub mood, try the **Lass O' Gowrie in the Southern Quarter (36 Charles Street, 0161 273 6932)** Monday to Friday, 2.30pm–4.30pm; pints from £1.95, bottles of wine from £4.95, hotpot-and-ale for a fiver. Then move on to **Snook in Fallowfield (317 Wilmslow Road, 0161 248 0546)** for cheap, inventive cocktails between 5pm and 8pm. If you prefer a more leisurely, sophisticated approach, we recommend Manhattan-themed **Obsidian in the city centre (18–24 Princess Street, 0161 238 4348)**: every night, 5pm–8pm; cocktails for £3.95, Peroni at £2, bottles of house wine for £7.95 (and it's decent stuff). Then try not be sick on your shoes.

Top five cocktail bars

Cloud 23 @ The Hilton, Deansgate
Drink titles themed on Manchester. Over 2.5 times better than Cloud 9.

Grill on the Alley, Deansgate – Get sloshed before chowing down on a bloody big bloody steak.

Restaurant Bar + Grill, Deansgate
Table service means no Tom Cruise wannabes showing off to you.

Socio Rehab, Northern Quarter
It's all sweet and boozy here.

Rodeo, Northern Quarter – You won't find a better Margarita this side of Mexico.

Top five most notable toilets

Baa Baa, Deansgate – *Ally McBeal's* unisex toilets were cleaner than this.

Temple of Convenience, Southern Quarter – Small and great. Toilets: small and rancid.

Satan's Hollow, City Centre
Black urinals. We will say no more.

Lime, City Centre – An illuminated running-water wall is a lovely way to disguise a urinal, but it will leave you wondering where to piss.

Revise, Chorlton – Two cubicles: one unusable; the other struggling.

How to make your pint last all day

ARD UP, BUT LIKE NOTHING MORE THAN WHILING AWAY TIME IN A BOOZER? FEAR OT. A TRIP TO THE PUB NEEDN'T BREAK THE BANK

eep the pint cool – Get yourself ne of those chemical ice-packs for juries. After an hour or so, crack open, and wrap it around your everage. Hey presto: it's like you've st bought it.

o minesweeping – Some people st don't understand the value of the st two sips. Wait 'til these wasteful 'pes have left the pub, then nip over nd finish their backwash. Take the ass to the bar afterwards, and the ar staff'll love you so much they'll t you carry on all day.

reate fake identities – Running erilously low on that pint? Quick, retend it's your birthday and befriend the nearest person who looks like they might have full pockets. Drunk that one too? Tell someone you're about to become a parent. Necked that one as well? Well, there's no helping you then...

Play coin football – Fact: if you're not actually drinking, your drink lasts longer. Indulge in a nice game of coin footie instead. Place three coins in a triangle formation, then flick them forwards one by one, using the coin that's furthest back, sliding it between the other two. The target is the makeshift goal your opponent has made with his fingers

Get a job there – Hey, we've given you four top tips already. What more do you want from us? If you can't make a pint last all day with these gems, you're going to have to ask the landlord for a job.

Illustration by Si Clarke

Drink

ACADEMIC DISTRICT BARS

Big Hands

296 Oxford Road, Academic District
(0161) 272 7779

Flanked by Abdul's takeaway and the tiniest flower stall known to man lurks Big Hands, the diminutive unofficial stop-off for semi-famous musician types after Academy gigs. Even if you don't get to rub shoulders with the next big thing, it certainly ranks amongst the über-cool of Manchester bars. Regardless, it serves a damn fine selection of continental beers; and the kudos of bagging the window seat is worth the price of booze alone – despite the eventual replacement, a few years ago, of what was rumoured to be a bullet-holed pane.

Varies depending on Academy gigs

ACADEMIC DISTRICT PUBS

The Footage

137 Grosvenor Street, Academic District
(0161) 275 9164

The main battle here is trying not to insert a pool cue into the ear of the nearest tone-deaf fresher who's paid an ill-advised trip to the video jukebox. That aside, The Footage brings together students from all the worthy Oxford Road institutions – and the drinks are cheap. A Scream Yellow Card makes them even cheaper. And, Itchy admits begrudgingly, sometimes the tacky songs can brighten up your night. Depending on your intentions for the evening, an added bonus is the small dance floor.

Mon–Sat, 11am–2am;
Sun, 12pm–10.30pm

Kro Bar

325 Oxford Road, Academic District
(0161) 274 3100

Located directly opposite the Univers of Manchester's main campus are Kro's existence depends on luring students who feel they've outgrown th nappy-and-bib security of the unic bar – and are ready to step into th pseudo-trendy, Huggies pull-ups of th real world. The original of Manchester Danish-inspired Kro venues, the menu somehow both delicate and hearty – ar on sunny days the front terrace bulge Come to think of it, there is a shockir scarcity of beer gardens on Oxford Roa

Mon–Thu, 8.30am–12am; Fri, 8.30am–1am; Sat, 10.30am–1am;
Sun, 10.30am–10.30pm

Jabez Clegg

2 Portsmouth Street, Academic District
(0161) 272 8612

Like so many venues in Manchester, Jabe tries to take on too much – like eking o scrapings of butter over an enormou piece of toast. This results in a bare moistened mouthful. It puts on a bizar range of events, ranging from tasteful ne live music to downright tacky club night Apologies, Bop fans. On the other hand you could say it impressively straddle the spectrum of light entertainment. Th clientele is odd too – anyone from th thriftless student to the middle-aged lawye (probably in denial and hiding from his wife

Mon–Sun, 11am–11pm

The Bop club night, 10.30pm–3am; entry, £5

he Phoenix

ecinct Centre, Oxford Road, Academic District

161) 272 5921

ne Precinct Centre is dingy, sticky and a tle depressing – and so can is this place if ou're in the wrong mood. These features e unusual for a Scream pub, as most m for an open, bright layout – but this fference is actually a good thing: giving e Phoenix some character. The chain is s prominent in Manchester as anywhere ith a student population, so you know hat to expect. Big-screen footy, tunes ou've heard a million times already, omfy yet sweaty sofas and beermats at cling to your glass. Less predictable, owever is the jazz on Sunday lunchtimes.

Mon–Fri, 11.30am–11pm;
at–Sun, 12pm–11pm

ukes 92

3–25 Castle Street, Castlefield

161) 839 3522

ukes 92 and next-door restaurant lbert's Shed are part of the same peration, which makes it extremely andy if you fancy a meal with only a short tumble next door afterwards to continue ne evening with a few swift ones. Let's e honest, the last thing you want when ou're full of pizza or pasta (and possibly a queur coffee or two) is to trek all the way o the Northern Quarter. Or anywhere, for hat matter. There's plenty of room inside nd out (take note, smokers) – and the analside location is the icing on the cake.

Mon–Sat, 11am–11pm; Sun, 12pm–
0.30pm; food, Mon–Sun, 12pm–9pm

Prawn linguine, £7.50

CASTLEFIELD BARS

Barca Bar

Arches 8 & 9 Catalan Square, Castlefield

(0161) 839 7099

Mick Hucknall used to own this, or still part-owns it, or something. Actually, we think he might have sold it when money was too tight to mention. Old arches and canals weave around it and in summer the outdoor seating is unbeatable for atmosphere. Best visited when busy, as many of the staff tend to look bored the rest of the time, or maybe they're just pining for the Hucknall glory days. They do, however, seem to think you want to hear their taste in CDs FAR TOO LOUDLY.

Mon–Thu, 12pm–11pm; Fri–Sat,
12pm–2am; Sun, 12pm–10.30pm

CASTLEFIELD PUBS

The Ox Hotel

71 Liverpool Road, Castlefield

(0161) 839 7740

The good things about The Ox include the Sunday night pub quiz (where you can win a decent bottle of wine); the bedrooms that serve as its hotel function; its location; and its nice old-fashioned pub styling. The bad things... Well, the one thing that really lets it down is the service. The staff aren't too friendly (unless you're part of the Corrie cast) and the food takes longer to reach you than the formation of an oxbow lake. Sorry. You'd think it'd be easy to be funny about an Ox. But, apparently not...

Mon–Thu, 11am–11pm; Fri–Sat,
12pm–11pm; Sun, 12pm–10.30pm

CHORLTON BARS

The Bar

533 Wilbraham Road, Chorlton

(0161) 881 7576

The winner for most unoriginally named bar of all time. Chorlton has many, many drinkeries – and this one probably has the least tasteful sign of any of them. The décor isn't the best either, and don't get Itchy started on the toilets. But the buzz in The Bar, especially on a Friday night, is really quite special. The only downside is the crowding, but that's a small price to pay. If you're in the mood for a quiet night and a guaranteed comfy seat, you wouldn't be here in the first place, would you? No, exactly. So stop moaning.

Mon–Sat, 11am–11pm (approx); Sun, 12pm–3pm & 7pm–10.30pm

CITY CENTRE BARS

Billie Rox

106–108 Portland Street, City Centre

(0161) 228 2036

It may not be PC to say it, but, come on now, we were all thinking it. Those who frequent Billie Rox are essentially the trailer trash of Manchester. Menopausal women in sparkly boob tubes scrapping over white wine spritzers being egged on by fat, leery DJs who, for some unknown reason, take off their tops and want these harridans to do likewise. And for three nights a week you can see this all happening on wheels for their gouge-your-eyes-out-terrifying roller disco. Unless this kind of thing happens to turn you on, stay away.

Tue–Thu, 8pm–2am; Fri–Sat, 9pm–4am

CHORLTON PUBS

The Horse and Jockey

9 Chorlton Green, Chorlton

(0161) 881 6494

The last dying ember of the rave scei glows bravely on. On a Sunday afternoo the Horse and Jockey is the homing poi for legions of middle class bohemian type shaking off the remnants of the previou night's various intoxicants. Sometimes it hard to tell where the beer garden ends ar the village green begins as you elbow yo way through the white-man dreadlocks. fact, it's all so terribly middle class – yc get the feeling that if it rained, Cliff Richar might rock up to entertain the troop.

Mon–Thu, 12pm–11pm; Fri–Sat, 12pm–12am; Sun, 12pm–11pm

Fab Café

111 Portland Street, City Centre

(0161) 236 2019

Descending into Fab feels much like a vis to one of those musty, retro collectors dens. But here, instead of geeks gettin sweaty over back-issues of Flash Gordo you're greeted by a merry, down-to-eart clan, many of whom have obviously enjoye all three of the happy hours. Proud 80 children will delight in accompanying the pint with a game of Pac-Man; or boogyin to The Smiths next to a life-size Dalek Happily, leg-warmers and Princess Lei bikinis are not mentioned in the dress code

Mon, Wed & Thu, 4.45pm–2am; Tue, 4.45pm–1am; Fri–Sat, 4pm–2am; Sun, 6pm–12.30am

Fri–Sat, free before 10pm, £2 after

ribeca Bar & BED

) Sackville Street

)161) 236 8300

/ith a swanky Manhattan loft-style bar bove, and a luxurious dinner/drink/dance enue below, Tribeca and Bed excels s an unusual but infinitely stylish place ɔ spend an evening. Bed calls itself an underground ultra lounge and restaurant' that may sound like something from *'laderunner*, but it's an advanced concept vhich works wonders for the party-loving Manc crowds. With a damn fine menu, a st of champagnes and cocktails to please ven a Hilton sister, and a 'clean sheets nd stiff drinks' policy, this place prides self on being a little bit different and a ut above the rest. Manchattan's arrived.

Mon–Sun, 12pm–2am

Tiger Lounge

5 Cooper Street, City Centre

(0161) 236 6007

Boasting a variety of events from clubnights and cabaret to live music, Tiger Lounge is also beloved for holding one of the happiest hours in the city, with pints a mere £1.50 and bottles of wine just £5 before 8pm. And that's just for starters. As cult films flicker on vintage TV screens and burlesque lovelies smile down from the furry walls, you soon realise Tiger Lounge is not like other bars. It has a uniquely retro feel and situates itself proudly in the past, which is emphasised further by its kitsch, eclectic music policy. This place is naughty but very nice, which is just how we like it.

Mon–Thu, 12pm–2am; Fri, 12pm–2.30am; Sat, 3pm–3am; Sun, 5pm–2am

CITY CENTRE PUBS

Mr Thomas's Chop House

52 Cross Street, City Centre

(0161) 832 2245

Brilliantly old-looking, the peculiarly long-and-thin layout, the rare city centre exterior drinking area – and great food and drink. Yes, there are many things to like. As an example: one of Itchy's visits was on a rammed Saturday night. The restaurant, which takes up half the whole space, sat empty. Inches from the bar tables, no barrier of any kind. yet out-of-bounds. Unless you were the manager's mates, of course. Nice.

Evenings, Mon–Sun, 5.30pm–9.30pm; daytime, Mon–Fri, 11.30am–3pm; Sat, 11.30pm–4pm; Sun, 12pm–4pm

The Waterhouse

67–71 Princess Street, City Centre

(0161) 200 5380

A well-presented member of the Wetherspoons clan (yes, they really exist), The Waterhouse is named after the architect of the town hall (located opposite). On the down side, despite it being one of Manchester's first smoke-free pubs (that means no smoke), there's something stifling about The Waterhouse (sorry, we're just enjoying using brackets). There are lots of heavily-furnished rooms (that means lots of furniture) and a definite lack of fresh air or natural light (both desirable to most human beings in most situations). And the on-tap wine tastes distinctly of past-best Ribena (it shouldn't).

Sun–Thu, 9am–12am; Fri–Sat, 9am–1am

DEANSGATE BARS

Cloud 23

01 Deansgate, Deansgate

(0161) 870 1600

Cloud 23 is situated, surprisingly enough, on the 23rd storey of the Hilton Hotel in the Beetham Tower. A celebrity magnet and nemesis to anyone with a fear of heights. Or peculiar pinkish lighting. The upsides: it's a unique, exciting Manchester drinking experience. The downsides: the service makes you feel more like a shabby inconvenience than a welcome guest. The table service is improving, but still slow. And the place doesn't even open until evening. What a waste of a superb view.

Mon–Thu, 5pm–2am; Fri, 5pm–3am; Sat, 2.30pm–3am; Sun, 12pm–12am

Loaf

Arches 3a–5 Deansgate Locks, Deansgate

(0161) 819 5858

Rumour has it (well, the 'Spotted' pages of Heat) that this little gaff is a favourite haunt of the *Corrie* and *Hollyoaks* lot. Maybe in its heyday that might have been true, but as your granny will always tell you, 'Nowt's like it were in my day.' Now it's too tatty, too naff and too packed at the weekend with orange tans and cheap aftershave to attract even the soap crowd. Oh, and on Itchy's most recent visit, they were turning their noses up at hen parties as well. Talk about not using your Loaf.

Mon–Wed & Sun, 12pm-late;
Thu–Sat, 12pm–2am

Chicken club triple decker, £4.50

£11.95

The Living Room

80 Deansgate, Deansgate

(0870) 442 2537

Fancy rubbing shoulders with Justin Timberlake, or perhaps Posh and Becks? Well, nowadays at the Living Room you might have to settle for a D-list WAG, but it's still good for a cheeky cocktail or a bit of decent grub if you're out to impress. This Deansgate branch is exactly what you'd expect: passé (but comfy) leather sofas, and booths where the footballing lot try to hide. Nothing particularly stunning, but an all-round safe bet.

Mon–Tue & Sun, 10am–12am; Wed–Thu, 10am–1am; Fri–Sat, 10am–2am

Classic cheeseburger with mushroom and onion, £9.75

£13.95

Mojo

19 Back Bridge Street, Deansgate

(0161) 839 5330

Mojo is everything you'd expect from a rising star on the Mancunian rock scene: elusive and cool, you want to be its friend, but it couldn't give a toss. Despite the cocktails, you won't find any pretension here – though you couldn't blame it for blowing its own trumpet a bit. Its older brother in Leeds has seen the likes of Irvine Welsh and Liv Tyler mingle with a crowd of trendy students and musos. The Manc populace is similar, but you're more likely to be fighting your way through hordes of faux-hemians and scenesters. Nevertheless, Mojo is doing a great job of filling a very big pair of blue suede shoes.

Sun–Thu, 5pm–2am; Fri–Sat, 5pm–3am

Drink

Prohibition

2–10 St Mary's Street, Deansgate

(0870) 220 3026

Sister bar to the Living Room chain, but decidedly more intelligent in conception and reality, Prohibition is – yes, you guessed it – dedicated to the period of alcohol illegality in the US. It's an original concept for what's essentially just another themed bar, and it does a pretty good job. You don't actually believe you're in the 1920s, but then again, assuming you're not ridiculously impressionable, it would be hard to make you believe that anyway. And besides, it's far better than most themed bars, which offend with bland overkill. Walkabout, anyone?

Thu–Sat, 11am–2am; Sun–Wed, 11am–11pm

DEANSGATE PUBS

Moon Under Water

68–74 Deansgate, Deansgate

(0161) 834 5882

Boozer trivia: formerly a cinema, this is apparently the largest pub in Britain. Sad fact: size is not directly proportional to quality. The clincher: it's a Wetherspoons, and not one of the modern ones. Cheap lager, an eerily morgue-like ambience, and a no-music policy. It is packed at weekends, and should you enter, you will wait ages to be served, all the while looking nervously behind you, lest a wayward pint pot should approach at speed. Can't beat the prices, though.

Mon–Sat 11.30am–11pm; Sun, 12pm–10.30pm

The Restaurant Bar & Grill

14 John Dalton Street, Deansgate

(0161) 839 1999

Yeah, we know that several other cities now have one, but this is the original – and best. It does appear rather posh at first, but falling victim to inverse snobbery would be depriving yourself of a decent drinking experience. The staff are relaxed and polite and Itchy has never, ever seen anything kick off in here. And the table service is a godsend in busy periods. Fair enough the drink prices aren't quite as nice, but certainly no more than Deansgate's other aiming-for-posh-but-actually-a-scally magnet venues – where what your money has bought will end up all over your clothes.

Mon–Thu, 12am–11pm; Fri–Sat, 12pm–12am; Sun, 12pm–10.30pm

The Old Grapes

Little Quay Street, Deansgate

(0161) 839 4359

If you're a fan of Vera Duckworth, this is definitely the bar for you. The walls are adorned with pictures of her (plus a few other celebrities). Hmmm... Why should that be..? Could it possibly be because actress Liz Dawn owns the pub? Just up the road from Granada Studios and the Manchester Opera House, you're actually quite likely to run into a star or two. Alright it's hardly Hollywood, but don't say that to some of the posers. Aw, it's no good. We just can't get through this review without pointing out the obvious double entendre of Vera's Old Grapes. Yummy.

Mon–Sat, 12pm–11pm; Sun, 12pm–10.30pm

DIDSBURY BARS

The Metropolitan
Lapwing Lane, West Didsbury
(0161) 374 9559

The other venues of West Didsbury seem tiny beside this sprawling mansion of a place. The Met is all about making yourself feel more important. By the end of the evening, you're thinking of getting yourself a brandy and a cigar. The restaurant offers a range of bistro-style food including a fantastic Sunday lunch. That cigar is definitely in order, old chap.

Mon–Wed, 11.30am–11.30pm; Thu–Sat, 11.30am–12am; Sun, 12pm–11.30pm; Food, Mon–Thu, 12pm–9.30pm; Fri–Sat, 12pm–10pm; Sun, 12pm–9pm

Sunday lunch, £10.95

£15

DIDSBURY PUBS

The Didsbury
852 Wilmslow Road, Didsbury Village
(0161) 445 5389

The beer garden of The Didsbury used to be a village green, and you'll feel immersed in South Manchester's semi-rural history as your pint is pulled in the rustic bar. Mainly because of ye olde wood panelling and crumbly artefacts adorning every surface, but sometimes also because of the relaxed attitude of the bar staff. Now we know that sounds like we're having a bit of a dig, and we kind of are, but it's a bit like criticising Angelina Jolie for having slightly big lips. Sure it's a criticism, but at the end of the day, it would hardly stop you, would it?

Mon–Sun, 11am–11pm

Dog & Partridge
667 Wilmslow Road, Didsbury Village
(0161) 445 5322

Once upon a time, there lived a dog and a partridge. One day, the partridge really got on the dog's nerves, so the dog ate him. Then the dog wished he hadn't, and cried for days, even though dogs can't cry. The End. Hmm... Ok that story was pretty poor. Moving on, this pub would be the ideal place to take a visiting American friend who wants to see a ye olde English pub. Steer them away from the streamlined, soul-sucking chains and into this cavern of proper ales, proper old men, proper wooden beams and even a proper pub name. But ideally not when the football is on.

Mon–Sat, 12pm–11pm; Sun, 12pm–10.30pm

FALLOWFIELD BARS

Glass

258 Wilmslow Road, Fallowfield
(0161) 257 0770

Smack bang in the middle of the student ghetto, this three-tiered boozer is like Deep Heat slapped on the thigh of a rugger player – a cheap way to warm up for a scrum (but without quite the same hint of homoerotic frisson, sadly). Get your frugal little hands on a loyalty card and stretch those drinking muscles as far as your money. You can also survey the talent trawling past the entirely-transparent frontage, or strike your best pose and get yourself a cheeky wink to boost your confidence for the night.

Mon–Sat, 12pm–12am; Sun, 12pm–10.30pm

Sofa

236 Wilmslow Road, Fallowfield
(0161) 248 4820

In the middle of Fallowfield's busiest student ghetto, Sofa puts a comforting arm around those wide-eyed freshers still to be taught the ways of nightlife in Manchestershire. Drink offers and the odd well-chosen club night poster create an ideal middleman venue for a big night out. The quirky décor and chilled-out vibe also make this a suitable place to fall into the morning after the night before. Its matronly charms present plentiful nosh and coffee to soothe those sore, naive heads.

Mon–Sat, 12pm–11pm; Sun, 12pm–10.30pm

Revolution Bar

311–313 Wilmslow Road, Fallowfield
(0161) 225 7529

Revolution sports enough types of the clea stuff to impress a Russian army – but with serving staff infinitely better-looking than Stalin. Becoming a Privilege cardholder means that you get deals on food and drinks that would make David Dickinson go weak at the knees. Great cocktails abound too, and will almost certainly ensure that your night is unforgettable. Or very forgettable. Oh, and drinking chilli vodka is not big or clever. It's rank.

Mon–Sun, 11.30am–1am

Fully-loaded flatbread, £5.95 (with Privilege card friends eat free)

£8 (with Privilege card); £6.50 for two cocktails (with Privilege card)

Trof

2a Landcross Road, Fallowfield
(0161) 224 0467

Trof is essentially a student living room without the slug trails and mouldy socks. Random crap adorns every surface of this converted house's ground floor, which somehow accommodates seating room, a bar, kitchen, (a small person's) toilet and a DJ booth. Daytimes see the Trof Royal Brekkie littering every table as students crawl in after a night out and continue drinking. A more grown-up, (yet still quirky) version has been launched in the Northern Quarter.

Mon–Sun, 9am–12am

FALLOWFIELD PUBS

The Drop Inn

389–393 Wilmslow Road, Fallowfield

(0161) 286 1919

Walking into this place is like walking into a Bulgarian youth hostel in the off season – but instead of over-friendly Europeans wielding table tennis bats, there are nicotine-yellow Mancunian divorcees. The décor looks as if it was found in a skip outside an office block in Trafford, while the curious 'room of sofas' indicates poor map reading by a delivery truck driver on the way to a DFS summer clearout. If you are very local, a borderline alcoholic and have the loyalty of a well-trained Basset hound, this could be the pub for you.

Mon–Sun, 11am–11pm

The Orange Grove

304 Wilmslow Road, Fallowfield

(0161) 224 1148

'STUDENTS ONLY' should be emblazoned across the entrance – but that would deprive the door staff of the pleasure of turning away people old enough to know better. But believe Itchy, being an undergraduate is part of enjoying this place, so don't feel left out. Cheap drinks, popular music, pool tables, quiz machines and the like. If it's sunny, there's the grassy beer garden with a view of Fallowfield. It really couldn't be any more stereotypical. Nothing wrong with that, though, it's all part of the experience.

Mon–Sat, 12pm–2am; Sun, 12pm–12.30am

Mon–Sat, £1 after 10pm

Friendship Inn

353 Wilmslow Road, Fallowfield

(0161) 224 5758

The last bastion of (sort of) civilised drinking in the student jungle of Fallowfield. A mini-Utopia free from the horrors of Sambuca-coated Scream bars. If your only wish is to drink and chat with a group of mates, without shite conversation-stopping music putting a damper on your evening, here's the promised land. Locals and students alike can quaff a reasonably-priced ale side-by-side without a hint of animosity. It's also an ideal place to watch the footie, as screens are in plentiful supply. Calling the ref a wanker has never been such a relaxed passtime.

Mon–Sat, 12pm–11pm; Sun, 12pm–10.30pm

Queen of Hearts

256 Wilmslow Road, Fallowfield

(0161) 249 0271

Don't forget your student ID and beer goggles. Like so many of its type, the massive Scream pub affectionately known as the Queen of Tarts is a student hive combining cheap drinks, cheap thrills, pool – and quite possibly one of the best nights out in Fallowfield for NUS types. During the day you can relax and have a beer with friends in the tree-lined garden. Into late evening you'll find yourself dancing and flirting with anyone and everyone. Why oh why does that always feel right at the time?

Mon–Tue, 11am–11.30pm; Wed, 11am–1am; Thu–Sat, 11am–2am; Sun, 12pm–10.30pm

Fri–Sat, £3 after 10pm

MILLENNIUM QUARTER BARS

Paparazzi

2a The Printworks, 27 Withy Grove, Millennium Quarter
(0161) 832 1234

Brings together the style and glamour of Manchester and mixes it up in an r 'n' b and hip hop dance mix. Or thinks it does. You'd better be wearing smart shoes or you'll be home with a nice cup of hot chocolate, courtesy of the strict door policy. Yup, Paparazzi is one of those places. The entrance fee isn't cheap; and neither are the drinks. Also, watch out for the money beggars in the toilets. The old mobile trick works a treat.

Mon–Tue, 9pm–2am; Wed, 10pm–2.30am; Thu & Sun, 9pm–2.30am; Fri, 10pm–3am; Sat, 10pm–4am

Free before 10pm; £5 after; £7 after 11pm

Waxy O'Connors

The Printworks, Corporation Street, Millennium Quarter
(0161) 835 1210

No, you're not mental. There actually is an Irish voice booming away at you while you're in the toilet. A sort of far less useful version of those Learn Italian tapes you get in places like Frankie and Benny's. There's also the twisty, tree-like, cubby-hole-filled layout and décor; which is either cosy or claustrophobic, depending on your mood. On the whole, not bad at all... just a shame it's a chain in the Printworks instead of a genuine pub. Fake ancient woodwork isn't too convincing in an old printing press building in the middle of Manchester.

Mon–Wed, 12pm–11pm; Thu, 12pm–12am; Fri–Sat, 12pm–1am; Sun, 12pm–10.30pm

Tiger Tiger

Units 5–6, Printworks, Millennium Quarter
(0161) 385 8080

A venue strictly for the shirt-and-shoes brigade, Tiger Tiger is to be avoided at all costs unless you're (a) a *Big Brother* loser, (b) a teenage footballer with bad hair and acne, or (c) someone who aspires to be either (or both) of the above. At weekends it's packed out, mostly with punters who fit into category (c). If you do have the misfortune to end up in here, don't worry – the bar staff are having even less fun than you. Mind you, they're not paying a ridiculous price for the privilege. And if you think we've missed a category, don't hesitate to compile a list of your own.

Mon–Sat, 12pm–2am; Sun, 12pm–12.30am

MILLENNIUM QUARTER PUBS

Sinclair's Oyster Bar

2 Cathedral Gates, Millennium Quarter
(0161) 834 0430

A bit of old England in the middle of the Millennium Quarter. It may not look like the most robust of buildings, but this pub has an action-story past that Indiana Jones himself would be proud of. Sinclair's and its neighbour The Old Wellington – known as The Great Survivors – have been moved twice, brick-for-brick: once when the Arndale was built in the 1970s, and again after the 1996 bomb, when Manchester's ill-conceived shopping square The Shambles was blown to bits. Visit it before it gets taken apart again.

Mon–Sat, 11am–11pm; Sun, 12pm–10.30pm

Why not
advertise
in
Itchy?

NORTHERN QUARTER BARS

Bluu

Smithfield Market, Thomas Street, Northern Quarter
(0161) 839 7195

Bluu combines some of the tastiest bar grub Itchy has had the pleasure of eating ,an amazing cocktail menu and nice big comfy leather couches. The perfect venue to meet your mates and whine about the office bitch while slowly getting plastered. Better watch the evil colleague in question isn't also hiding in a leather seat nearby (and complaining about you).

Sun–Mon, 12pm–12am; Tue–Thu, 12pm–1am; Fri–Sat, 12pm–2am; food, Mon–Sun, 12pm–6pm

Homemade fish finger buttie with tartar sauce, £5.50

Common

39–41 Edge Street, Northern Quarter
(0161) 832 9245

Actually, we say it's rather uncommonly good. There's a certain playground charm to Common, with its plastic chairs and cartoon-style walls. One of the better alcohol-toting establishments in the area, the atmosphere is less oppressive than the nearby competition, combining a light and airy café feel with a quaint Eastern European bar vibe. It serves everything from frankly silly continental fruit beers to top-shelf absinthe for the more thrillingly bohemian among you. Oh, and read the small print on the menu; it's good for a chuckle.

Mon–Wed, 12pm–12am; Thu, 12pm–1am; Fri, 12pm–2am; Sat, 1pm–2am; Sun, 2pm–12am

Cafe Bar Centro

74 Tib Street, Northern Quarter
(0161) 835 2863

What do a table of young professionals, a tramp, three scallies and some generic indie boys have in common? Nothing at all, you may say, apart from providing a handy cross-section of modern society. But you'd be wrong. The answer is that apparently they can all eat under the same roof and not feel out of place. It's easy to love Centro for this alone; it gets away from the almost-mandatory über-chic scene of the Northern Quarter – and allows for all to eat fresh ciabatta and some extraordinary hummus for pocket change. Character without pretensions: always a bonus.

Mon–Wed, 12pm–11pm; Thu–Sat, 12pm–1am; Sun, 12pm–10.30pm

Cord

8 Dorsey Street, Northern Quarter
(0161) 832 9494

If navigating around the Northern Quarter wasn't already like solving the *Crystal Maze*, some bright spark decided to conceal a beaut of a bar like Cord down a non-event of a side street. You'd never know it was there until, come 9pm, the place suddenly reappears like a desert mirage. Visit with those who know its whereabouts, or you'll end up wandering around in circles and getting asked if you want business by the same prostitute for the third time in 15 minutes. Oh, and yes, the walls really ARE covered in a putrid shade of brown cord. Ps. Good luck finding a seat.

Mon–Thu, 12pm–11pm; Fri–Sat, 12pm–1am; Sun, 4pm–10.30pm

Dry Bar

28–30 Oldham Street, Northern Quarter

(0161) 236 9840

The shaggy-haired, bandy-legged regulars of Dry Bar look rather like the ghosts of Manchester past. They sit at the minimalist tables, nursing their pints of Stella and gazing misty-eyed into the middle distance, thinking back to the good old days when this place was the setting for all kinds of shenanigans, Shaun Ryder, gunshots et al. All this makes the place feel more like a museum than a bar. Give it another decade, and the city council will have renamed it The Official Madchester Experience and be charging a fiver in on the door. Oh hang on – they do that anyway.

Mon–Thu, 11am–1am; Fri–Sat, 11am–2am; Sun, 12pm–10.30pm

Lammars

57 Hilton Street, Northern Quarter

(0161) 237 9058

Itchy isn't being lazy here, but this place really does try its best to deny categorisation. Blissfully snuggled at the end of a seemingly redundant alley in the Northern Quarter, Lammars boasts décor which could be described as semi-art nouveau... And semi-car-boot-sale clutter. Relying on word-of-mouth publicity, it remains a well-kept secret. But now, you too can enjoy its live jazz bands and jams on Wednesdays and Thursdays, and Fat City DJs at the weekend. The chunky sofas and well-filled glasses of wine aren't too bad either.

Mon–Sun, 12pm–1am; happy hour: Mon–Fri, 5pm–7pm

Odd

30–32 Thomas Street, Northern Quarter

(0161) 833 0070

Firmly established in the Northern Quarter family of bars, but still retaining enough character to set it apart, Odd is like the bar equivalent of your cousin with the weird haircut who's actually alright once you chat to him. The range of food and booze on offer is vast and the staff are so friendly you want to wrap them up in a hanky and smuggle them out of the door with you. Although you should be aware that human trafficking is still illegal, apparently. A new addition to the concept, Odder, has so far flaunted itself successfully on Oxford Road in the city's southern quarter.

Mon–Sat, 11am–11pm; Sun, 11am–10.30pm

Rodeo Bar

Edge Street, Northern Quarter

On paper, the concept of Rodeo is fantastic: setting up a Mexican-style Margarita bar in an area which thrives on being retro and alternative. However, Itchy is sorry to report that Rodeo is somewhat disappointing and it's largely due to service issues. The layout resembles a dentist's waiting room and the decidedly warm beer (though that may be authentically Mexican; we're not sure) served by the ultra-surly, disinterested bar staff tops off the feeling of discontent. Unless you love tequila, of which they have many varieties, then you're better off heading next door.

Sun–Wed, 12pm–12am; Thu–Sat, 12pm–4am

Socio Rehab

100–102 High Street, Northern Quarter

(0161) 832 4529

David says cocktails make you hard. Well, according to the menu, anyway. And the bartenders at Socio Rehab are not shy about sloshing in the Zubrowka with vigour, sliding the drinks down the bar in a slick free-flowing relay race of cocktails. It's not cheap and the music smacks a little of 90s girl band, but the feel is stripped-down, no-nonsense and good value for money; while maintaining the feel of a darkened living room in a Spanish villa. If rehab's this much fun, then it's no wonder Lindsay Lohan et al can't stay away.

Sun–Thu, 5pm–12am; Fri–Sat, 5pm–1am

Trof

5–8 Thomas Street, Northern Quarter

(0161) 832 1870

If the name seems familiar, it's because this is a city centre offshoot of the Fallowfield student favourite. And with its range of foreign beers, good solid bar food and its occasional live band nights, this place makes a welcome addition to the extended Northern Quarter family. Three floors offer wooden simplicity or plush comfort, depending on where you prefer to plant yourself. Itchy has also on occasion witnessed some of the most original and hilarious graffiti we have ever seen in the bogs here.

Mon–Sat, 9am–2am; Sun, 9am–12am

NORTHERN QUARTER PUBS

Bar Fringe

Swan Street, Northern Quarter

(0161) 835 3815

Considering the cosmopolitan district in which it finds itself, Bar Fringe is a true anomaly. In one corner, grumbling old men nurse pints of John Smiths; in the other, lonely men in their mid 30s slump in their post-work suits and ties. Bar Fringe is the epitome of the 1970s English pub. It's like *Life On Mars* without the cool soundtrack and little hope of returning to the present. For the young professionals who stumble in to get half a Früli and listen to Mr Scruff, it's a slight shock to the system. But it'll probably do 'em good.

Mon–Sun, 11am–11pm

Marble Arch

73 Rochdale Road, Northern Quarter

(0161) 832 5914

Stepping into the Marble Arch is like stepping into a Victorian drinking den, and you half expect to see a couple of rakes loitering in the corner with frock coats and top hats. Or at least it would be like a Victorian drinking den, were it not for the organic beers – brewed on the premises – and a whiff of gastropub in the bar menu. But these nods to the 21st century are well balanced by splendid tiled walls, panelled ceilings and engraved glass lampshades. Disconcertingly, especially after a few, the floor follows the slope of the hill beneath it. The beer's lovely too, and being organic, almost counts as a health drink. Surely?

Mon–Sun, 12pm–12am

The Bay Horse

35–37 Thomas Street, Northern Quarter

(0161) 661 1041

Is it a pub? Is it a bar? Well, it's sort of both, actually, but somehow manages to offer the best of both worlds. Aside from an outrageously expensive pool table (a pound a game, in this district?), The Bay Horse is a decent halfway house between the established boozers and the trendy bars of the Northern Quarter. Like most hybrid pub/bars punching successfully above their weight division, they manage to draw in their potential punters with a crafty and alluring mix of pub quizzes and acoustic nights on different evenings throughout the week.

Mon–Fri, 12pm–11pm; Sun, 12pm–10.30pm

SOUTHERN QUARTER BARS

Cornerhouse

70 Oxford Street, Southern Quarter

(0161) 228 2463

It's actually ok to go in here without being an indie cinema luvvie. The number of floaty scarves in the bar might suggest otherwise, but the Cornerhouse is a Manchester institution. Quiz nights, DJ sets, culture deals and decent, well-priced pizzas on the bar menu are all on offer – and it's flanked on all sides by bus stops, a railway station, a taxi rank, shops and alternative eating and drinking venues. Now that may sound practical and boring to some of you, but it's actually very bloody handy.

Mon–Wed, 9.30am–11pm; Thu–Sat, 9.30am–12am; Sun, 11.30am–10.30pm

Drink

Font Bar

7–9 New Wakefield Street, Southern Quater

(0161) 236 0944

With a huge menu of freshly-cooked grub at bargain prices (including hangover-repellent Sunday roasts), great music, free wifi and a dazzling selection of real ales and continental beers, it's not surprising Font's incredibly popular. Especially with their delicious range of fontastic cocktails, served all day every day for only £2. If you opt for some smart–mouthed shooters, you've got an evening of wisecracking fun lined up with the bartender: start with a 'slippery nipple', move on to a 'toilet cracker' and wind up with a 'brain haemorrhage'. See, you too can be just like Elvis.

Mon–Sat, 12pm–1am; Sun, 12pm–12.30pm

Odder

14 Oxford Road, Southern Quarter

(0161) 238 9131

Odder, sister venue of the Northern Quarter's Odd, opened without much fanfare. Some were sceptical about its prospects, but naysayers must now be spluttering into their cocktails. Odder is buzzing at weekends, with an attractively kooky interior, bars on both floors, a small dance floor and a cracking menu. The bad bit: due to the venue's popularity and a slack attitude by some staff, you might find yourself waiting for longer than you'd like. Upside: almost everything else – especially the food.

Mon–Wed, 11am–12am; Thu–Sat, 11am–2am; Sun, 11am–12am; food: Mon–Sun, 11am–9pm

Rain Bar

80 Great Bridgewater Street, Southern Quarter

(0161) 235 6500

Rain Bar is the type of grand spacious pub with maze-like Victorian-style rooms that gets the balance just right between Sunday afternoon hangover haven and Friday night piss-up port. If there were a downside to the place, it would possibly be that it's located annoyingly near the financial and conferencing part of town, so as well as the usual range of sauce artists it does tend to get a lot of those slightly-desperate post-work yuppie-types looking to drown their accountancy-related sorrows; but it manages to keep its authentic feel all the same.

Mon–Thu, 12pm–11pm; Fri–Sat, 12pm–12am; Sun, 12pm–6pm

Retro Bar

78 Sackville Street, Southern Quarter

(0161) 274 4892

By day, Retro Bar is a great, dependable place for a pint, some greasy food and a game of pool. But by night, it certainly knows how to let its hair down and have some fun. With a clutch of cool club nights that play anything from rockabilly and punk to brand new indie, there's something for everyone. And if the great music isn't enough, you'll also find a dirt-cheap doubles bar and the friendliest dance floor in Manchester, where trampling on people's feet and shouting drunken abuse at everyone who 'gets in your way' is not looked upon kindly.

Sun–Thu, 9am–2am; Fri–Sat, 9am–3am

£5 between 4pm and 7pm

Temple of Convenience

Great Bridgewater Street, Southern Quarter

(0161) 228 9834

This venue is a toilet, quite literally. It's a converted public convenience at the top of Oxford Road. It contains one of the best jukeboxes, one of the smallest bars, and two of the most rancid cubicles in the whole of these islands, which is hardly surprising given that at one stage everywhere in the place was fair game for taking a piss. One cubicle was wallpapered with pages from Fear And Loathing In Las Vegas last time Itchy visited, which was praiseworthy – but in no way made up for the dankness. Definitely a good pub overall, for the 50 per cent of us who wee standing up anyway.

Mon–Sun, 4pm–11pm

SOUTHERN QUARTER PUBS

The Thirsty Scholar

50 New Wakefield Street, Southern Quarter

(0161) 236 6071

There's definitely a peculiar attraction to the Scholar. Tucked underneath Oxford Road Station, it's a compact, ramshackle old place with awkward seating arrangements. But it's cosy, brilliantly situated and the bar staff do their best to slice through the swathes of students – none of whom seem to know that ordering one drink each is REALLY IRRITATING for everyone behind them. Check out the gigs in the Attic upstairs.

Mon–Sun, 12pm–12am

Sandbar

120–122 Grosvenor Street, Southern Quarter

(0161) 273 3141

This is a typical postgrad place. Why does Itchy say that? Well, the wispy beards of the eternal students are out in full force here. But these older academic types often have surprisingly excellent taste in bars. We suppose they need a haven where they can escape from all the harrowing amounts of reading they have to do. It's as if they've intellectually examined the merits of every venue in reach, with meticulous, quiet observation – then made this their own, even encouraging the evolution of a thoroughly satisfying jukebox.

Mon–Sun, 11am–12pm

WITHINGTON BARS

Fuel Café Bar

448 Wilmslow Road, Withington

(0161) 282 6040

When Fuel is full, you'd think they were trying to force a game of sardines. But on a lazy Sunday morning, it's great. The venue is just over the road from another Withington student haunt, Solomon Grundy's, but is a slightly less formal experience – if that's possible. Colourful art adorns the walls and the whole place oozes ramshackle chic. Fuel is also a vegetarian paradise – the menu is excellent – and they serve what are probably the best homemade chips in town.

Mon–Sat, 10am–late; Sun, 10am–11.30pm; food, Mon–Sun, 12pm–9pm; breakfast, Mon–Sun, 10am–4pm

Pleasure

489 Wilmslow Road, Withington

(0161) 434 4300

Despite its name and rather suggestive red curtains, Pleasure isn't some kind of seedy smut den waiting to corrupt your little sister. While it is vaguely possible that you might come across some sleazy-looking men letting their bulldogs run amok around the tables, Pleasure boasts a relaxed buzz and cheap drinks. Their food menu is an elusive creature, but if you happen to be there at the right time – God knows when that is – they'll sort you out with the best four quid steak and chips you'll ever have. Perhaps that's the sort of pleasure that's on offer.

Mon–Thu, 12pm–12am; Fri, 12pm–1am; Sat, 11am–1am; Sun, 11am–12am

WITHINGTON PUBS

The Red Lion

532 Wilmslow Road, Withington

(0161) 434 2441

The Red Lion feels immediately familiar. There's an exact replica in every village/small town/hamlet, and they're all probably called the Red Lion too. Slightly grimy leather seats that have seen better days, averagely-priced drinks, a quiz night and array of small, confusing rooms. It's a little off the beaten track, but this doesn't keep people away by any means – families, students and locals all cluster here throughout the week. Definitely more welcoming in character than any other 'traditional' pub in Withington, especially its white-titled counterpart.

Solomon Grundy

447–449 Wilmslow Road, Withington

(0161) 445 6722

Come in. Chill out. Fancy a burger? Or just a coffee maybe? They'll be right with you... In about 15 minutes. But hey, what's the rush? Just soak up the eclectic mix of bohemian and rustic décor, chat with your mates over large wooden tables, decide which continental beer to have with your steak ciabatta, or maybe share a chocolate fudge cake with your best friend. Most of all, take your time. Weird name aside, Solomon Grundy is all about the relaxed atmosphere, friendly staff and good food.

Mon–Thu, 11am–11pm; Fri–Sat, 10.30am–12am; Sun, 10am–10.30pm; food, 'til 5pm

Pork & leek sausages with mash, £6.90

£12.60

OTHER

Arch Bar

2 Hulme Walk, Hulme
(0161) 227 7550

If airports had security like Arch Bar, Al-Qaeda wouldn't have a prayer. It's allegedly the preferred watering hole of the area's bad boys. But maybe, just maybe, this is where the toughs go when they want to drink Babycham, chat about who's had a baby, who's getting fat, who had the best haircut on *Friends*, etc. Once you're past the Tyson lookalikes and metal detectors, the atmosphere is actually rather jolly. The most intimidating thing about the place is the external blue tiling, which makes it look like a massive public bog.

Mon–Sat, 11am–11pm; Sun, 12pm–10.30pm

The Rampant Lion

17 Anson Road, Victoria Park
(0161) 248 0731

If there's one thing you don't want a lion to be when you come face to face with one, it's rampant. Looming like some haunted gothic inn you would be forgiven for expecting the clientele here to send you away, advising you to 'stick to the roads'. Once you're in though, this cozy boozer is as inviting as it is bohemian. The prices seem to contradict the obvious student appeal, but the beer garden, warm atmosphere and mini-festivals make it a great place to relax with a cold one – especially in summer.

Mon–Thu, 12pm–1am; Fri–Sat, 12pm–2pm; Sun, 12pm–12:30am

Sunday roast, £7.95

£7

Hardy's Well

257 Wilmslow Road, Rusholme
(0161) 257 0450

Finding a pub in Rusholme is no easy task, but you can't miss this one. As it's visible from the bus route, it has a white exterior, and on top of all that there's a Lemn Sissay poem painted in black lettering on the side. There's no getting away from the fact that it's bleak, with its beer garden of pure concrete and neon curry house surroundings a positively depressing experience, but then beggars can't be choosers. If you live in Rusholme this is a safer bet than some of the pubs located further away from mainstream eyes. Seriously, don't even think about it

Sun–Thu, 4pm–11pm; Fri–Sat, 5pm–12pm

The Apsley Cottage

Apsley Grove, Ardwick
(0161) 273 3657

Just as you wouldn't wade into a pool of hungry alligators with a Pepperami, don't underestimate the good-time potential of this petite firecracker of a pub. Nestled behind performance arena The Apollo, it's busiest on show nights and perfect for a pre-gig pint or even a game of sardines. With a musical history that puts Live Aid to shame, it's worth a visit on quieter nights to peruse walls adorned with backstage passes and famous faces. The Guinness is great, the wine best avoided; no airs or graces, cash only. A nice honest slice of rock and roll.

Mon–Sun, 12pm–11pm (late licence at management's discretion)

Dance

INTRODUCING A NEW WAY TO SAVE POTS OF CASH

Imagine a world where food and booze is free, where you can walk into a nightclub for nothing, and where cinemas don't charge you to watch the latest flick...

Ok, so that's slightly wishful thinking, but we've got the next best thing. With discounts of up to 50% off your bill, the Itchy City Card lets you enjoy the best of Manchester's bars, pubs and restaurants for less. And in our book, that means twice as much fun...

Other wallet-friendly offers include 2-for-1 deals at cinemas, comedy venues and theatres, as well as discounts at gyms, beauty salons, shops and many other venues all over town.

All you need to do to get involved is to get yourself on the internet, log on and sign up for your card at **www.itchycitycard.co.uk** and start saving oodles of wonga. See the page opposite for a taster of participating City Card venues.

Get up to 50% off at venues including...

RESTAURANTS

nk Bar and Grill
Choice Bar and Restaurant
Didsbury Village Restaurant
The Northern Quarter Restaurant
Sapporo Teppanyaki
Beluga
Try Thai
East
Hanaan
City Café
Sweet Mandarin
Villaggio
Relish
La Tasca
The Ox
Linen
Numero
Livebait
Brasserie Blanc
Yang Sing
Palmiro
Dilli
Obsidian
Opus One

BARS & CAFES

Simple Bar
Piccadilly Lounge
Slug and Lettuce
Sweet Mandarin
Beluga
Rice bar
Bar Est
Tribeca

ENTERTAINMENT

AMC Cinemas
The Comedy Store
The Palace Theatre
The Opera House

HEALTH & FITNESS

GL14 Health Club
Fitness First
Theraphysique Sports Massage
Sunshine Studios

SALONS & SPAS

Sienna Spa
The Gentry Grooming Co
Terence Paul Hairdressing
Nicky Clarke Salons
Heaven Spa

SHOPS & LIVING

Selfridges Moet Bar
Selfridges Food Hall
Eliotts Prestige Car Rental
The White Company
Stuart Jones Styling Opticians
The Mall Dental clinic
Bang & Olufsen
Innerform
Strictly Bespoke Personal Tailoring
Martine Alexander Personal Shopping
Sunshine Photography Studios

Right on Queue!

DO YOU EVER FIND YOURSELF STANDING IN A LONG LINE TO ENTER A CLUB, GET A DRINK OR GO FOR A PEE? THEN YOU'LL FIND ITCHY'S Q-TIPS ON WAYS TO AMUSE YOURSELF WHILE YOU HANG ABOUT WORTH THEIR WAIT IN GOLD

Get the party started before you even hit the floor. Just bring a bag of thick elastic bands to hand out to fellow queue-tey pies, and get everyone to pluck a different note. When you're at the bar, try blowing over the tops of bottles to entertain the other punters. If you're good enough, they might throw you enough loose change to pay for your drink.

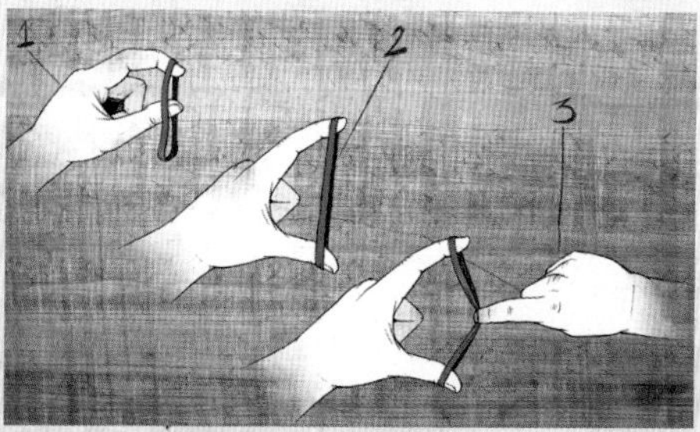

Illustration by Si Clarke

Before striding out, get down to the pound shop and buy a big bottle of the foulest perfume you can find, or even better, nip to a fishing shop and get your mitts on a bottle of lobster essence used for scenting baits. When waiting for a loo cubicle, pretend to be a toilet attendant, and offer exiting punters a free spritz of 'fragrance'. Every pongy person you zap with your minging musk is one fewer rival to compete against in the pulling stakes.

Or you can try the following trick. Start your evening at home by chowing down on beans and bhuna. Later, when you find yourself so far back in line that the folk at the front are in a different postcode, let the gas go. Watch the crowds shrink as they run from your stink, and try to figure out who it was who let rip. Don't strain too hard though, unless you fancy wandering home with the contents of your bowels sloshing around your smalls.

CLUBS

42nd Street

Bootle Street

(0161) 831 7108

42nd Street is a curious compromise between a trendy indie club and a chavtastic drunken ruckus. Every night threatens to descend into complete Redbull-charged carnage, yet somehow the music pulls people back from the abyss. Passionate 'Madchester' types ensure a semblance of structure to the evening, as 90s indie classics provide the backbone to the club's identity. Best of all, you can cover the night's festivities with a tenner – including a kebab and the bus ride home.

Times vary; doors open at 10pm

£3 before 10.30pm, £4 after

The Brickhouse

6 Whitworth Street West

(0161) 236 4418

Those who never got over the loss of the Hacienda can find a home here, as tunes from the Madchester era are the mainstay. It's an odd place; all kind of black and dusty, but with a high main ceiling and mezzanine level (complete with tables covered in spills from others' drinks – but that's all part of the atmosphere). It's plenty of fun, as long as you're not really bothered what you're drinking and are happy to get dirty while you dance. And we mean that in a literal sense, not in a Patrick Swayze sense. Although you can choose to dance like that if you so wish.

Fri–Sat, 10.30pm–2.30am

Prices vary

The Attic

59 New Wakefield Street, Southern Quarter

(0161) 236 6071

No ghosties in this lofty space – none that Itchy knows of anyway – but that doesn't stop it getting a bit scary sometimes. For starters there's the treacherous and windy staircase up to the entrance, and once you're up it, you'll be shrieking at a completely different kind of bumping in the night. Oooh, cheeky. The Attic is moodily-lit and intimate (read 'dark and small'), but despite its diminutive stature the attic is no shrinking violet. It consistently offers a range of the best to be had on the rich and varied Manchester music scene, with their DJ sets and gig evenings ranked highly on all levels.

Thu–Fri, 11pm–2am; Sat, 11pm–3am

Jilly's Rockworld

65 Oxford Street, City Centre

(0161) 236 9971

To sum up the kind of place this is, imagine a short, skinny indie kid trying to chat up a 6'5", leather-clad goth girl. Yes, optimistic, but also odd and proud of it. Emo kids cry into their reasonably-priced beers, while some are fuelled purely by their sense of melancholic self-indulgence. The TARDIS of Manchester's alternative clubs, Jilly's is a veritable labyrinth of goths, ravers, metalheads and scenesters; the modest exterior giving no hint of the vast, bizarre bounty that lies beyond.

Thu & Sat, 9pm–3am; Fri, 9pm–7am

Thu, £1.50 (free before 10.30pm with flyer); Fri–Sat, £5.50 (£1 off before 11pm with flyer); £4 concs

Joshua Brooks

106 Princes Street, Southern Quarter

(0161) 273 7336

Often overlooked as just a pit stop for those on the Oxford Road circuit, Joshua Brooks manages to draw in the 5th Ave-bound with its laid back upstairs bar. It also embraces underground scenes, quite literally; its basement club nurturing a whole host of Manchester's burgeoning nights. A diaspora of musical styles and scenes happily clash from night to night. But let's be honest... It's mired deep in student-ness and as such revolves heavily around pissed-ness (or inebriation for those of you who prefer real words). Still, that's fine with us.

Last Friday of the month, 11pm–3am

£8.95

M2

Peter Street, City Centre

(0161) 839 1112

Itchy thought about avoiding bein judgemental, but it's impossible. The girl here tend to be those who've grabbed the best wannabe outfit from the back of the wardrobe – the tartier, the better. Thos who haven't stick out like Paris Hilton i a prison cell. This may explain why th male clientele outnumber the female b about three-to-one. Drinks are expensiv and so is the entry fee, but if you're int mainstream, new-style r 'n' b and danc (and cattle markets), you'll have an absolut whale of a time. And by 'whale' we don' mean the girl/guy you'll end up with

Wed–Thu, 10pm–2am; Fri–Sat, 10pm–late

£3–£5, 10.30pm–11.30pm; £7 after

Mint Lounge

46–50 Oldham Street, Northern Quarter

(0161) 228 1495

Some Mancunians believe 46 Oldham Street stands on cursed ground. In the early 2000s, clubs opened and closed at such a rate that the discovery of an ancient Indian burial ground beneath it would have been no surprise. But in 2004, the dingy basement magically transformed into Mint Lounge. DJ residencies from a bunch of local heroes have replaced the nipple tassles and it's made a name for excellent music, plus a good-looking, fun-loving crowd. So it looks like all those superstitious souls were wrong. Or maybe all the other clubs were crap.

Fri–Sat, 10pm–3am; other nights vary

Fri–Sat, £5; other nights vary

The Music Box

65 Oxford Road, Southern Quarter

(0161) 273 5200

Underneath one of the busiest roads in Europe lies a hidden cavern filled with musical gems. Perfectly positioned, The Music Box is not hard to find – but once trapped in its devilish depths, you'll find it incredibly difficult to leave. Making up for its cramped interior with atmosphere and music, this venue changes music policy like a chameleon, offering a Pick 'n' Mix selection to sweeten any tooth. Home to monthly nights such as Electric Chair and Mr Scruff's Keep it Unreal, it stays fresh and refuses to be neatly packaged.

Wed–Thu, 8pm–12am;
Fri–Sat, 10pm–3am

Prices vary

One Central Street

Central Street, City Centre

(0161) 211 9000

If you're seeking a quiet pint and deep conversation, this ain't the place. Youngsters with scissor-sharp barnets and flashy rags; a music policy almost as strict as the dress code; and cheeky flirting by loan spenders – that's more the flavour here. One of Manchester's trendier venues, One Central is lucky enough to boast a weekly Romp – its most popular club night. So, if you're feeling in need of escape from the city's rougher spots, and the world in general, lose yourself in admiring the chic interior. Who needs current affairs discussions when you've got eye candy?

Thu–Sat, 10pm–3am

£4–£7

Pure

Withy Grove, Printworks, Millennium Quarter

(0161) 819 7770

A lot of money has been ploughed into Pure to make it the swankiest bar in the Printworks. That it is – when it's empty. The problem with the Printworks bars is that they cater for the lowest common denominator. They're big places and huge sums have been invested into making them very attractive, but to recoup this, they'll fill them with virtually anybody. Pure attempts to be selective but is still full of alcopops, those new to social drinking, work dos, stag dos and hen dos. If you've got any self-respect, just don't.

Mon & Wed, 10pm–3am; Fri-Sat, 10pm–4am

£5–£8 (£4 NUS)

Po Na Na

42 Charles Street, Southern Quarter

(0161) 272 6044

Don't Stop 'til You Get Enough. That was the tune playing on Itchy's latest visit to this underground lair of dancing and disgraceful behaviour. It's hard not to obey, actually, seduced by incense burning through wooden slats as you descend a wooden staircase to a cosy Turkish palace, filled with a juxtaposition of luxurious bedseats and a thriving dance floor. But some people really should know when to stop, especially early-year students. Children, if you keep chucking down that Sambuca and those cocktails, you'll ruin the cushions. Mark our words.

Mon–Thu, 8pm–2am; Fri–Sat, 8pm–3am

Free–£5

The Ritz

Ritz Ballroom Whitworth Street West, Southern Quarter

(0161) 236 4355

Despite looking rather like a dodgy old hotel that you'd cross the street to avoid, The Ritz is actually a great gig and club night venue. Drunken disasters abound thanks to the sloping floor – but, as it angles towards the stage, that's just a handy way to discover Manchester's emerging band talent. The surrounding balcony really sets the venue apart from more conventional club layouts – and the atmosphere is uniquely electric, thanks in part to a long music history. But the most popular night is Love Train. We'll say no more, but we're sure you can use your imagination. Choo choo, here comes the... ok, we'll stop now.

Times and prices vary

Robinskis

5–7 Wilbraham Road, Fallowfield

(0161) 248 1931

It's 9pm on a Tuesday night in Fallowfield. Should you escape the banality of the so-called student hub? Or else follow the hordes of mindless drones to Robbos, where for a measly amount of money you can drink neon-green piss water which purports to be a vodka-Redbull? Oh, ok, there is something to be said for VodBull Tuesday: mainly that it's always packed, that you WILL get hammered, and that the friends you make in the toilets while sat in a pool of your own vomit probably WILL be your friends for life. Isn't that what you go to uni for?

Mon–Sun, 12pm–12am

VodBull, £3/£4

Ruby Lounge

28–32 High Street, Northern Quarter

(0161) 832 1392

Club Ohm's profile and popularity wen into overdrive when the owners hit on a brainwave. They installed poles, rename it Ruby Lounge, and started a studen lapdancing night, complete with super cheap student prices. Now all thos studious Mancs brimming over wit pent-up sexual energy can finally acces the pleasures which were previously ou of their rather limited price range. Loca feminists are up in arms, but frankly, th publicity can only be doing the plac good. No one had really heard of it before

Mon, 10pm–2am; Wed, 9pm–2am; Sat, 10.30pm–4am; Sun, 6pm–12am

Prices vary

Sankeys

Radium Street, Ancoats

(0161) 236 5444

Those who think Madchester regained its sanity when the Hacienda spun its last vinyl need to take a trip to Sankeys. The city's most adventurous clubbing establishment has dropped the Soap affix from its name, and has also given itself a right good scrub down – still just as mad, but cleaner and with extra-swirly wallpaper that's guaranteed to mess with already sketchy vision. Every weekend, DJs from across the world and exuberant clubbers from all walks of life get together to mash it up in the three rooms of this electric venue. Not for the fainthearted – and certainly not for the sane.

Times and prices vary

Satan's Hollow

101 Princess Street, City Centre

(0161) 236 0666

Sort of like a puppy wearing a Hallowee costume, this place is innocent fu cloaked in an evil façade. After the initia surprise, on closer inspection, the devils and gargoyles that adorn the walls look as if they were borrowed from a cheap ghost ride in Blackpool. And yet, the ponderous quasi-horror décor gives the club a curious charm. After a few beers, dancing next to a mock gravestone becomes perversely entertaining... Your style may struggle as the tunes deviate wildly from Metallica to Girls Aloud. Bizarre in every way.

Mon–Wed, 10.30pm–3am; Thu, 10.30pm–4am; Fri–Sat, 9pm–3am

£2/£5; Sat, free before 10pm with flyer

›tar and Garter

›8–20 Fairfield Street, Ancoats

›161) 273 6726

›mid the seediness of one of Manchester's ›famous red light districts lies a club ›hat looks like a pub, where the clientele ›ppear to have covered their bodies › superglue and rolled around in the ›earest vintage clothes store. There are ›lso boys in waistcoats and cravats, ›vho think 'I'm from Salford' justifies their ›oorly-placed cockiness. Posing album-›over style in a vaguely cool and/or bored ›nanner on the dance floor sidelines is ›ractically a prerequisite. And if you can't ›hout the words to Le Tigre, why are you ›ven there? Shouldn't you be at 42s?

Times vary

£4 with flyer/£5 without

South

4a South King Street, Deansgate

(0161) 831 7756

If you're wondering why such an incredibly northern club is called South... Well, it's located on South King Street and is underground – so there you go. Dave Haslam (Hacienda/Xfm) and Clint Boon (Inspiral Carpets) are residents on Fridays and Saturdays – and there's nowhere better for some good, hard dancing. Gets really full after 10.30pm, so don't leave it too late. And don't expect to sit down, either... Itchy has never seen a single chair, occupied or otherwise. The floor is therefore popular for more than just dancing. Oh, and that's not the toilet; it's the DJ booth.

Fri–Sat, 10pm–3am

Prices vary

ubspace

New Wakefield, Southern Quarter

61) 236 4899

very city needs a club like this. A place r those who prefer holding a can of ed Stripe to a Cosmopolitan – and ve no style more than the understated, ependable T-shirt. Like the popular attire its clientele, Subspace suits anything. usic, not fashion, is always the passion. is lack of fussing allows it to comfortably ost a wide range of nights, from electro 80s, and hip-hop to punk rock. Leave our airs and graces at the door, and ubmerge yourself in the fun. Oh, and ere's a roof garden on top – handy r smokers and fresh-air seekers alike.

Sun–Wed, 12pm–12am; Thu, 12pm–30am; Fri, 12pm–3am; Sat, 12pm–3.30am

ramp @ North

flecks Palace, Oldham Street, Northern Quarter

161) 236 1807

fter two years at The Bierkeller, Tramp as upped sticks and dragged its ungry and homeless' placard and tatty ardboard box of delights to the basement f Affleck's Palace, where it maintains its Vednesday night tradition of churning out thy underground electro. Tramp tends attract the alternative elite, so arrive ecked out in the relics of your mother's ardrobe if you want to fit in – and be ure to only hang out in the darkest nd coolest corners of the room when ou're not busting out the rave hand to e latest MSTRKRFT remix. Like a pro.

Wed, 10pm–2am

£4/£5

The Zoo

126 Grosvenor Street, Southern Quarter

(0161) 236 3786

If it weren't for the huge, colourfully-painted title reaching across the brick wall of a dimly-lit side street, this club would remain tucked away in the armpit of Manchester's hefty body of clubs. And it doesn't get any more glamorous upon entry. But what it lacks in frills, it makes up for with wild animals, so watch out for romance-hungry mooses (of both sexes). More jungle adventure than tame captivity, The Zoo is mainly known for its boozy student nights on a Thursday, but has started to host more underground events.

Mon–Fri, varies from 9.30pm; Sat, 9.30pm–2.30am

£6/£4.50 concs

Gay

Drag Kings: A Very British Affai

MEN WHO DRESS AS WOMEN ARE OLD HAT. ITCHY'S MUCH MORE OF A FAN OF TH NATION'S NEWEST GAY CRAZE – WOMEN DRESSING AS MEN. MOVE OVER DRAG QUEENS: HERE COME DRAG KINGS

Following its brief moment in the spotlight during Victorian music hall performances, drag king shows – where women dress as men – may have pretty much vanished, but they're just about to make a comeback.

Some king performers take on realistic male personas on the stage by strapping down the chest area, 'packing' (typically created by sock-filled condoms), and adding realistic facial hair. Performances are usually mimed comic songs, performed as a 'troupe' of band members. However, solo performers, who take the act into wilder and more feisty territory, are becoming increasingly common.

Worldwide, 'kinging' has moved on from the days of old, but backward Britannia is still dragging her high heels. Drag queens have long been accepted in the gay scene, and more recently in mainstream entertainment, but sadly drag kings are yet to gain the same widespread popularity.

Illustration by Si Clarke

There is some hope though. Th annual Transfabulous Festival is big showcase for drag kings, and th Wotever World group hosts a variet of different drag king-packed nights If this risqué revolution does tak hold, we reckon there's no reaso drag kings shouldn't have as muc stage-space as their long-successfu queen counterparts. Perhaps the a of female cross-dressing is about t come home...

BARS

All Aboard

Canal Street, Gay Village

161) 236 9003

ke its name, this is a plush and elaxed venue – with plenty of unique ouches. Among them is the soundtrack the hetero/homo-split toilets. Yes, a oundtrack. Falling rain, chirping birds, that ind of thing. A minor problem is the large, ometimes-private, sometimes-not area ear the entrance. It can be a bit awkward if ou glide in early evening with your bottle of ouse red (cheaper than separate glasses), nly to be turned away by a member f staff or snooty private-area guest.

Mon–Thu, 11am–11pm; Fri, 11am–12am; at, 11am–2am; Sun, 12pm–10.30pm

Eden Bar

Brazil Street, Gay Village

161) 237 9852

Ve all remember the story of Adam and Eve. The take-home message of the whole Garden of Eden saga seems to be: 'Don't ake advice from talking snakes.' Sounds ogical to us. Still, we're glad that eating ere isn't a sin, as they have some damn ood food on offer. And if you don't want o eat, then don't panic. There's a DJ on weekends playing camp/cheesy classics, lounge area, and outside there's even a oating barge you can chill out on. Seriously.

Mon–Wed, 11am–12am; Thu–Sat, 11am–am; Sun, 11pm–12am; food, Mon–Sun, 1am–9pm

21 day hung fillet steak, £18.95

£9.95

AXM

10 Canal Street, Gay Village

(0161) 236 6005

You can tell that AXM is pretty damned proud of itself. Then again, it kind of has a right to be. Winning awards for best bar in Manchester, best gay bar in Manchester, best acronym for a bar ever (ok maybe not that last one), AXM is the bar of choice for Manchester's gay community. There are events on every night, there's a hi-tech video jukebox (because normal jukeboxes just don't cut it any more), there's free internet access and it even serves up some mean cocktails. One quick thing, you best look stylish and chic, or you're going to look like a bit of a twazzock.

Mon–Thu, 12pm–1am; Fri–Sat, 12pm–2am; Sun, 12pm–12.30am

Taurus

1 Canal Street, Gay Village

(0161) 236 4593

There's nothing more disappointing than rocking up to some trendy new 'in' bar only to find that it's a bit pants, and that the wooden chairs are so uncomfortable they give you back ache. Thankfully, Taurus is nothing like this. Think comfy sofas, friendly service, good food at a reasonable price and friendly, attentive staff. We could make some joke about it making other places look like a load of bull, but obviously we'd never dream of sinking that low.

Mon–Thu, 12pm–11pm; Fri–Sat, 12pm–1am; Sun, 12pm–10.30pm; food, Mon–Sat, 12pm–10pm; Sun, 12pm–9.30pm

Square of braised belly pork, £9.25

£10.75

Via Fossa

28–30 Canal Street, Gay Village

(0161) 236 6523

This gothic staple of the gay village somehow cavernous and cosy at th same time, revelling in its salvage architectural charms. A modern bar the guise of a treehouse village, Via Foss has a largely young, friendly and attractiv clientele. The bar staff aren't half ba either. However, the chaotic layout ca play with your brain when utterly trolleye If you're not careful you'll end up trappe in a nook or cranny, praying there' still enough God left in the old church derived furniture to grant you rescu by a friend. Consider yourself warned

Mon–Thu, 11am–1am; Fri–Sat, 11am–2am Sun, 12pm–12.30am

:LUBS

:lique @ Joshua Brooks

06 Princess Street, Southern Quarter

161) 273 7543

chy rarely uses the word 'shiny' when eviewing a club, but we reckon it could e applied to Clique. Held in the bowels of tudent favourite Joshua Brooks, it attracts swarm of bright young things who come omplete with excellent skew-whiff fringes ut, fortunately, minus the attitude the ight's name might suggest. The music s described as 'digital dance-pop' and ne combination of fun tunes and overspill om the rammed dance floor ensure you'll pend the night bopping about. Whether ntentionally or not is another matter.

Last Friday of every month, 11pm–3am

Essential Nightclub

loom Street, Gay Village

0161) 236 0077

They've kind of forced our hand by choosing a name like 'Essential', but this is an essential listing for gay clubbers. It's so gay in fact, and its door policy is so strict, that it's not unknown for gay people to get turned away for looking too heterosexual. Nights include 'Chav Bender', 'Bad Drag Flip', 'Kinky Bender' and 'Disco Bender' (so every kind of bender really), and then it's all topped off with 'Morning Glory' every Sunday. Expect gay, camp and loud nights, and maybe someone waggling a plastic willy in your face.

Tue & Sat, 11pm–3.30am; Thu, 11pm–4am; Fri, 10.30pm–4am

Prices vary

Club Alter Ego

105–107 Princess Street, Gay Village

(0161) 236 9266

This place was formerly Mutz Nutz and Equinox, aka home of Manumission. Now they've pumped a wallet-shattering £250k into the place, and it looks pretty swanky after the refurb, with a new bar, sound system and plasma screens. Which you'd kind of expect after forking out that much. Whether the new name's cool or a bit up its own arse we're not exactly sure, but either way, it's just around the corner from Canal Street, and that means it's gay-friendly. Check out Poptastic on Tuesdays and Saturdays. It's... err... well, poptastic.

Tue & Sat, 11pm–3.30am; Thu, 11pm–4am; Fri, 10.30pm–4am

Prices vary

Homoelectric @ Legends

56 Swan Street, Northern Quarter

(0161) 819 2898

With a marketing cry of 'homos, heteros, lesbos, don't-knows and disko asbos', Homoelectric is home to those who'd rather stick needles in their eardrums than endure the unalterable high-camp, handbag-house sound synonymous with Canal Street. The night is all about music and experimentation, and a wander around the labyrinthine chambers of Legends should see you encounter all manner of objects and individuals weird and wonderful. The line-up varies but it's consistently packed, so make sure you get there early to avoid disappointment.

Times vary, check website for details

£10

SHOP

Clone Zone

36–38 Sackville Street, Gay Village

(0161) 236 1398

If you're like us here at Itchy, then yc probably thought you'd seen it all. As turns out, we were being slightly naive Clone Zone has such marvels as th 'horse tail buttplug whip', 'alligatc adjustable tit clamps' and 'the Bosto pump works system'. We're sure you ca use your imagination for all of these things Essentially, if it's depraved, related to se and you can imagine it, then Clone Zon probably has it. It certainly makes a chang from doing your weekly shopping at Tescc

Mon–Thu, 11am–8pm; Fri–Sat, 11am–11pm; Sun, 12pm–7pm

Shop

Shop

Welcome to shop

When choosing your designer togs, you can do it in compact style in **Selfridges (1 Exchange Square, 08708 377 377)** and **Harvey Nichols (21 New Cathedral Street, 0161 828 8888)**, or with fresh air and a walk on **King Street (M2, DKNY, Armani, Agent Provocateur, etc)**. If alternative style is more your thing, opt for the Northern Quarter, where you can find not only fantastically individual gear at the likes of **Rags to Bitches (60 Tib Street, 0161 835 9265)** and **Oi Polloi (70 Tib Street, 0161 831 7870)** – but also some of the UK's best record shops. We particularly recommend Oldham Street's finest: **Vinyl Exchange (18 Oldham Street, 0161 228 1122)** and **Piccadilly Records (51 Oldham Street, 0161 834 8789)**. Manchester is also amazing for food. You really can't afford to miss Chorlton's fishmonger, **Out of the Blue (Wilbraham Road, 0161 881 8353)** and butcher, **WH Frost (12–14 Chorlton Place, 0161 881 8172)**.

Top five bits of tourist tat you can buy in Manchester

Vimto – Vim Tonic was invented here in 1908. Or there's Cheeky Vimto, a mix of port and Blue WKD.
Bee keyrings – The busy bee is the mascot of Manchester.
Snowglobes – They should be rainglobes, but we're not picky.
Rusholme postcards – Curry-tastic. Oklahoma in the Northern Quarter has the most kitsch ones.
T-shirts – 'And on the eighth day, God created Man-CHESTER'.

Top five shops to bag a bargain in

Primark City Centre - Yeah, it makes your soul feel a bit grubby, but can you imagine life before it?
Affleck's Palace Northern Quarter
The cultural antithesis of Primark.
Quality Save, Piccadilly – Classier than pound shops, but just as cheap.
T K Maxx City Centre - Try to stay sane as you fight through the rails.
Selfridges, Millennium Quarter
Forget Next on Boxing Day; the sales here can save you hundreds.

MALLS AND MARKETS

Afflecks Palace

52 Church Street, Northern Quarter

(0161) 834 2039

A kaleidoscopic hoarder's paradise and a self-consciously 'alternative' social shopping experience, Afflecks Palace attracts folk from scenesters to goths, and just about everyone in between. Its several storeys are a treasure trove for items that simply can't be bought elsewhere. Get pierced, tattooed or blue hair extensions, blow your hard-earned loan on some handmade tailoring, or simply sit in the café on the top floor. Jewellery, music, vintage, fetish – Afflecks is a cultural beacon in the city's creative history.

Mon–Fri, 10.30am–6pm; Sat, 10am–6pm

The Arndale Centre

Market Hall, Market Street, City Centre

(0161) 832 9851

Until very recently, much of the Arndale was marked on the Manchester map as 'here-be-dragons' territory. The main bit was just scuzzy; the market was downright scary. But then, someone in the city's planning department realised that if you're going to give over a vast swathe of your city centre to an indoor shopping complex, it's best not to let it turn into a mini Moss Side. After a massive refurbishment project, the new market area and extension are essential ports of call on any Manchester shopping spree. But unless you're after cut-price sportswear, 15 lighters for a quid and knock off perfume, the Market Street side is still best avoided.

The Triangle

37 Exchange Square, Millennium Quarter

(0161) 834 8961

Like a futuristic Malteser, the Triangle's traditional outer shell doesn't match its contemporary, sleek interior. With a crisp selection of shops, you'll wish it was bigger. But fear not, Calvin Klein will package any package and The Titchy Coffee Co will stimulate you so you're ready for more. Despite claims of being 'the new retail heart of Manchester', with an atmosphere more clinical than the sterilised chairs in your doc's waiting room, you get the feeling you're in *The Truman Show*. But when the shopping's this good, we'd happily be stuck here for ever.

Mon–Wed, 10am–6pm; Thu–Sat, 10am–7pm; Sun, 11am–5pm

FOOD

Barbakan Delicatessen

67 Manchester Road, Chorlton

(0161) 881 7053

An award-winning Polish deli selling every foodstuff you can possibly imagine. It can be rather daunting on the first few visits, but once you get past the huge queues and discover there's a ticket system, it gets a lot easier. Boasting delicacies from eastern-Europe and beyond, Barbakan's freshly-baked bread is especially famous. It's far too easy to clean out your wallet in here – but you'll eat like a prince even if you leave as a pauper. In summer it's also a great place for an informal al fresco lunch, but you might have to be nifty grabbing a table.

Mon–Fri, 9am–5.30pm; Sat, 8.30am–5pm

Hang Won Hong Supermarket

Connaught Building, 58–60 George Street, Chinatown

(0161) 228 6182

Remember when you were a kid and you used to build mini cities on the breakfast table out of Weetabix boxes? The Hang Won Hong Supermarket is like a grown-ups' version, except fashioned from packets of noodles and cans of coconut milk. A maze of tiny aisles lined with teetering stacks of stock, it's usually rammed, and you get the feeling everyone is praying they won't be the one to send everything toppling like edible dominoes. This is also a top place for fancy veg – you'll find everything you need to whip up an authentic oriental dish.

Mon–Tue, 10am–8pm; Wed–Sun, 10am–7.30pm

Burton Road Bakery

165 Burton Road, West Didsbury

(0161) 445 5316

18 months ago this place was more of a tribute to nasty 70s décor than a sandwich shop, but its new owners have given it some much-needed attention on the aesthetics front and come up with a winning menu to match. And though it sits comfortably alongside the ultra-chic bistros and delis of Burton Road, The Bakery manages to remain down-to-earth in an inimitably Manc way. Freshly-made butties to take away, with impressive breakfast and lunchtime menus. Everything is homemade, and reassuringly inexpensive.

Mon–Fri, 8am–5pm; Sat, 9am–5pm; Sun, 9am–4pm

Full breakfast, £4.95

Hotel Chocolat

Arndale Centre, New Cannon Street, City Centre

(0870) 444 8384

This is no ordinary chocolate shop. This is a Hotel Chocolat shop. A place that commands chocoholics to rush from far and wide for a taster of its delectable delights. Choose from humungous chocolate slabs, Jack-and-the-Beanstalk-style chocolate beans, or a gooey dipper to dunk in your afternoon tea. Or how about some of the countless variations of truffles, all presented in packaging every bit as delicious as the sweet stuff itself, to make you feel that extra bit special? It's incredible that Itchy managed to leave to write this review.

Mon–Fri, 9am–8pm; Sat, 9am–7pm; Sun, 11am–5pm

SHOES

Oi Polloi

70 Tib Street, Northern Quarter

(0161) 831 7870 or 7781

To get anywhere in Manchester, you have to have a fantastic pair of trainers. Trust us, it's like a religion here, and it simply won't do to have any old pair from JJB. But where does one find such a vital fashion product in this characterless modern age? As ever, we know best: Oi Polloi, a nifty little needle in the haystack of porn merchants that is Tib Street. It's a magical fountain of one-off designs, that rather distressingly come with less-than-magical price tags. But hey, who are we to question the price of cool?

Mon–Sat, 10am–6pm

BOOKS

Waterstones

91 Deansgate, Deansgate

(0161) 832 1992

Waterstones is quite frankly the king of all book stores. Full of every text you could ever want or need, it's pretty easy to find what you're looking for. Okay, for books on a student budget, it can be expensive – but if you've left that essay until the last minute and everyone else on your course has already raided the uni library, Waterstones will be your saviour. The charting system of the newer releases gives you a taste of what's hot, which saves you digging through the shelves for a decent read.

Mon–Fri, 8am–9pm; Sat, 8am–7.30pm; Sun, 11am–5pm

CLOTHING

East

18a The Triangle Exchange Square, Millennium Quarter
(0161) 839 5102

Is your mum, or any other older female in your life, a former hippy, forced into sophistication by her age and peers? Point her to East to put a smile on her face. Actually, even if you're a young slip of a thing, East will thrill you like Duncan from Blue did when you were a bit younger. Devour racks of glossy, glass-beaded necklaces and deliciously detailed and surprisingly flattering skirts. Look as trendy as possible, beating off the mutton hints with chunky bangles, and leave others green with envy.

Mon–Sat, 10am–7pm; Sun, 11am–5pm

Karen Millen

48 King Street, Millennium Quarter
(0161) 834 0653

If you're a sexy secretary type – or even all fur coat and no knickers – Karen Millen will be right up your well-pruned street. With overpriced pencil skirts, satin bustiers and backless tops galore, this is the place for girlies with a few extra pounds (and we're strictly talking sterling – which they probably saved up by living on raisins for a month prior to the shopping trip) to spend on clothing. However, with shoes and bags as awe-inspiring as KM's, it's worth buying those raisins in bulk. Or perhaps that's a bit extravagant. Maybe best not to spend money on luxuries like food at all, and save up for just the essentials.

Mon–Sat, 10am–7pm; Sun, 11am–5pm

La Senza

Unit 20–23 The Arndale Centre, West Didsbury
(0161) 839 9765

For women who want to treat themselves – or perhaps men who want to treat their ladies (but really themselves, sly dogs) – La Senza is a welcome answer without breaking the bank. It caters for all shapes and sizes. Yes, even those who, as Alan Partridge might say, weren't 'at the front of the queue when the Lord gave out chests'. Itchy particularly recommends it for morale-boosting in the wake of a failed relationship. Alright, it may not be as satisfying as wilful destruction of property, (anatomical or otherwise), but at least it won't land you in jail.

Mon–Fri, 9am–8pm; Sat, 9am–7pm; Sun, 11am–5pm; bank holidays, 10am–6pm

Pearl

238 Burton Road, West Didsbury

(0161) 434 9067

Badly fitting bra? Fed up of Primark's endless selection of bargain basement undies? Well, pleasingly, a solution to all your problems has arrived in the form of recently-opened Manchester shop Pearl, selling the finest and sexiest yet affordable lingerie and swimwear around. Proud owner Amy (who henceforth we shall refer to as 'Mother of Pearl') certainly knows her balconettes from her plunges and offers a professional fitting service, along with friendly advice. Whether you resemble an ironing board or a space hopper, you're guaranteed great service and fabulous lingerie from a woman who cares.

Tue–Sat, 10.30am–6pm

Vicky Martin

Unit 31, The Triangle, City Centre

(0161) 832 8234

Cinderella, you shall go to the ball. Hot Salford designer Vicky Martin still chooses to sail her flagship store in the Triangle Centre – great news for all you downtrodden and sooty Manc lasses. Her party dress creations are much-loved by local female celebs, and are reasonably-priced enough for us normal types to splash out on for special occasions. You'll be in a whole different fashion league to the ugly sisters down on Deansgate Locks. Now will you look at that. We managed to make it through the whole review without our customary reference to *Livin' La Vida Loca*. Oh, wait...

Mon–Sat, 10am–6pm; Sun, 11am–5pm

Rags to Bitches

60 Tib Street, Northern Quarter

(0161) 835 9265

In search of a little something fabulously individual? Or perhaps something ever so slightly naughty? Then Rags to Bitches is a must. Offering one-off pieces from yesteryear and collections from up-and-coming local designers such as Lauren Clowes, Rags to Bitches has everything but the girl. Tucked away in the Northern Quarter, it is more than just your standard vintage shop or boutique, providing customers with a quirky and friendly environment in which to hunt out those essential pieces. And to top it all off, if you are lucky, you might even get free cake on Fridays.

Mon–Sat, 11am–6pm

Selfridges in the City

1 Exchange Square, Millennium Quarter

(0800) 123 400

If our experience of the similarly-titled TV show is anything to go by, then this place will be a horrendous experience for all men. If you're a woman, your heels may slow you down in getting here, but you'll be excited enough by this ensemble not to care. Bedazzling Kurt Geiger shoes sit alongside over-produced Topshop dresses, with Paul's Boutique thrown into the mix to add some colour. Ok, so it's shamelessly cashing in on a certain fashion-obsessed HBO series of old, but in a way that suckers us in even more. We want to be fabulous, dagnammit.

Mon–Fri, 10am–8pm; Sat, 9am–8pm; Sun, 10.30am–5pm

Urban Outfitters

Market Street, City Centre

(0161) 817 6640

Students surround Urban Outfitters like children with noses pressed up to the glass of an amazing toy shop, before their mother impatiently pulls them away. Each time Itchy sees a student shedding a tear at all the nice clothes their overdraft can't stretch to we think: 'Well, they should learn to budget, shouldn't they?' Though it could be argued it wouldn't help much in this case. Perhaps every time they sell a pint of blood in order to afford that beautiful pair of tights with the price tag worthy of a small country, they rationalise that beauty is pain. Money can buy happiness.

Mon–Wed & Fri–Sat, 10am–7pm; Thu, 10am–8pm; Sun, 11am–6pm

Vivienne Westwood

47 Spring Gardens, King Street, City Centre

(0161) 835 2121

Paying a visit to this King Street boutique feels more like looking round a stately home than going shopping. The dark wood fittings and ornate gilt mirrors make you feel as if you're trespassing on an ancestral pile, rather than finding ways to pulverise your credit card, and most of the customers amble round in wonderment as if they've found the arc of the covenant. Everything is so lovingly laid out that, if it weren't for the price tags, it'd be hard to believe the clothes are actually for sale. But there's no better place for just looking: the staff are friendly, the clothes are compelling – and the smell of beeswax is strangely alluring.

Mon–Sat, 10am–6pm; Sun, 12pm–5pm

Zara

2 New Cathedral Street, Millennium Quarter

(0161) 831 0940

This chain is far cheaper in Spain, but the flight ticket out there makes that pretty much irrelevant. Unless you happen to be on holiday there anyway, in which case, go mad. In the UK, the odd item is on the pricey side, but nothing that'll induce a heart attack. Zara looks far more expensive than it is, which makes it ideal for workwear. Whether sitting behind a desk all day or running around, it's generally practical not to waste hundreds of pounds on designer gear for either. There's some casual stuff too. Oh – and the basics (ie, cheap) range is particularly good for all thriftier readers.

Mon–Wed & Fri–Sat, 10am–6pm; Thu, 10am–8pm; Sun, 12pm–6pm

VINTAGE CLOTHING

American Graffitti

Hilton Street, Northern Quarter
(0161) 228 3677

Wonderfully kitsch and jam-packed with clothing from every era imaginable (we're yet to find a set of Anglo-Saxon chain mail), American Graffiti is a one-stop wonder for all your vintage and costume needs. Leather jackets, 70s platforms and an impressive array of beads, belts and bags to match, this shop makes vintage chic an almost effortless experience. Expect to leave and find, blinded by daylight, that an hour has passed since you went in and your wallet has taken a beating.
Mon–Fri, 10.30am–6pm; Sat, 10am–6pm; Sun, 12pm–5pm

Oxfam Originals

11 Smithfield Buildings, Oldham Street, Northern Quarter
(0161) 839 3160

If you like the convenience of having it all laid out for you, Oxfam Originals finds the vintage gems and puts them all in one convenient, root-free shop. Often, they will customise the odd T-shirt or add a certain je-ne-sais-quoi to that amazing bag you've been eyeing up. Sadly, they seem to have forgotten about the 'Oxfam' part of their name, as instead of charging you dirt-cheap amounts for good clobber, you shouldn't be surprised to find that the price tag mirrors that of the high street, which somehow defeats the object of a 'charity shop'. Pay the price for individuality or scoot on over to H&M? Tough call.
Mon–Sat, 10am–6pm; Sun, 12pm–5pm

Pop Boutique

34–36 Oldham Street, Northern Quarter
(0161) 236 5797

Fear not – if all the hunting for those must-have 1920s shoes becomes too much, just chill out, (man), in the café downstairs. Walk into Manchester's Pop Boutique and you are transported back to an era when pretty much anything went. The vibe is as warm and welcoming as the food and drink. When you've recovered sufficiently, go back upstairs and flick through rails of timeless vintage pieces and you're guaranteed to fall in love with at least one item. Probably more if you're not careful (after all, who are we to put limits on the power of love?). Then it'll be time for you to get your bank manager to chill.
Mon–Sat, 10am–6pm; Sun, 11am–5pm

Retro Rehab

91 Oldham Street, Northern Quarter

(0161) 839 2050

Amidst the hordes of vintage shops in the Northern Quarter, it is rare to find one that is just right. At one end are the massive barn-like emporiums demanding several hours' rummaging through heaving rails; at the other, smaller boutiques staffed by fashionable yet humourless young things, for whom your very presence seems a major inconvenience. Retro Rehab stands out like a sparkling diamante hat pin. The shop is small, the clothes carefully arranged and the staff actually seem pleased by your custom. Keep an eye out for the kitsch kitchen pinnies and fab metal pendants, handmade by a local designer.

Mon–Fri, 11am–6pm; Sat, 10am–6pm

Ryan Vintage

Oldham Street,

Northern Quarter

Tucked away at the end of the famous Oldham Street, Ryan Vintage is nothing less than a pirate's treasure stash of beautiful vintage and retro booty (how we love to use that word), enough to satisfy even the most dedicated of bargain hunting buccaneers. This shop boasts a massive variety of clothes and accessories, with prices starting at just a paltry £7 for an eminently tasteful polka dot skirt. If you're looking for a present, they even sell gift vouchers. However, be warned, Ryan Vintage is absolutely massive, so you'll need to roll those sleeves of yours right up and get digging if you don't want to miss anything.

OTHER

Cast

49–51 Thomas Street, Northern Quarter

(0161) 832 5100

Named after what you'll end up in if you try and use any of their products, Cast is a skate shop by day and a rave venue by night. Someone must have realised it's a bit of a waste having a full-sized skate ramp in your premises if it only gets used during the day. So what started as a series of semi-legal parties on weekend evenings has now turned into the beast Cast is best known for: offering the city's clubbers the chance to get messy on a seriously slanted dancefloor. There's only one toilet, so be prepared for queues.

Mon–Sat, 10am–6pm; Sun, 12pm–4pm

Magma

22 Oldham Street, Northern Quarter

(0161) 236 8777

The ridiculously pretentious selection of arty books in Urban Outfitters aren't really doing it for anyone. Well, not unless their wildly trendy tea-towel scarf is cutting off the circulation to their brain. So, as an alternative, Magma is an indispensable part of Manchester city centre. This bookshop on Oldham Street caters for fans of art, fashion, graphic design and photography; ranging from Banksy's street art, to middle-America photography, and interior design. And, if *Heat* and *Grazia* just aren't doing it for you these days, there's also a great collection of unusual magazines to take away with you.

Mon–Sat, 10am–6.30pm; Sun, 12pm–6pm

Heals

11 New Cathedral Street, Millennium Quarter

(0161) 819 3000

Even if you lived in Buckingham Palace you'd wish it was twice as big just so you could justify buying more from this amazing home store. From couture-like chandeliers to funky plates and mugs – plus scented candles powerful enough to make the local landfill smell heavenly – Heals has it all. If you only write one thing this year make sure it is a very neatly-written letter beginning 'Dear Father Christmas, I have been extra-good this year, so...' The only downside is that once you've been here, everything in your house that's not from Heals will seem tawdry and cheap

Mon–Fri, 10am–6pm; Sat, 9.30am–6.30pm; Sun, 11am–5pm

MUSIC

Fat City Records

20 Oldham Street, Northern Quarter

(0161) 237 1181

If you're looking for something to move to that isn't the standard crap that ends up in the charts, then pay a visit to Manchester's Fat City Record Shop. Of course, there are the usual DJ-wannabes posing while their decks go dusty at home, but let them. There are worse hobbies – like, er, wannabe popstars. Specialising in hip-hop, funk, jazz and soul, Fat City opened as a small stall in Manchester's Affleck's Palace in 1993, and is now a company that includes a record label plus its famous Friends and Family club night (residing at Mint Lounge).

Mon–Sat, 10am–6pm; Sun, 12pm–5pm

Music Ground

2 Oxford Road

0161) 237 5815

Music Ground lays claim to a range of amous customers, from George Harrison, Jimmy Page and Keith Richards to, err... Menswear. They certainly cater for all budgets; while struggling local musicians will find plenty of reasonably-priced options o choose from, Music Ground's real bread and butter comes from dealing vintage guitars and amps, some even boasting amous previous owners. A few items bear he scary label 'POA': We understand this to stand for 'price on application'; the closest we'll ever get to owning one of them is to ake a picture and make a huge cardboard cut-out to play in front of the mirror.

Mon–Sat, 10am–6pm

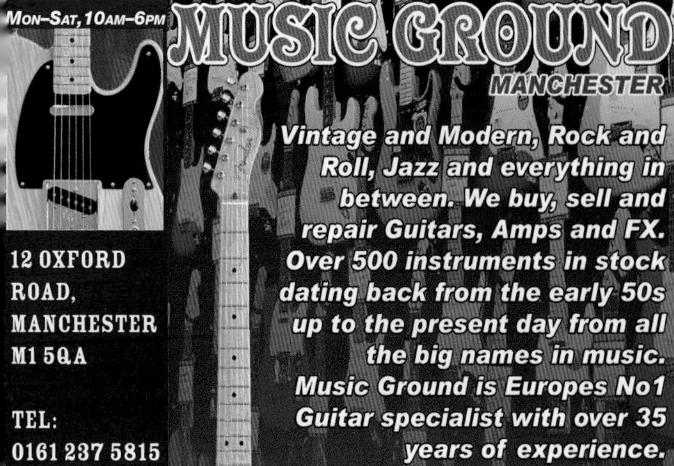

Shop

Newspoint

33 Oldham Street, Northern Quarter

(0161) 832 1583

No shop truly sums up the maverick spirit of the Northern Quarter like the newsagent formerly known as Best One. Barmy though it may sound, this place really is both a visitor attraction and an indispensable resource for the local community. Situated just off Piccadilly Gardens, its unassuming exterior belies the inspired, TARDIS-esque hybrid of grocery store, off-licence and cut-price DIY warehouse that awaits the intrepid within its walls. Search long and hard enough, and you can find absolutely whatever you are after on the shelves – fact. But watch you don't trip over the dog near the till.

Mon–Sun, 8.30am–6pm

Octopus

8 Market Street, City Centre

(0161) 832 8722

This shop was conceived either by an extremely business-orientated eight year old, or else some overgrown, hyperactive fellow with a very vivid imagination. Easil mistaken for a surreal toy shop, Octopus is a manically colourful little store stocking everything from hairbrushes to lighters to toasters with the jewellery, watches and cufflinks (our favourite were the Bogey and Bacall ones) being particularly unique. Several times we bemusedly picked up an item, before exclaiming 'Oh, it's a pen/lighter/bracelet'. Ingenious

Mon–Wed & Fri, 9.30am–6.30pm; Thu, 9.30am–7pm; Sat, 9am–7pm; Sun, 11am–5pm

Thunder Egg

22 Oldham Street, Northern Quarter

(0161) 235 0606

Welcome to the Northern Quarter's home for the weird and wonderful world of Japanese imports. With two locations boasting more anime-related items than you can shake a stick at – although why you would want to shake a stick at a pile of Hello Kitty paraphernalia is questionable – the newest site on Oldham Street stocks up on larger items and packs in the tiny stocking-fillers to the ceiling. In particular, the hand-crafted, quirky jewellery and cutesy notebooks generally fulfil the last minute birthday present panic-buy, and will have definite amusement value if nothing else.

Mon–Fri, 10.30am–6pm; Sat, 10am–6pm; Sun, 12pm–5pm

radiohead

Out & About

Welcome to Out & About

If you want a good laugh, there's nowhere better (or cheaper) than **XS Malarkey @ Bar XS in Fallowfield (Wilmslow Road, 0161 257 2403)**. It's on every Tuesday, with a combination of upcoming talent and seasoned stars, and not a tumbleweed in sight. Just make sure you get there early to defeat those tight types who spread their coats over chairs and nurse one pint for four hours. If you're lucky enough to have a free day and are in need of some excitement, try **Chill Factor-e in Trafford (7 Trafford Way, 0161 749 2222)**. It's as real as a synthetic Alpine skiing experience can get. Or you may prefer a relaxing option. Providing it's not raining (which, we confess, is rare), give one of Manchester's many parks a try. **Ardwick Green, Chorlton, Fletcher Moss** (Didsbury) and **Wythenshawe** were among 21 Mancunian Green Flag award-winners in 2007.

Top five summer activities

Twit-spotting – Score points for fake tans, whitened teeth, lipo bruises and stupid bags.

Park trips – Renting a row boat after a boozy picnic is not advised.

Eating outside – Don't forget a cardie or a trusty cagoule.

Drinking outside – Beer gardens rule, though plastic chairs on tarmac don't count as a 'garden'.

Drinking inside – We're not living in fairyland, but Mancland, so this is inevitable now and again.

Top five winter activities

Christmas markets – Don't go for the shopping; it's all about the mulled wine and pancakes.

Iceskating – Great fun, but watching people crash and burn from the sidelines is even better.

Chill Factor-e – Real snow all year round, so you can pretend it's Christmas all year round.

Eating inside – Forget the diets. This is about surviving the cold.

Drinking Inside – Because beer is nicer than driving sleet.

Itchy's Dictionary of *Dahling!*

EVER FELT THAT THE CULTURE-SAVVY SEEM TO DWELL ON A HIGHER INTELLECTUAL PLANE THAN THE REST OF US? WELL NEVER FEAR – BEHIND THEIR LUVVIE LINGO, REFINED-SOUNDING FOLK HAVE THE SAME THOUGHTS, HOPES AND FEARS AS US CRUDE PROLETARIANS. HAVE A PEEP AT ITCHY'S THESP THESAURUS TO FIND OUT WHAT THEY'RE REALLY ON ABOUT.

ON THEATRE

'I found the final act deeply moving.' *The end was just like* Last of the Mohicans.

'His sense of comic timing left something to be desired.' – *I've had funnier episodes of food poisoning.*

'I felt the costumes were rather avant-garde.' – *I could almost see Juliet's nipples in that corset.*

ON MUSIC

'I don't much care for their notion of ensemble.' – *I'm going to piss in a bottle and throw it at the drummer.*

'I've always had a sense of vocation about the arts.' – *Why don't we start a band? I've got an old cowbell I stole from school and you could play the harmonica.*

ON DANCING

'Oh my, I'm all left feet this evening!' *We both know that I was dry-humping your leg just then, but let's never speak of it again, eh?*

'Nothing like a foxtrot to aid one's constitution.' – *I'm shagged. Where's the bar?*

ON WINE

'This wine's really got legs.' – *And I won't when I've had enough of it.*

'A young and bold number, with zesty notes of rosemary and field mushroom.' – *This one was the second cheapest on the menu.*

ON ART GALLERIES

'I find the figurative liberties of proto-classical sculpture highly diverting.' – *Hee hee, look at the massive wanger on that statue. I wonder if they sell replicas in the shop.*

CINEMAS

Cineworld

Parrswood Entertainment Centre, Wilmslow Road, Parrswood

(0871) 200 2000

The Parrswood complex is a strange place. A bleak island between major roads, minutes from Didsbury Village. It's not a bad option for dates or friends, providing you don't end up stuck to the foyer floor in Cineworld with its carpet of popcorn. Upsides include comfortable seats, a massive range of treats on the way in and a bar upstairs. And you might need a drink if you've been foolish enough to go and see a Will Ferrell flick.

Mon–Sun, 11am–11pm

£4–£6.50

Odeon @ The Printworks

27 Withy Grove, Millennium Quarter

(0871) 224 4007

The Odeon towers over other cinemas in the area and, in this case, bigger is better. The IMAX screen's wider than Kirstie Alley after a week in a doughnut factory – and any celebrity crushes will immediately vanish on close-up shots, as you're privy to a display of disconcertingly long nose hair. The Gallery gives you VIP treatment, but unlimited food and drink unfortunately means you'll get stuck next to bloaters whose crunching, chewing and wheezing muffles the sound from the screen.

Daily, 12pm–1am

£6/£4 concs; gallery, Mon–Thu, £13; Fri–Sun, £16 (includes unlimited soft drinks and snacks)

The Cornerhouse

70 Oxford Street, Southern Quarter

(0161) 200 1500

A specialist in all things artsy, independent and foreign, The Cornerhouse has Manchester's alternative film scene wrapped up in a slightly chaotic parcel on the corner of Oxford Street. Its odd layout is spread either side of the approach to Oxford Road Station, faintly romantic beneath the looming railway. The Whitworth Street West corner holds the main cinema, and a number of offices dedicated to educational outreach; while the other hides another two screens, masses of art exhibition space and – most importantly to any self-respecting citizen of Alternatopia – a superb café and bar.

Times and prices vary

COMEDY

Frog and Bucket

96–102 Oldham Street, Northern Quarter

(0161) 236 9805

Smokers in the know will have heard of smirting – the art of seduction while inhaling noxious breath-wrecking vapours, having been banished from polite, tar-free society to the overcrowded and butt-strewn streets. Well, Itchy would like to introduce smeckling, as practiced outside Manchester's most intimate comedy club, The Frog and Bucket. It's much the same, except you get insulted by the evening's performers as you have a puff. Worst thing is, you can't even blow smoke in their face.

Thu–Mon, doors open 7.30pm, all shows start 8.30pm

The Comedy Store

Arches 3–4, Deansgate Locks, Deansgate

(0161) 839 9595

It's Manchester's best-value comedy night, especially if you're in possession of an NUS card. The 'Best in Stand Up' show on Friday and Saturday nights will make you laugh until a little bit of wee comes out. The experience is finely balanced between utter hilarity and seat-squirming embarrassment. While the seasoned pros provoke guffaw after guffaw, the stand-up virgins stammer and sweat as they grope for any hint of laughter from the 500-strong crowd. Hilarious.

On show days: doors open 12pm, evening food from 6.30pm, shows start 8pm

£11.50

£4–£16

LIVE MUSIC

Hop & Grape (Academy 3)

Manchester University Oxford Road, Academic District
(0161) 275 2930

Cramped, dark and with only about two coloured lights, it's hardly the Evening News Arena. But if you want to keep tabs on the burgeoning music scene in the city, Academy 3 has a history of booking those up-and-coming bands that in six months time are headlining Academy 1 and leaving you feeling silly for not going to see a bunch of kids from the seaside called The Kooks on the cheap when you had the chance. Yep, that was us. Like many such no-frills establishments, has bags of atmosphere and generally draws a great crowd.
Times and prices vary

Manchester Apollo

Ardwick Green, Stockport Road, Ardwick
(0161) 273 6921

Unless you enjoy the Britishness and camaraderie of queuing, don't be a numpty and get here hours before the doors open. The raised floor means you can usually get a good spot minutes before the main act appears, even if you don't have the stealth tactics and rolling capabilities of a ninja. More intimate than the MEN and more epic than the Academy, the 3500-capacity Apollo is the undisputed middle-weight champion of Mancunian venues. Taking in its history (every artist worth an encore has played here) can be crippling. Mind you, for gig-goers, so can the beer prices.
Box office, Mon–Sat, 2.30pm–show; Sun, 5.30pm–show; shows, 7pm onwards

Matt & Phred's

64 Tib Street, Northern Quarter
(0161) 831 7002

Get your jazz face on, hepcats. Welcome to Matt and Phred's jazz club – grrreat. That crazy character lurking in the corner could produce a trumpet from his trousers at any given moment and perform an impromptu fusion solo. Or he could be a random booze hound. Either way, expect your pizza served with a generous helping of finger-clicking, funk-based improvisation. The spirit of jazz lives on inside this smouldering, secret hideaway of bohemian musical cool. The overall ambience encapsulates the musical movement it embraces – spontaneous yet really quite beautiful.
Mon–Sun, 7pm–late

Night + Day

26 Oldham Street, Northern Quarter

(0161) 236 4597

Despite boasting a brand new menu and even toying with the term 'restaurant', Night + Day appears to think itself above such servile matters as feeding customers. Sticking to its well-oiled guns seems advisable, laying on spankingly good gig nights with its powerful sound system. A jolly old knees up with bells on, whether you want to see a low-key established name or the next big thing. Just be sure not to ask for an ice bucket for your wine. This is service with a scowl and a general look of disgust.

Mon–Sun, 7pm–2am; food, Mon–Sun, 10am–6.30pm

£5–10 on gig nights

The Roadhouse

8–10 Newton Street, Northern Quarter

(0161) 228 1789

The Roadhouse is an intimate little gig venue with a back catalogue including the likes of The Chemical Brothers and The Verve. It's also refreshingly free from inhibitions on its club nights – seriously, 'the twist' is still a legitimate shape to pull on this dance floor, which makes us love it all the more. Monday night's Revolver plays 60s classics, while Tuesday's Sex With Robots drops the latest electro beats. The Roadhouse is for genuine music lovers of every persuasion: an alternative to 42nd Street without the soul-sapping, sobering queues.

Doors open: club nights, 9pm; gigs, 7pm

Club nights £5 max

THEATRE

Contact Theatre

Oxford Road, Academic District

(0161) 274 0600

If the Contact hits a boundary, it eats a boundary. If it sees convention, it flies in the face of it. It has more edge than the remains of a china shop after an incident with a bull. Inevitably, this forceful approach leads to the odd bit of self-indulgence and pretension, so, cynics: brace yourselves. But, despite the copious amounts of artistic hot air emanating from the building's curious turrets, an occasional diamond emerges from the theatrical rough.

Sun–Thu, 10am–11pm; Fri & Sat, 10am–2am

£5–£10

Library Theatre

Central Library, St Peter's Square

(0161) 236 7110

Founded in 1952, the Library Theatre Company is situated underneath the historic Manchester Central Library in St Peter's Square. This friendly 312-seat theatre presents contemporary drama and modern interpretations of classic plays, and also stages occasional one-night poetry, comedy events and special talks. The Library's popular singles' nights, for those who like to go to the theatre but don't want to go alone, comprises a meal at a nearby restaurant, an interval drink in the theatre's private bar, and on some productions, the chance to go and meet the actors afterwards.

Times and prices vary

USEUMS

he Gallery of Costume

tt Hall, Wilmslow Road, Fallowfield

61) 224 5217

it a jumble sale? Is it an oversized essing-up box? No, it's The Gallery of ostume. No interactive, computerised tivities or spot-lit animated exhibits here. ut along with having to ring a bell to gain ntrance, this makes a refreshing change. e array of wardrobe additions ranges from ntastically psychedelic 1960s dresses, elaborately embroidered 18th-century owns. It's an enjoyable rainy afternoon tivity... If an overload of plastic mannequins ithout eye sockets won't creep you out.

Mon–Fri, 10am–4.45pm (depends on affing, call first)

anchester Museum

xford Road, Academic District

161) 275 2634

rst-off, it's free. Secondly, there are so any rainy days in Manchester, you must ave at least one spare for the Manchester useum. Or at least one day when you're ee and you don't feel too hungover to ove that far/show any appreciation r anything cultural whatsoever. This is delightful opportunity to spend time the company of lizards, mummies, arcophagi, a giant golden Buddha, ewellery and a huge range of other xcavated and rescued artefacts. And a ad of other bits of civilisation and culture at we don't have room to go on about.

Sun–Mon & bank holidays, 11am–4pm; ue–Sat, 10am–5pm

The Greater Manchester Police Museum

57 Newton Street, Northern Quarter

(0161) 865 3287

It turns out watching *Life on Mars* isn't the only way to indulge a passion for police history. Relive the glory days of thumbscrews and birch rod lashings, and peruse the copper-speak information panels: 'He explained to officers that he could not believe how difficult it had been to actually kill his girlfriend with a Martini bottle'. This museum houses a Victorian Magistrate's Court, as well as original cells complete with wooden pillows and ball-and-chain restraints. Tip: bag yourself a volunteer retired policeman as a guide.

Tue, 10.30am–3pm

Free

Urbis

Corporation Street, Cathedral Gardens, Millennium Quarter

(0161) 605 8200

Yes, it's another shapely deposit of glass and metal. You either love them or you hate them. Urbis is on a mission to explore the urban environment in an accessible way. And it works in that you don't bore here as quickly as you might at a more traditional presentation. Art, architecture and grafitti illustrate the culture and dynamics of city life. The interactive exhibits make you feel a bit like you're on a school trip but planned future events are a city beach, tai chi lessons, and flash mobbing.

Mon–Wed, 10am–6pm; Thu–Sat, 10am–8pm; Sun, 10am–6pm

Free

GALLERIES

Castlefield Gallery

2 Hewitt Street, Knott Mill, Castlefield

(0161) 832 8034

On paper, this venue has a lot going for it. It's run by the UHC Collective, renowned for artistic comment on social issues, and is in one of the most green and pleasant parts of the city centre. Unfortunately, it can be so 'niche' as to be a bit inaccessible. On Itchy's recent visit, a single exhibition displayed a bundle of televisions playing several nonsensical (sorry, art) films. All at the same time. And all with full sound. It was like being trapped inside a headache. Hopefully, it'll be gone when we next go.

Wed–Sun, 1pm–6pm;

Free

Manchester Art Gallery

Mosley Street, City Centre

(0161) 235 8888

Grand and old, sleek and modern in equal measure, the Manchester Art Gallery boasts a collection as diverse as the city itself. Elegant portraits of Lord Whatshisname and images of daily life in the 17th century sit alongside new and contemporary work. In particular, the CIS Manchester Gallery captures some fantastic creativity. Far from just photos of Oasis – as the unsuspecting visitor might assume – it shows how deep art and creativity run in Manchester, beyond that rather colourful and kebab-filled chunky pool of sick which you walked past the other day. A lovely image for you there.

Tue–Sun, 10am–5pm

CUBE

113–115 Portland Street, City Centre

(0161) 237 5525

You'll find The Centre for Urban Bu Environment quietly nestled in amor the blaring traffic nightmare that Portland Street. Set on two floors, hosts architectural exhibitions and even with consistent aplomb. They also hav a specialised bookshop where staff a happy to offer advice and informatic or just let you browse to your hear content. CUBE has the usual white wa and wooden floors you'd expect to fir in any modern gallery (is that a seat? an exhibit?), but it also manages to fe friendly. The free admission certainly help

Mon–Fri, 12pm–5.30pm; Sat, 12pm–5pm

Free

The Whitworth Art Gallery

University of Manchester, Oxford Road, Academic Distri

(0161) 275 7450

This elegant Victorian mansion wa probably once owned by some aloc Darcy type, who would shift uncomfortab in his grave if he knew of the ghast indecencies occurring among the tree in the grounds these days. Well, that what happens when a university spring up on your doorstep. Inside, beside som conceptual exhibitions and a worl renowned William Blake masterpiece, th immense textile collection can answe some truly important, glove-relate questions, then you can swing by the caf with its organic, locally-grown produce

Mon–Sat, 10am–5pm; Sun, 2pm–5pm

Free

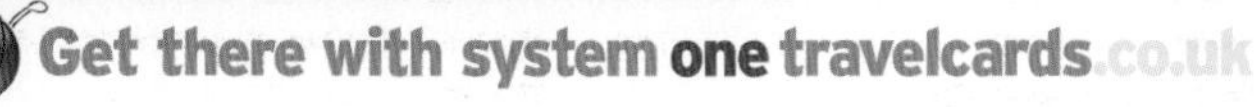
Get there with system one travelcards.co.uk

SPORT

Manchester Aquatics Centre

2 Booth Street East, Academic District

(0161) 275 9450

It may be international standard, with its two swimming pools, diving pool, gym and health spa; and the vending machines may sell drinks intimidatingly named 'Powerade' and 'Relentless', but look closer and you'll notice that maintenance hasn't been of a winning standard since the 2002 Games. So please join Itchy in a nagging crusade, and you never know, they might fix some broken stuff. Or even clean the changing rooms sometimes.

Mon–Fri, 6.30am–10pm; Sat, 7am–6pm; Sun, 7am–10pm

Gym, £4.60; swim, £2.80 (concs, £1.70)

Copacabana

Sevendale House, Dale Street, Northern Quarter

(0161) 237 3441

Females beware: The question 'Would you like to dance?' is commonly overheard above Copa's merengue rhythms. Expect to be whisked and whirled into a frenzy of hip-swaying and dizzying turns by an enthusiastic, well-gelled male, whose trousers are so high up his waist that his chin nearly nestles in the crotch. This is pretty fun if you can bear the neon wallpaint and sweaty aromas. If you can't, just have another sangria.

Tue–Sat, 10pm–2am; Salsa classes, 7pm

Fillet steak medallions with rice, £8.50

£10.50

Thu, £2, £1 concs;
Fri–Sat, £5, £3.50 concs

Chill Factor-e

Off M60 J10, Trafford

Why not break your legs in style here Mancland, instead of spending a fortu to fly out and do it on real mountains? C at least, you can practise. Price-wise, i not really much different to a few game of tenpin bowling – except there you g minging shoes that a thousand peop have worn before you instead of shir skis. That's just one of the points th makes Chill Factor-e a brilliant day ou In the imaginatively-titled 'cold' area, th attractions include real (manufacture snow, three slopes and a tobogga run; while the, er, 'warm' area takes th shape of an 'alpine village', with shops bars and restaurants. So even nor sporty types can be dragged alon

Cycle Routes

Cycling in Manchester is an adrenalin junkie's paradise. A plethora of pavement hoppers imitating Bart Simpson' skateboard escapades are testimony tha most would rather dodge pedestrians an prams than double-deckers and trams Lock-up stands are plentiful everywher and cycle lanes sandwich the mai routes into the centre. Once there, yo either need Tour de France confidenc or firm knowledge of the back alleys On Oxford Road, sharing the bus lane i the perfect challenge for thrill-seekers Try overtaking at bus stops before the driver pulls out again. Eek. Rusholme's traffic system matches its chaotic décor while the Fallowfield Loop is a safe and pleasant ex-rail track leading to Chorlton

Monty's Health and Fitness Club

1–23 Oldham Street

(0161) 831 9997

Mercifully nothing to do with the predatory uncle from *Withnail and I*, Monty's is in fact a cheap – very cheap – gym, and it's located slap-bang on Oldham Street. The downside is that you have to step into the bright lights of the Northern Quarter to get there, which invariably means you'll get sucked into a spot of shopping or a cheeky pint, instead of actually going to the gym. Or, you'll find yourself trying to break in for a workout as you gallivant home from a night on the piss. Either way, not the desired outcome.

Mon & Wed, 7am–9.30pm; Tue, Thu & Fri, 10pm–9.30pm; Sat & Sun, 10am–4pm

TOURIST ATTRACTIONS

Fletcher Moss Gardens

Wilmslow Road, Didsbury Village

(0161) 434 1877

'If you're going to Fletcher Moss Gardens, be sure to wear some flowers in your hair.' When the noise and bustle of the city centre becomes too much – or if you just really enjoy unleashing your inner hippy – escape to these green, idyllic and historical gardens, easily accessible by the number 42 bus. Those with the tender heart of a flower child can frolic in pretty Victorian greenery or run wild in the huge open grassy space that runs down to the banks of the great River Mersey. And when your enthusiasm for all things green and natural begins to wane, The Didsbury pub is right next door.

Green Spaces

For a city reputed for diagonal, umbrella-phobic rain and generalised grey bleakness, Manchester has nurtured many a fine green park. Take your gran to Heaton Park for cream tea in the mansion house, or to Tatton Park to see other old deers. Fletcher Moss, on the River Mersey banks in Didsbury, has a botanical flair, while Chorlton Water Park's wild beauty attracts people from far and wide. The cream of the turf crop is Platt Fields Park in Fallowfield, with space for undisturbed sunbathing. Not that the sun's out all that often, but it's a nice idea anyway.Tennis players, hoop-shooters and contemplaters are all catered for – and boats can be rented on the lake in summer for those who think that rowing is actually enjoyable.

Lyme Hall and Park

Disley, Stockport

(01663) 762 023

Yes, this is it. This is where THE wet shirt scene of the 1990s BBC adaptation of *Pride and Prejudice* was filmed. Cue swooning etc, etc... The poo droplets scattered on the ground spoil the romance a little. Someone really should alert Mr Darcy's gardener. Ignoring that tiny grumble, Lyme Hall and Park are nothing short of stunning. If you want to escape the hustle and bustle of city life, it's perfect for snow sledging in winter and relaxing in summer. But the lake is cold all year round, so don't even think about it.

Approx: Nov–Mar, 11am–6pm; Apr–Oct, 8am–8.30pm

Hall and gardens, £5.50; Wider park, free

Manchester Town Hall

Albert Square, City Centre

(0161) 234 3157

Bees. Everywhere. Apparently the wides range of bee-themed paraphernalia i the UK. Not the home of some obsessiv insect collector – like the transvestite kille in *Silence of the Lambs* – but Mancheste Town Hall. In case you hadn't worked th out from the Boddingtons logo, the bee i the official symbol of Manchester. And wha busy bees they must have been to build th imposing neo-gothic building, with staine glass and creepy gargoyles. Architecturall acclaimed since its birth in 1887, th intricate interior is both a powerfull atmospheric and educational experience

Mon–Fri, 9am–5pm

Free

Manchester United Football Club

Sir Matt Busby Way, Old Trafford

(0161) 868 8000

There's no disputing that Old Traffor is one of the most exhilarating footba stadiums in the world. But as a visitor, let's be honest, food is darned important too Yet, catering for fans is not high on MUFC's list of priorities. The spotty adolescents in charge of dishing out the overpriced lukewarm pies and pasties stare in wide eyed wonderment at the huge crowds as if surprised they always get busy afte some bloke in black blows his whistle Remember to bring a packed lunch

Mon–Sun, 9.30am–5pm

Match tickets, £25–£35; museum and tour, £8.50

URTHER AFIELD

lderley Edge

here's so much bling scattered about is part of Cheshire, it looks like there's een an explosion in David Beckham's ewellery box. But if you have simpler (and ome might say better) taste, there's the ctual Edge itself – very scenic, steeped n legend, and the original reason why eople made the effort to trek out here rom Manchester. But it's hard not o be distracted just a tiny bit by the nultitude of footballers' mansions in the rea. It's surprisingly easy to while away n afternoon with a drive-by version f *Through The Keyhole*. Just don't oiter for too long, or you'll have to take some meat to placate the guard dogs.

TRAVEL

System One Travelcards

www.systemonetravelcards.co.uk

Having a System One Bus Saver in your wallet is more likely to save your life than a donor card. Ok, so it can't provide you with a pair of shiny new kidneys, but it can get your long-suffering liver back to base on any Greater Manchester bus until 4am, then trundle you to work the next day so all you have to worry about is trying not to breathe your noxious fumes on people. New customers need to take along a passport-sized mugshot (of your face, not your coffee, smart arse) to a GMPTE Travelshop to get a membership card, and after that you can top it up at over 800 PayPoint retailers.

Chester Zoo

Upton, Cheshire

(01244) 380 280

Are we at a Justin Trousersnake gig surrounded by young teens? No, it's a zoo, and there are young children everywhere, shrieking at pigeons trying to look exotic next to a rare, three-eyed Maori lizard. This is actually a fantastic daytrip, though the placing of two-dimensional cardboard cut-outs of 'tribal' people around the rhino enclosure is a bit disconcerting. An optional supplement on the entry fee contributes to Chester's conservation projects, and the animals look content. Well, as content as a meerkat can look, anyway.

Feb–Mar, 10am–4pm; Mar–Apr, 10am–6pm; Apr–Oct, 10am–5pm

£10.95/£9.95 concs

OTHER

John Rylands Library

150 Deansgate, Deansgate

(0161) 275 3764

If you've been wondering what on earth that scary-looking building on Deansgate is, the answer is not as cool as you might hope. It's a library. It was opened in 1900, in commemoration of John Rylands. A mill owner. We were hoping he was some kind of gothic lord rumoured to have stored his many wives in the basement, too. Recently re-opened with a new wing, it is home to special collections and rare books, and the chance to view such a cool building shouldn't be missed.

Mon & Wed–Sat, 10am–5pm; Tue & Sun, 12pm–5pm

Chanel Facials @ House of Fraser

Ground Floor, House of Fraser, Deansgate

(0161) 839 6985

If you've never been this nice to your skin before, we recommend the luxury option, as there's a full consultation – followed by the long, relaxing treatment itself. This includes cleansing, toning, moisturising, exfoliation, a mask and even massage (of the face AND scalp). That's right: you can do a hell of a lot more to your face than you might think. Plus, if you really can't justify the full works – the express option is a darn good second. Treat yourself to a pampering morning out.

The Basement

24 Lever Street, Northern Quarter

(0161) 237 1832

Those who want to make love, not war and save a tree in between peac rallies – tend to frequent The Basemer instead of the usual carbon-copy coffe shops. The atmosphere here is infinitel more copacetic (that's our new favourit word – look it up) than its soulles countorparts, absolutely everything i Fairtrade, and you can even recline i a comfy rocking chair while samplin the quirky library. Check your emails meander through the exhibition space o spend ten minutes absorbing the notic board by the door, which always come up a treat with bizarre local events

Wed–Fri, 12pm–3pm; Sat, 12pm–6pm

Laters

You Snooze, You Lose

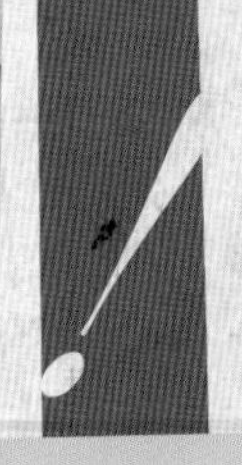

MISSING OUT ON LATE-NIGHT FUN BECAUSE YOUR GROOVY TRAIN IS STUCK IN LAZY TOWN? WANNA BE A MEMBER OF THE WIDE AWAKE CLUB, BUT YOUR DOZY HEAD FEELS HEAVIER THAN MALLETT'S MALLET? YOU NEED ITCHY'S MINI A-TO-ZED OF WAYS TO STAY AWAKE FOR DAYS...

If you don't want to set foot in the Land of Nod for a whole 24 hours, preparation must begin at breakfast time. If, like us, you like to kick your day off with a Weetabix or two, you'll know that dried-up cereal is one of the stickiest, most viciously viscous substances known to man. Smear a little porridge onto your eyelids and press them up towards your brows. Next, hold your head over the toaster to accelerate the drying process. Result: your peepers will be glued open permanently, or until it rains.

Worrying is a great way to stave off the sandman. Want to stay wired throughout a week-long holiday or festival? Go for an STD test just before things kick off. It'll be an agonising seven days before your results come through, during which time you won't sleep a wink.

Threadworms are known to be more active at night. Pick up your own wriggly-ass infestation by babysitting for your neighbourhood's grubbiest kids, then enjoy hours of sleeplessness courtesy of an intensely itchy bum. It's guaranteed you'll still be up at the – ahem – 'crack' of dawn.

Or, watch that kinky home video you discovered in your ma and pa's camcorder collection. Better than any horror film for making sure you'll never sleep again.

Illustration by Si Clarke

LATE-NIGHT SHOPPING

You've got two options: city centre, mostly open until about 8pm; or **The Trafford Centre (0161 749 1717)**, mostly open until 10pm. The first option features the big shops of **The Arndale (High Street, 0161 833 9851)**, **The Triangle (37 Exchange Square, 0161 834 8961)** etc. – plus department stores like **Marks and Spencer (7 Market Street, 0161 246 9085)** and **Selfridges (Exchange Square, 0161 838 0619).** The second... well, the same, only less spread out. Pros of the city centre: attractive in places; access to fresh air; nice places to eat and drink. Cons: a bit of a trek between some quarters; roads to cross. Pros of the Trafford Centre: extremely handy for mass emergency shopping (i.e. Christmas). Cons: the usual synthetic drawbacks – heavy air con and lights comparable to living inside a dentist's surgery or a fruit machine.

FAGS AT 4am

NOT vending machines. They're just muggers in disguise. If you're near the Southern Quarter, the 24-hour **Spar (2–4 Oxford Road, 0161 228 0355)** is indispensable. Or, alternatively, why not try taking advantage of the smoking ban side effect and try bumming ciggies off the crowds of smokers outside bars and pubs across the city.

LATE-NIGHT DRINKING

In the Southern Quarter, in the cobbled cavernous area under Oxford Road Station, lurk **The Thirsty Scholar (50 New Wakefield Street, 0161 236 6071)** and **The Salisbury (2 Wakefield Street, 0161 236 5590)**. Both old, characterful and crammed; yet with the possibility of a seat if you stay sharp and look lively and aren't afraid to turn to intimidation. If a backdrop of studenty metal music isn't your thing, try **Fab Café (111 Portland Street, 0161 236 2019)**, **Tiger Lounge, (5 Cooper Street, 0161 236 6007)**, or **Manto (46 Canal Street, 0161 236 2667)** in the Gay Village. Or pretty much anywhere in the Northern Quarter, where irregular opening times are part of the charm.

POST CLUB ACTION

In Manchester, post-club venues are viewed as being more pretentious than cool. Late-night revellers fall into the following categories: those who dance feverishly in Manchester's top clubs until morning, all weekend, every weekend; those who have a quick dance then return to talking-while-drinking at a relaxed bar or pub; and those who always choose a late-night meal in Chinatown or Rusholme over a club. For most, if it's summer, you're likely to be in the same garden you arrived at 12 hours earlier; and in winter, the takeaway-taxi-home-tunes-bed combination wins hands down.

FOOD NOW!

It's an unwritten law in Manchester that every residential address must have 20 takeaway menus. But on the late-night journey home, name and design are of secondary importance. "The kebab shop near the Spar on Oxford Road" is revered by many friends of Itchy, namely for its red chicken kebab; thing of legend. Its real name is Monsoons **(2 Oxford Road, 0161 237 5557)**. Other popular choices include **Finger Licking Chicken (422 Wilmslow Road, 0161 4451070)** in Withington, **McTucky's (36 Canal Street, 0161 236 1700)** in the Gay Village, and **Janam (78 Portland Street, 0161 228 2485)** in the city centre.

OTHER LATE-NIGHT INDULGENCES

Entertainment beyond the 9–5 grind doesn't have to consist of watching strippers work their way through med school (although there's nowt wrong with that). Casino membership at **Manchester 235 (Watson Street, 0161 828 0300)** can have you living the life of a Vegas high-roller 'til rosy fingered dawn does her thang. Or prove your devotion to cinema at the **Printworks Odeon (27 Withy Grove, 0871 224 4007)**. Laugh the night away at **The Comedy Store (Whitworth Street, 0161 839 9595)**. But why not be creative? Hop on the night bus. We guarantee you'll see sights you won't see anywhere else, not to mention the smells.

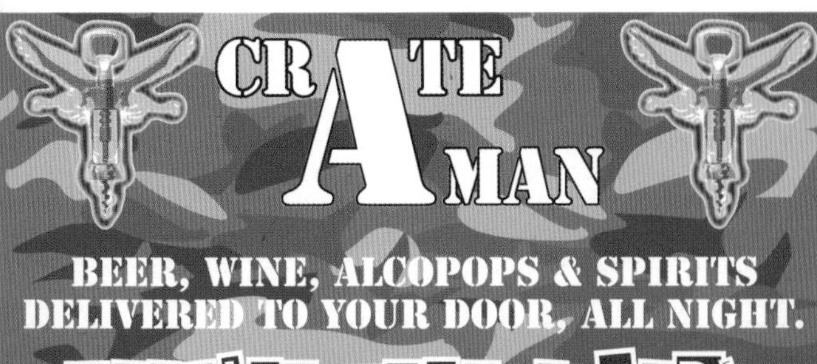
CRATE MAN
BEER, WINE, ALCOPOPS & SPIRITS
DELIVERED TO YOUR DOOR, ALL NIGHT.
KEEPING MANCHESTER'S
PARTY PEOPLE WET
0870 950 1525 07976 CRATES 07976 272837
www.crateman.co.uk
You must be 18 to purchase alcohol. We do not charge for delivery.

Sleep

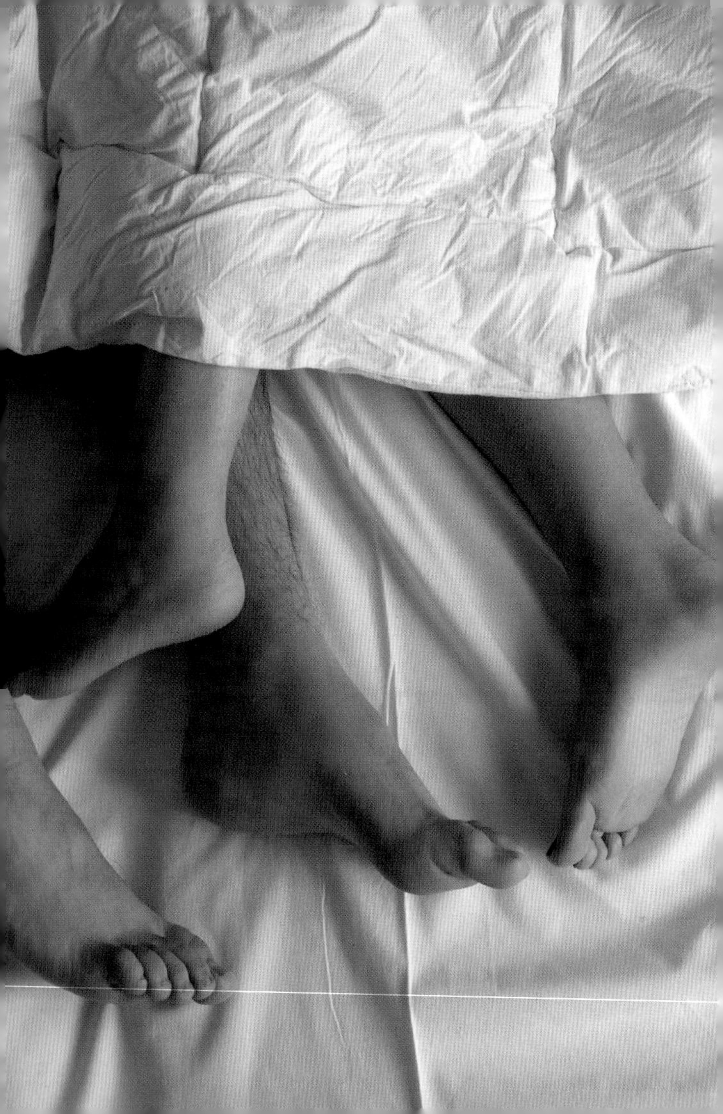

CHEAP

YHA

Potato Wharf, Castlefield

(0870) 770 5950

No running around in towels here. All rooms are en-suite – yes, really. Clean and airy with pleasant views.

Dormitory beds, from £16

SWANKY

The Lowry

50 Dearmans Place, Chapel Wharf, Deansgate

(0161) 827 4000

You wouldn't think the River Irwell could look pretty – but when you're on a balcony, with a glass of wine in your hand, it does.

£215–£315

MID-RANGE

Campanile Hotel

55 Ordsall Lane, Salford

(0161) 833 1845

A strange green-neon-and-red-brick island of a building, the Campanile screams 'business trip on a budget', but is ok really.

From £60

Gardens Hotel

55 Piccadilly Gardens, City Centre

(0161) 236 5155

Ow ow ow, shield your eyes. Blaring and tasteless, the pink neon 'hotel' sign can be seen from miles away. However, if you get past these initial impressions, the Gardens is a clean, reliable and reasonable option.

Doubles, £55–£65

Useful info

BEAUTY

Didsbury Beauty Clinic

715a Wilmslow Road, Didsbury

(0161) 445 4147

If you can't make yourself look beautiful, let these guys do it for you instead.

Tue–Thu, 10am–8pm; Fri, 10am–6pm; Sat, 9am–4pm

The Lowry Health Spa

Lowry Hotel, Dearmans Place, Chapel Wharf, Salford

(0161) 827 4034

If that guilt at your third takeaway of the week is starting to play on your mind, then take matters into your own fat, stubby hands and come here.

Mon–Fri, 7am–10pm; Sat–Sun, 8am–8pm

HAIRDRESSERS

Toni and Guy Academy

Queens House, Queen Street

(0161) 832 8282

Three-hour appointments aside, this place is the key to accessibly posh hair. And it's safer than letting your mate do it.

Mon–Fri, 9am–5.30pm

Nicky Clarke

Triangle, Hanging Ditch, Millennium Quarter

(0161) 833 3555

One of only four in the country. It also has some of the best hair stylists and 'colour technicians' in Manchester. Still, being pretentious now and again can't do you any harm, can it?

Mon–Fri, 10am–7pm; Sat 9am–6pm

Bannatyne's Health Club

Regency House, 38 Whitworth Street, City Centre

(0161) 236 6864

In or oot? Shake it all aboot at Bannatyne's. An express gym, cardio room, steam room, sauna, sunbeds, pool and spinning studio – whatever the feck that entails.

Mon–Fri, 6.30am–10pm; Sat–Sun, 8am–9pm

Spindles Health Club

Brittania Country House Hotel, Palatine Road, Nothenden

(0161) 434 3411

Sounding a bit like 'spinster', but without the loneliness, Spindles offers hair care, beauty treatments and fitness. In a hotel.

Mon–Fri, 7am–10pm; Sat–Sun, 8.30am–8.30pm

Redds Hair Design

329 Wilmslow Road, Fallowfield

(0161) 224 0546

Oddly for a hairdresser, über-trendy snottiness definitely isn't on the menu here. The staff are friendly and the service simple, reliable and well-priced.

Mon–Wed, 9.30am–5pm; Thu, 9.30am–5.30pm; Fri, 9.30am–6pm; Sat, 9am–4.30pm

Olivier Morosini

98 Tib Street

(0161) 832 8989

The great thing about this place is... Well, everything really. Cups of tea or coffee, amazing haircuts, friendly stylists, and even a biscuit if you're lucky.

Mon–Wed, 9am–6pm; Thu, 10am–8pm; Fri, 9.30am–6pm; Sat, 9am–4pm

ANNING

he Sun Room

7 Mauldeth Road

161) 224 4330

Vhen you start to look so pasty that eople could mistake you for the living ead, come here to brown yourself up.

Mon–Sat, 9am–5pm

op Tan

22 Barlow Moor Road, Chorlton

0161) 862 9898

Grab some free goggles, lock the door, strip off, put your coins in according to your safe limit, step in – and get a tan. Don't end up looking like Dale Winton though.

Mon–Fri, 9am–9pm; Sat, 9am–5pm; Sun, 9am–4pm

TATTOO

Holier Than Thou

105a Oldham Street, Northern Quarter

(0161) 839 3737

We don't think this is what 'holier' really means, but we like the name anyway.

Mon–Wed & Fri, 10.30am–6pm; Thu, 10.30am–7.30pm; Sat, 10.45am–6.30pm

Rambo of Manchester

42 Shudehill

(0161) 839 0090

If there's one person who you probably don't want a tattooist to model himself on, it's Rambo. Well, either Rambo or Patrick Bateman. Still, we reckon you should go to this place just so you can say you got a tattoo from Rambo. Sounds cool, dunnit?

Crateman

(0870) 950 1525

(07976) CRATES/272 837

Was there ever a more ingenious invention than a man and a crate of fags and booze delivered to your door at stupid o'clock? Itchy likes to think that, like Father Christmas, there is only one Crateman, who makes his rounds delivering goods to excited revellers, who sit swigging the last drops of vino and toasting their cigs around the stove in anticipation of his arrival. Most brilliantly, the clever elves in the workshop have put their thinking caps on and drummed up some party packs, so you don't have to worry those wasting braincells on whether you're going to keep on Carling or pass the Courvoisier.

Fri–Sat, 11pm–6am; Sun–Thu, 11pm–4am

TRAVEL

GMPTE Information Line

(0161) 228 7811

As far as acronyms go, GMPTE hardly rolls off the tongue. Still, this is the place to call if you want to know the movements (or not) of Manchester's public transport.

Mon–Fri, 7am–8pm; Sat–Sun, 8am–8pm

System One Travelcards

www.systemonetravelcards.co.uk

The guys at System One Travelcards make travelling around Manchester a hell of a lot easier. Get passes for a day, a week or a month and never worry about not having enough cash to buy a ticket again. The cards work on any train, bus or tram in Greater Manchester.

TRAINS

National Rail Enquiries

(08457) 484 950

If you want to know why your tra hasn't shown up/station is shut/there chewing gum on your seat, then thes guys might be able to help. Possibl

Mon–Sun, 24 hours

Virgin Trains

(08457) 222 333

If you don't want someone to sit next t you on the train, simply look into the eye of anyone walking past, smile at then suggestively, and then gently pat the sea next to you. It should work. Having sai that, if they smile back and sit next to you they might expect you to put out. Ooe

BUSES

National Express

Chorlton Street

(08705) 808 080

Make sure you get the seat at the front, so you can play Itchy's favourite game and pretend to be the driver.

Enquiry line, 8am–10pm

Piccadilly Bus Station

Piccadilly Gardens

(0161) 228 7811

The thing about Piccadilly Bus Station is that it isn't so much a bus station as a road. Still, if you're staggering around drunk looking for a bus and aren't sure where to go, this place is probably a good bet.

Mon–Sun, 8am–8pm

INTERNET CAFÉS

L 2 K Internet Gaming Café

32 Princess Street

(0161) 244 5566

L 2 the K. It almost sounds cool, but for the fact that you know these guys are dedicated to getting their level 38 wizard a new magic staff and a hat with +10 dexterity.

Mak's Internet Café

65 Blackfriars Road

(0161) 835 1899

Mak's place is the talk of the town. Well, maybe not, but head here if you need to check your emails when the internet has broken in your flat. Again.

Mon–Fri, 10am–9pm; Sat–Sun, 10am–6pm

CAR HIRE

Hertz Car Rentals

Manchester Airport, Terminal One

(0870) 850 2677

Itchy got a cut on our knee the other day, and it really Hertz. What does that have to do with this? Absolutely nothing, but we felt like making a pun anyway.

TAXIS

Avenue Cars

16a Victoria Avenue

(0161) 740 3030

Manchester Cars

4a Whitworth Street

(0161) 228 3355

LAUNDRETTES

Granada Dry Cleaners

71–73 Bridge Street

(0161) 834 8947

Ensuring we all go to work, weddings and movie premiers looking snazzy and suave, with same day service for the disorganised.

Mon–Sat, 9am–5pm

The Laundry Room

839 Wilmslow Road

(0161) 445 6264

Coincidentally, The Laundry Room was also the name of the least popular room in Willy Wonka's Chocolate Factory. But with all those kids getting chocolate on their clothes, you have to have one right?

Mon–Sat, 9am–5pm

ESTATE AGENTS

M1 City Apartments

68 Whitworth Street West

(0161) 228 1877

www.ls-1.co.uk

If pads really did come padded, the plush apartments this city centre specialist offers would be the snuggliest, fluffiest cashmere comfort blankets ever. The excellent M1 'life agents' cater for those who want to rent or buy right in the heart of Manc's chest. Live somewhere with proper interior design that extends beyond putting a poster over the hole in the wall you where you whacked it with the door handle, and a bowl of mouldy pot pourri on top of the bit of sideboard you accidentally burnt with a joss stick.

Mon–Fri, 9am–6pm; Sat, 10am–4pm

Jordan Fishwick

217 Deansgate

(0161) 833 9499

Manchester@JordanFishwick.co.uk

Jordan Fishwick; master of disguis secret agent, private investigator, licenc to kill. Or possibly none of these things but Jordan Fishwick is still a goo name for an Estate Agents regardless

Kings Residential Estate Agents

46 Edge Street

(0161) 832 3641

mail@kings-residential.co.uk

We reckon you should buy property fron here just because they have a cool logo It's a knight (or a king perhaps), sat on a horse. Clad in armour. With a sword. Cool

TAKEAWAY CURRY

Abduls

33–135 Oxford Road, All Saints

(0161) 273 7339

We advise against trying to eat a chicken korma out of your lap when you're rip-roaring drunk. Seriously, you should see our trousers.

Spicy Hut Restaurant

35 Wilmslow Road

(0161) 248 6200

Takeaway from a tasty Rusholme curry house. Perfect if you fancy a night in front of the television or luminous fish tank. Plus, they do free delivery within one mile of the restaurant. Perfect if you've lost one of your shoes.

TAKEAWAY FISH AND CHIPS

Armstrong's Fish and Chips

486 Bury Old Road

(0161) 773 6023

When Itchy was a youngster, we had a toy called Stretch Armstrong. A flexible rubber Hoff-alike filled with cornflour. We presume there is no connection.

Taylor's

7 The Precinct

(0161) 430 6319

Eating fish is a bit of a minefield these days. You're not supposed to have cod because we're fishing out natural stocks, while farmed fish is apparently naughty, You will forget all such moral quandaries on tasting the award-winning goodies here.

TAKEAWAY PIZZA

Buy The Slice

2 Chapel Street

(0161) 832 5553

Grab a monster 19" pizza, get some mates around and pretend you're in *Friends*. Without the naked guy opposite or the relentlessly incestuous romances.

Domino's

224 Wilmslow Road

(0161) 257 3832

Crawling with lazy students who forgot to buy dinner, Domino's does your typical, greasier-than-your-average takeaway fare. They also deliver if you can't be bothered to dig out your coat from underneath the dog.

TAKEAWAY CHINESE

Buffet Metro

59a–59b Piccadilly

(0161) 238 8686

Sometimes only a shameful pig-out on MSG-laden goodies will do the necessary, and when such urges strike, Buffet Metro is there for you.

The Treasure Pot

101 Manchester Road

(0161) 881 3609

Recently we were watching the fine cinematic work of Warwick Davis in *Leprechaun*. We can't help thinking that there would have been a whole lot less trouble if old Warwick had just settled for a takeaway from this place.

TAKEAWAY KEBAB SHOPS

Abdul's

324–326 Wilmslow Road

(0161) 248 7573

Yes, we all know it's a bad thing, and we did once know a kebab shop owner who refused to serve doner meat to his family, but it just tastes so good.

Kebabish Original

170–172 Cheetham Hill Road

(0161) 834 4544

So apparently this was the first kebab shop in the history of the world, father of them all. We wonder whether perhaps their kebabs are so special that they are now only an approximation of those sold elsewhere. A kebab(ish).

TAKEAWAY CHICKEN

The Chicken Run

6 Yarburgh Street

(0161) 231 0153

Mel Gibson, Jane Horrocks, Julia Sawalha and Miranda Richardson star in this stop motion escape caper from the creators of *Wallace and Gromit*. Oh, hang on...

Roosters Fried Chicken

582 Ashton New Road

Mud in the eye to all those beguiled by wholesome-looking TV ads featuring glowing families bonding over buckets of greasy chicken and litres of sugary pop to a banging Motown soundtrack, it's nice to see a chicken joint that wears its heart on its sleeve.

Support

Brook Advisory Centre
Commonwealth House, Lever Street
(0161) 237 3001

Greater Manchester Police
(0161) 856 0905

Manchester City Council
Town Hall, Albert Square
(0161) 234 5000

Manchester Drug Service
The Bridge, 104 Fairfield Street
(0161) 273 4040

Manchester Royal Infirmary
Oxford Road Manchester
(0161) 276 1234

Manchester University Police Liaison Officer
(0161) 275 7042

Manchester Visitors Centre
Lloyd Street, St Peter's Square
(08712) 228 223

NHS Direct
(0845) 46 47

Samaritans
72–74 Oxford Street
(08457) 909 090

Trafford Alcohol Services
Cornhill Clinic, Cornhill Road
(0161) 747 1841

Chapel Street
Travelodge
Booth Street
Blackfriars Street
River Irwell
Victoria Street
Cathedral
Cateaton St
Hanging Ditch
Corporation Street
Arndale Shopping Centre
St Mary's Gate
Market St
Exchange Street
Royal Exchange Theatre
Parsonage
College Land
Deansgate
Barton Sq
St Ann's Sq
Cross Street
New Market
Market St
Norfolk St
Old Bank St
Pall Mall
Back South St
St Mary's St
St Mary's Parsonage
St Ann Street
Brown Street
Chapel Walks
Marsden St
Southgate
King St West
Butter Ln
Back Bridge St
Police St
St Ann's Church
King Street
South King Street
King Street
Essex St
Tib Ln
Spring
John Dalton Street
Four Yards
Ridgefield
Wood Street
John Rylands Library
St Mary's Church
Booth St
Brown St
Kennedy Street
Fountain St
Brazennose Street
Albert Square
Registry Office
Queen Street
Lloyd Street
Princess Street
Town Hall
Mosley St
Jordell St
Jackson's Row
Lloyd St
Little Quay St
Southmill St
Central St
Mount Street
Bootle Street
Jerusalem Pl
Marron Pl
Peter Street
Central Library
International Convention
Cinema

Craft Centre
GREAT ANCOATS STREET
Copperas St
Edge Street
Oak Street
High Street
Back Turner St
Turner Street
Market
Union St
Red Lion St
John St
Hilton Street
Tib Street
Oldham St
Spear Street
Church Street
High Street
Tib St
Bridgewater Pl
Dale Street
Coach Station (Temporary)
Lever Street
Faraday St
Hilton St
PO
Postal St
Dean
Little Lever St
Police Museum
Newton Street
ANCHESTER
Back Piccadilly
Little Lever
Dale St
Brewer Street
Hilton St
Piccadilly
Tariff Street
China Lane
Dale Street
Piccadilly Gardens
Mosley Street
Parker Street
Piccadilly
Paton St
Lena Street
Hope St
Chatham St
Gore St
Ducie St
George Street
George St
York Street
Chain St
Charlotte St
Faulkner St
Portland St
Aytoun Street
Silver Street
Minshull Street
Crown Court
Auburn St
London Road
Oriental Arch
Chorlton St
Bloom St
Coach Station
Street
Get there with system one travelcards.co.uk

Index

Index

Dan Colwell

CONTENTS

MAPS

This Way Australia

The Great Outdoors

An exhilarating mix of ancient land and modern nation, Australia is not a place for sitting back and letting things happen. Rather, it demands that you go out and experience the excitement of the ultimate "great outdoors". Just inland from the sparkling cities which cling to the coast, you will find a vast, majestic expanse of uninhabited land which stretches 4000 km (2500 miles) from Sydney to Perth.

Famous for the awesome "outback", burnt red under the relentless sun, this dramatic land is large enough to encompass tropical rainforests and snow-capped mountains. What is more, it is encompassed by over 36,000 km (22,000 miles) of coastline, a paradise for surfers and swimmers. Australia is the size of the USA, but has a population of a mere 18 million people—which guarantees that its boundless national parks and endless, empty beaches remain unspoiled.

The First Australians

For the indigenous peoples who lived here for 40,000 years before the first European set eyes on the place, the land has a mystical significance. Every rock, creek, animal and bird is part of what is known as the Dreamtime, a complex vision of the world which has profound spiritual, artistic and environmental resonance. The Aboriginal peoples believe that the spirits who created the land and its inhabitants during the Dreamtime also created the laws by which they themselves live. The Dreamtime is present in every aspect of Aboriginal life, be it hunting, painting or daily chores, continually re-creating the relationship between the spiritual world, the land and the people.

The loss of their land after the British arrived, therefore, was not just a territorial disaster, but a spiritual one as well. It is only through their strong sense of cultural identity that they have managed to survive at all. But there are signs that things might be changing for the better. Recent moves have seen ownership of certain important spiritual sites restored to the Aborigines—Uluru (Ayers Rock) and the Kakadu National Park are now owned and jointly managed by the local Aboriginal tribes.

City Life

The majority of Australians today are city-dwellers. Nevertheless, their cities give them many opportunities to enjoy an al fresco lifestyle. With oceanside locations, a glorious climate and plenty of space at their disposal, they have made their cities remarkably pleasant places to live in. The suburbs may sprawl for miles, but the city centres of Perth, Darwin, Brisbane and Adelaide offer a surprising variety of experiences to choose from, with numerous subtropical parks and gardens, first-class museums and art galleries, radically modern architecture and a range of international restaurants. Atmospheric Hobart in Tasmania still retains the flavour of its early days as a whaling port, while Melbourne buzzes with the excitement of a big city. The capital, Canberra, is an interesting example of a planned city, and boasts some fine modern architecture and the unmissable National Gallery of Australia. The jewel in Australia's urban crown, though, is Sydney. With the stunning Opera House and beautiful harbour, it is one of the world's greatest cities.

Wildlife

Australia is the smallest, driest and flattest continent on earth, levelled out by several million years of weather-beating. Its animal and plant life has developed in its own unique direction. The vegetation ranges from the paperbark swamps of lush tropical wetlands to the hardy ghost gums and spinifex grasses of the central desert, and there are vast forests of the distinctively Australian eucalyptus, whose vapours tinge the air blue.

However, it is Australia's animals which capture the imagination. The duck-billed platypus and spiny anteater (echidna) are the only surviving egg-laying mammals. Saltwater crocodiles, tiger snakes and funnel-web spiders all hold a certain deadly fascination. But the marsupials, ancient mammals who carry their young in pouches, are Australia's real success story. Evolving into wonderful improbables like the kangaroo, koala and wombat, the marsupials colonized every corner of the continent. There are more than 120 different species alive today.

World Heritage

Among its thousands of national parks and reserves, Australia has 13 World Heritage Sites. Most are easily accessible from the major cities.

The most famous are the Rock and the Reef: Ayers Rock, the huge, mysterious monolith in the centre of Australia, now known by its Aboriginal name of Uluru; and the Great Barrier Reef, a vast living chain of coral stretching for

Most of Kakadu is owned and managed by Aboriginal communities.

2000 km (1200 miles) and dotted with gorgeous coral islands.

The lesser-known marvels include Kakadu National Park, near Darwin in the tropical north, an area of wetlands, ancient Aboriginal rock paintings, waterfalls, exotic birdlife and rivers full of crocodiles; Shark Bay, in Western Australia, where dolphins, dugongs, whales and turtles swim in the warm waters; and Fraser Island, north of Brisbane, the largest sand island in the world and home to a unique rainforest.

Gateways

The best way to approach a country of such epic dimensions is to divide it into digestible portions. Individual state capitals, such as Sydney, Melbourne and Perth, make ideal bases from which to explore the splendours of a particular region. Some of the most dramatic sights are remote from the big cities, however. For Uluru in the Red Centre, thousands of kilometres from the nearest metropolis, set off from characterful Alice Springs. Pleasant North Queensland towns such as Cairns are the best starting point for discovering the wonders of the Great Barrier Reef, while Broome is gateway to the isolated grandeur of the Kimberley, Australia's final frontier.

Flashback

Early Settlement

The first humans arrived in Australia at least 40,000 years ago, when sea levels were sufficiently low to allow migration from Asia. There was probably a much later wave of settlement from the north by people who brought with them the dingo, the Australian wild dog.

"Aborigine", the term used to describe indigenous Australians, suggests a degree of homogeneity among the population which did not actually exist. At the time of European settlement, up to 500 different tribes spoke more than 200 distinct languages, in an overall population which numbered between 300,000 and 500,000. They had spread across the continent to become coastal fishing communities, hunter-gatherers of the central desert, and rainforest dwellers.

However, two common characteristics were notable. The Aboriginal tribes developed complex cultures, with rich traditions of oral literature, art, sculpture and music, and yet they achieved virtually no technological advances except for the boomerang and the improvement of existing stone tools. This was largely because the population was already perfectly adapted to the conditions of the land, and cut off from all external spurs to development. Ironically, this meant that they were entirely unable to withstand European colonization when it came.

Dot paintings usually represent an aerial view of a Dreaming journey.

First Contact

Since the time of Ptolemy, European geographers had predicted the existence of a southern continent, *terra australis incognita*, the necessary counterbalance, they thought, to the land masses of the northern hemisphere. It is likely that the Portuguese, with their trading interests in Indonesia, chanced upon the continent sometime in the 1530s. However, the Dutch have the honour of being the first recorded Europeans on Australian soil: in 1606 Willem Janszoon reached the Cape York promontory, while in 1616, Dirk Hartog landed on the west coast at Shark Bay and famously left behind an old pewter dish as proof of his visit. In 1642, Abel Tasman rounded the southern tip of the continent, stopping briefly in the island later named after him, Tasmania. The monumental task of mapping the outline of Australia was well under way, but although the land was christened New Holland, the various reports of its barrenness and "miserably poor" natives soon led the Dutch to give up any hopes of establishing a trading base.

British Exploration

The British had become the most dynamic colonial power in Europe by the end of the 17th century, nurturing hopes of breaking into the Dutch, French and Portuguese markets in the Far East. The first Briton to reach Australia was William Dampier in 1688. However, his account of the country was so negative that the British were put off further exploration for some time. But fascination with the mysterious southern continent never completely died.

By the mid-18th century, the British were once again planning to pursue their interests in the region. Fired by suspicion of the French, and with renewed hopes of establishing an empire in the east, the British Admiralty sent a ship, the *Endeavour*, under Captain James Cook to explore the South Pacific. On April 20, 1770, land was sighted; over the next four months Cook discovered Botany Bay (so called because of the enormous range of new plants found there by the ship's botanist, Joseph Banks), and claimed the entire eastern coast for the British Empire, naming it New South Wales. The Aboriginal peoples' immense span of time alone on the southern continent was drawing to a close.

Colonization

In fact, colonization advanced no further for some years, until the loss of the American colonies in 1783 led the British government to consider a new destination for the country's overflowing prison population. At first reluctant to settle such a remote place, they finally decided on New South Wales. The First Fleet of 11 square-rigged sailing ships, under the command of Captain Arthur Phillip and carrying 736 male and female convicts, set sail from Portsmouth in May 1787 and arrived at what is now Sydney Harbour on January 26, 1788.

Things went badly in the first two years. Attacked by hostile Aboriginals and almost starving —the soldiers and urban convicts hadn't the faintest idea how to grow food crops in this alien environment—the colony nearly perished. It was rescued in the nick of time by the arrival of the Second Fleet at the end of 1790. Much to the amazement of sceptics back home, the colony of New South Wales would survive into the new century.

Expansion and Conflict

Following the enlightened rule of Governor Lachlan Macquarie from 1810 to 1821, free colonists poured into New South Wales, which became more of a conventional commercial colony, trading in wool and grain. As a result, the most recalcitrant convicts were sent to even more remote parts, conveniently opening up more territories to British settlement and legitimizing Britain's claim to the whole continent. New penal colonies were founded at Brisbane (1823) and Port Arthur in Tasmania (1830). Convicts were also sent to Perth, as too few settlers were willing to move to such a distant place. However, by the middle of the century, Australia was proving a popular destination for free colonists. The sorry chapter of transportation to eastern Australia finally closed in 1852, and to western Australia in 1868. In all, more than 160,000 men, women and children had been transported from Britain.

The newcomers' voracious appetite for land continued to have disastrous consequences for the Aboriginal population. Pioneer farmers and prospectors moved into all the main coastal areas of the country, inevitably bringing the two sides into further conflict. Contrary to popular opinion, the Aboriginals were never passive about their destruction. They fought back bravely, using guerrilla tactics and their greater knowledge of the bush, but ultimately they were no match for the settlers' guns and, even worse, their diseases. In Tasmania, the 4000 Aboriginals living there at the time of British settlement in 1803 were reduced to 187 within 30 years, and finally moved off the island altogether.

Explorers and Prospectors

The 19th century saw a rapid growth in British knowledge about the southern continent. In 1803, Matthew Flinders, a naval midshipman, had become the first person ever to circumnavigate the island-continent, and recommended changing its name from New Holland to Australia. By the mid-1800s, intrepid explorers of the outback, among them John Eyre, Ludwig Leichhardt, John McDouall Stuart and the doomed Burke and Wills, had demonstrated the colonists' desire and ability to reach across Australia's barren heartland.

In the wake of such expeditions came the prospectors. The second half of the 19th century was dominated by discoveries of huge mineral resources—the Victoria gold rush began in 1851, and subsequent gold booms occurred in Queensland in the 1860s and Western Australia in the 1890s. This fevered activity created a tremendous population explosion and saw huge influxes of settlers from as far away as China and the United States into the interior.

The land which had seemed as distant as the moon a century earlier was now an increasingly wealthy and confident set of colonies, with a cultural and political identity separate from the Mother Country. A strong nationalist movement developed towards the end of the century, and a change in the relationship with Britain became inevitable.

Federation

The Australian colonies shared two important concerns which outweighed their desire for individual autonomy: the need for free trade, and the perennial anxiety about threats from overseas. As a result, they saw the wisdom of joining forces to form one nation, and the Commonwealth of Australia came into being on January 1, 1901.

The new constitution created a federal system, with the states (as they now were) giving up certain powers, such as defence and immigration, to a federal government. The British monarch remained head of state, represented by a governor-general. Although the new nation remained loyal to Britain, the century ahead would see the ties gradually loosen.

The 20th Century

The first governments maintained an anti-Asian "White Australia" policy over immigration, coupled with an advanced social welfare system at home. By the beginning of World War I, women had obtained the vote, and a minimum wage and old-age pensions had been introduced.

The Great War was a defining moment for Australia. The remarkable courage shown by its troops at Gallipoli in 1915 was taken to symbolize Australia's arrival as an independent nation. On the other hand, it was a military disaster blamed on the failure of British tacticians, and led many Australians to criticize the country's unquestioning support of Britain and the use of its soldiers in such a distant war. Despite this, Australia followed the British into war again at the outbreak of hostilities with Germany in 1939.

This time Australia itself came under attack. When the Japanese bombed the northern coast in 1942, the 150-year-old fear of foreign invasion seemed about to be realised, and it was apparent that the British were more concerned with their own national survival than with protecting Australia. When Japan was finally defeated by American forces, it was inevitable that the Australians should become increasingly allied to the US. Unfortunately, this did not end the country's embroilment in foreign conflicts. Support for the Americans led to 50,000 Australian personnel serving in the Vietnam War during the 1960s.

Australia Today

Australia is now a very different country from the one which emerged from World War II. The most visible change is in the population itself. After the war, the prevailing slogan was "populate or perish", and immigration was actively encouraged from other parts of Europe as well as Britain. The White Australia policy officially ended in 1973, and immigrants from China and southeast Asia soon began to pour in. Indeed, Australia has recently begun to shift its geopolitical ties away from the US towards Asia, its most important trading area.

Nowadays Australia presents itself as a multicultural society, but the current major issues facing the country (other than the perennial ones of the economy and unemployment) have their roots in its colonial origins. The crucial Mabo Decision, handed down by the High Court in 1992, ruled that Aboriginal peoples had had a legitimate claim on the land prior to British settlement in 1788. This heated up the whole question of "native title". The implications of the decision, and the question of how the Aboriginal peoples' aspirations can be reconciled with the counter-claims of farmers and miners, will test the judgement of Australian politicians and judges for years to come.

At a constitutional level, the proposal to make Australia a republic and end its connection to the British monarchy was refused by 54.22 per cent of the people in the referendum of November 1999. In the new millennium, as this vast country enters its second century of nationhood, it will see many changes, but its fascination for visitors will undoubtedly remain as powerful as ever.

1

THE BEST PLACE TO PLAY WITH DOLPHINS

At **Monkey Mia**, a resort in Shark Bay, 850 km (528 miles) north of Perth, small groups of bottlenose dolphins swim into the shallows almost every morning. They take fish from visitors (under close supervision of rangers), nudge them playfully and charm one and all.

New South Wales and A.C.T.

Australia's oldest city was founded in 1788, when the commander of the First Fleet, Captain Arthur Phillip, wisely chose for his convict colony what he called "the finest harbour in the world" and named it after Lord Thomas Sydney, England's Home Secretary.

The capital of New South Wales is not the capital of Australia, however. For this rôle, Canberra, set within the 2,368 sq km (914 sq miles) of the Australian Capital Territory (A.C.T.), was custom-built in the early 20th century.

SYDNEY

The Rocks, Sydney Harbour, City Centre, Darling Harbour, Hyde Park, Macquarie Street, The Domain, Outside the Centre, Beaches

The city has gone from strength to strength since those first, harsh days. Some stately 19th-century buildings are testament to the riches which flowed through here after the New South Wales gold rush. Today, their Victorian elegance contrasts with the modernity of the famous Sydney Harbour Bridge and a spectacular forest of post-1945 high-rises, most visibly the gleaming Sydney Tower. The whole effect is crowned by the breathtaking Opera House, whose radical design of spinnaker-like segments is the ultimate symbol of Sydney's 20th-century confidence. The city continues to develop, as another flurry of building and renovation has been undertaken to greet the new millennium, following Sydney's selection as host of the 2000 Olympic Games.

Apart from its splendid sights, this vibrant, booming city of nearly 4 million people offers the most cosmopolitan urban experience on the continent. As both an important seaport and the nation's financial centre, it has attracted immigrants from all over the world. The result is that Sydney boasts the best in international cuisine, excellent shopping, a lively Chinatown and a nightlife which ranges from the sophisticated to the downright raunchy. And unlike many Australian towns, where the locals head back to the suburbs at night, here you will find that the smart Sydneysiders are out and about enjoying the delights of their glorious city 24 hours a day.

The Rocks

This hilly outcrop to the west of Circular Quay was the site which Governor Phillip selected to build the houses of the first English settlement in Australia. The Rocks proved to be an ideal port, but the area became sadly neglected during the 19th century. Today, following a major 1970s restoration project, the warehouses and wharves have been renovated as restaurants, shops and galleries. With its harbour setting and historic pubs, the Rocks provides the perfect atmosphere for sightseeing, shopping or socializing.

Call in first at the Rocks Visitor Centre on George Street, the former Sailors' Home. You can pick up a useful map of the area, and take in an interesting exhibition on the colourful local history at the same time. The modest sandstone house next door is Cadman's Cottage. John Cadman was transported to Australia with a life sentence for horse stealing, but he ended his days working as the government coxswain. Dating from 1816, the cottage is the oldest surviving dwelling in Sydney. When it was built it was just a couple of yards from the shore.

Across the road, Argyle Street takes you up to the famous Argyle Cut, a tunnel leading to Millers Point on the other side of the Rocks. Hewn out of solid stone by convicts using only pickaxes, the work began in 1843 and was still unfinished when transportation ended in the early 1850s. The tunnel was eventually completed by the use of explosives.

Millers Point

Once through the Cut, you may be forgiven for thinking you have entered another age. With its colonial houses, village green and delightful old pubs, picturesque Millers Point manages to retain the flavour of the past. The small 19th-century Garrison Church, which once served a nearby army barracks, sits peacefully at one end of Argyle Place. At the other end, hard-earned thirsts can be quenched at the Lord Nelson pub, licensed since 1842 and claimed to be the oldest in Australia.

On the nearby hill stands the Observatory, built in 1857 on the site of Fort Phillip. If you book in advance, its telescope is available for night-time viewing of the southern skies. The park outside is a delight, with welcome shade provided by Australian fig trees, and views over to the Harbour Bridge.

For a close-up of the bridge, head downhill to Dawes Point, a grassy, cannon-studded headland much favoured by photographers. Just around the corner at Pier One, the old shipping terminal has been renovated as a lively group of restaurants and shops.

Sydney Harbour

Officially known as Port Jackson, Sydney Harbour is a maze of headlands and inlets which stretches 20 km (12 miles) from the Pacific to the Paramatta River. The city is at its most picturesque seen from the water, so while you are at Circular Quay be sure to hop on a ferry—whatever the destination.

Sydney Harbour Bridge

Known affectionately as "The Coathanger", the gigantic steel-arch bridge rises up dramatically from the Rocks. Completed bang on schedule in 1932, the Harbour Bridge's span was a major feat of engineering—its 6 million rivets and 485,000 sq m (580,000 sq yd) of steel took eight years to put together. You can climb up the southeastern pylon (access from Cumberland Street) for excellent views of waterside Sydney. Halfway up, the Harbour Bridge Museum documents its history.

Circular Quay

This is the effervescent centre of the harbour. Ferries chug in and out of the docks, restaurants and cafes are filled with the chatter of commuters and tourists, and throngs of people stroll along the waterfront, stopping occasionally to watch buskers or read the bronze plaques of the Writers' Walk. Set in the pavement all around the quay, these are inscribed with quotations from Australian writers and famous foreigners on the glories of the country in general, and Sydney in particular.

CAPTAIN BOUNTIFUL

After the mutiny on the *Bounty*, the resolute Captain Bligh navigated his way across 5800 km (3600 miles) of sea in an open longboat and survived to become, eventually, governor of New South Wales. He clearly had a problem with people management, though. In 1808, just three years after his arrival in Sydney, the New South Wales Corps complained of his tyrannical behaviour, mutinied and placed him under arrest. However, Bligh lived a charmed life. The Sydney mutineers were captured and tried, while he ended his days as Vice Admiral of the Fleet.

Striking from any angle, the billowing sails of Sydney Opera House.

Sydney Opera House

The country's most spectacular modern structure juts out over Bennelong Point, a bold statement that its largest city had arrived on the world stage. It was originally designed by Danish architect Jørn Utzon, and construction began in 1959. By the time it was completed in 1973, the costs had escalated from an estimated $7 million to $102 million. Utzon resigned in 1966, and Australian architects finished off the plans, but the building immediately reveals the daring of his ideas—huge pre-cast concrete shells resting on narrow bases are covered with shining white roofs, clad in tiles whose anti-fungal surface never needs cleaning. The luxurious interiors are furnished in native woods and textiles, and the building contains not just an opera house but an entire arts complex, with two theatres and an enormous concert hall.

City Centre

George Street leads from the Rocks and Circular Quay right up through the heart of Sydney's business and shopping district, which is always a riot of activity on weekdays. Nowhere better represents this part of town than Australia Square, which serves as a lively lunchtime meeting place for office workers, to the north of the Wynard shopping complex. South along George Street, Martin Place is another busy pedestrian precinct, and contains the imposing Victorian general post office and a cenotaph commemorating Australia's war dead.

Sydney Tower

On Market Street, just off George Street, the southern hemisphere's tallest building is a 320-m (1050-ft) high needle topped by a striking gold spool. Inside, there is a revolving restaurant, and an observation platform from which you can see as far as the Blue Mountains to the west and Botany Bay to the south. The tower is open till 9.30 p.m. every night (11.30 p.m. on Saturdays).

Town Hall Square

A couple of blocks away, the heart of Victorian Sydney is dominated by the extravagant façade of the Town Hall, built in a mixture of French and Italian Renaissance styles during the gold-boom years of the late 19th century. Across the plaza, the Anglican St Andrew's Cathedral dates from 1868 and is the oldest in Australia, while that other passion of the Victorians, trade, is given a suitably grand showpiece in the nearby Queen Victoria Building. Starting life as a market hall, this grand, block-long structure has been beautifully restored to its earlier glory, and is now a very superior shopping centre.

Chinatown

Further south in the Haymarket area, Sydney's Chinatown centres on Dixon Street. The dragon-clad gates, the shops and restaurants fragrant with spices, all bring life and colour to an otherwise faded part of the city. The Chinese Garden, near Darling Harbour, was designed by architects from Guangdong province according to traditional principles dating back to the 5th century. It is small but has waterfalls, a lake, a pagoda and a teahouse, from whose balcony you can enjoy this oasis of calm.

Darling Harbour

During the 1980s, Sydney undertook one of the country's most important urban redevelopment programmes—transforming Darling Harbour from a run-down industrial area into a showcase of landscaped gardens, entertainment and convention centres, shops, restaurants, and exciting, new museums. Although it is only a 10-minute walk from the city centre, there are some interesting alternative ways to get there. You can take a ferry from Circular Quay, and there is the overhead monorail, which can be boarded in Pitt Street.

Australian National Maritime Museum

Housed in a huge, glass-walled building on the western side of the harbour, the museum recounts the story of Australia's ties with the sea, going back to the time of Captain Cook. Moored outside are vessels as diverse as a century-old racing cutter, a World War II destroyer and one of the rickety fishing boats which brought Vietnamese refugees to Australia in 1977.

Sydney Aquarium

On the other side of the harbour, you can come face to face with sharks, crocodiles, giant stingrays and other fearsome denizens of Australia's waters. The aquarium has an impressive underwater tunnel, which brings the sharks into unnerving close-up. There is also a display of brilliantly coloured fish from the Great Barrier Reef.

Powerhouse Museum

This snappy museum, based in an old power station, has thousands of exhibits covering industry, design, and science and technology —from an antique steam locomotive to the food used by astronauts. Its hands-on approach to the nuts and bolts of modern culture makes it one of the most popular of Sydney's museums with young and old alike.

Hyde Park

Smaller than its London namesake, but just as central, rectangular Hyde Park began life as a racetrack. The southern half contains the powerful Anzac Memorial, an Art Deco cenotaph housing an exhibition hall which documents the role of Australian troops in overseas conflicts. The northern half of the park is dominated by a splendid avenue of trees.

Australian Museum

Across the road from Hyde Park South, the museum occupies a vast neoclassical building of the mid-19th century. It houses an overwhelming collection of natural history and ethnology, perhaps the greatest in the South Pacific. There are major exhibits on Aboriginal history and culture, covering the vast period from the Dreamtime to the present. In addition, you can see artefacts from Papua New Guinea, such as spirit temples and costumes, and displays of Australian wildlife, minerals and dinosaurs.

St Mary's Cathedral

On the park's northeastern side, Sydney's monumental Catholic cathedral opened in the 1880s, and with its two lofty spires and large rose windows is very much a product of the late-Victorian heavy Gothic style.

Macquarie Street

Governor Macquarie set his stamp on the colony by commissioning convict-architect Francis Greenway, who had been transported for forgery, to set about designing the city's first major group of public buildings. These transformed Sydney from a penal settlement to a colonial Georgian town in just a few years.

Hyde Park Barracks

Outside the northern entrance to Hyde Park, the barracks were designed by Greenway as an overnight lock-up for convicts brought into Sydney as labourers. The building, dating from 1819, has been lovingly restored, and many of the objects found here are now included in a fascinating museum, which focuses on the story of the barracks and the lives of the convicts they once housed.

St James' Church

Opposite the barracks, and sharing with them the honour of being considered Greenway's finest surviving work, the oldest church in the city was originally intended as a courthouse. Completed in 1824, it reflects the architect's taste for Georgian classicism.

Mint Building

At 109 Macquarie Street, this two-storey colonial structure was once the southern wing of the Rum Hospital, so called because Governor Macquarie rewarded its builders with a highly profitable monopoly for the sale of rum. Built in 1816, it was turned into Australia's first mint in the 1850s following the New South Wales gold rush. It is still concerned with money: the museum has exhibits on gold, coins, mining and minting.

Parliament House

Occupying the northern wing of the old Rum Hospital, the elegant, colonnaded New South Wales Parliament has been home to the state's lower chamber since 1856. It is open to the public, and when parliament is sitting you can watch a debate from the visitors' gallery.

Museum of Sydney

Take a detour left down Bridge Street to a museum dedicated to the history of the city. A further point of interest is that it is located on the site of Captain Phillip's original Government House, built in 1788. Using sculptures, installations, digital-media technology and holograms, the museum leads you on a thought-provoking tour of Sydney's past, from the first encounter between Englishman and Aborigine to the bustling port town of a century later.

The Domain

The parkland of the Domain was reserved for the Crown by Governor Phillip and kept as an open space, for which picnicking, jogging and sunbathing Sydneysiders have been grateful ever since. It originally extended over the whole area from Bennelong Point to what is now Hyde Park, but in 1816 a large tract of land was set aside in order to establish the Royal Botanic Gardens.

Royal Botanic Gardens

The gardens' rolling green lawns are beautifully landscaped and cover more than 25 ha (62 acres). Perfect for admiring Australian and imported plants, they include a rose garden, a garden of succulents and a large palm grove on the site of Australia's first farm of 1788. Especially noteworthy features are the glass pyramid for tropical plants, the Moreton Bay fig trees and the statue honouring Governor Phillip.

Government House

Neo-Gothic Government House has been occupied by governors of New South Wales since 1845. Located entirely within the Botanic Gardens, it has a delightful garden of its own, which is open to the public.

Nearby, the castellated building which is now the Conservatorium of Music once served as the rather grand stables for the spoiled horses of Government House. Commenced in 1817, it was designed by the ubiquitous Francis Greenway.

Mrs Macquarie's Point

Governor Macquarie's wife was famously fond of this area, and her favourite spot from which to admire the city is now known as Mrs Macquarie's Point, at the tip of the Domain. Carved out of the rocky headland, Mrs Macquarie's Chair is still a place to sit and enjoy the view, though what the lady herself would have thought of the Opera House is anyone's guess.

Art Gallery of New South Wales

Situated in the southern part of the Domain, the gallery has an excellent collection of Aboriginal and Torres Strait Islanders art, as well as works by eminent modern Australian artists such as Sidney Nolan, Arthur Boyd and Russell Drysdale. There is also a collection of Old Masters, and modern Europeans from Picasso to Francis Bacon are well represented.

Outside the Centre

Sydney's suburbs have a flavour all their own, as well as some great attractions, so break out from the centre and discover another side to the city.

Kings Cross

To the east of the Domain, Kings Cross is Sydney's Jekyll and Hyde—by day it is an innocent-looking inner suburb, but at night its more lurid face is revealed. Strip clubs, dingy bars, and a thick sprinkling of dubious characters hanging around give it a suitably low-life atmosphere, but with so many sightseers checking out the scene it never feels particularly dangerous.

Fitzroy Gardens, at the heart of the district, boasts a curious dandelion-puff fountain commemorating the World War II battle of El Alamein. There is also an arts and crafts market in the square every Sunday.

Paddington

This area was a notorious slum earlier in the century. After a vigorous bout of gentrification, its Victorian houses, decorated with delicate, lacy grillwork, have been restored to their former glory. Oxford Street, Paddington's main drag, is one of the liveliest night-time hotspots in town, packed with bars and clubs. The famous Paddington Village Bazaar, held here on Saturdays, blends value-for-money shopping with a raucous street party. The old sandstone Victoria Barracks nearby are the most impressive military complex in Sydney and still in use.

Parramatta

This was the second site of European settlement on the continent, a mere 20 km (12 miles) upriver from Sydney, and developed by Governor Phillip as a farm, in a desperate bid to feed the new colony. To the east of the town centre, the colonial homestead at Elizabeth Farm dates from 1793 and is the oldest surviving house in Australia. It was built by the founders of Australia's wool industry.

Beaches

Australia's renowned beach and surfing culture began on the marvellous beaches around Sydney. Bondi is an institution in itself, and although its glamour has become a little faded these days it is still the place to go to experience the Australian dream at its rawest.

Several excellent beaches are to be found north and south of Sydney Harbour. If you fancy somewhere less touristic than Bondi, try the southern beaches at Tamarama, Coogee, Bronte and Maroubra. Vast, white-sanded and with great breakers, they will not disappoint. To the north, Manly is reached by an enjoyable ferry ride from Circular Quay. With the Manly Art Gallery and Museum and the shark-infested Oceanworld, there is plenty to do apart from fry on the beach.

AROUND NEW SOUTH WALES

Hunter Valley, Blue Mountains, Snowy Mountains, Broken Hill

Although the glamour of Sydney acts as a magnet for visitors, New South Wales has many other unexpected delights in store. You can sample the pleasures of the famous Hunter Valley wine region, lounge on miles of glorious beaches along the coast, look around the historic mining town of Broken Hill, or even go skiing in the Snowy Mountains.

Hunter Valley

Located 180 km (110 miles) north of Sydney, Australia's oldest wine-producing area is a must for all oenophiles, with tastings proposed at more than 50 vineyards centred around the rolling hill country near Cessnock. Many of them have tours, where you can learn more about the Hunter Valley's fruity Chardonnays.

Blue Mountains

Part of the Great Dividing Range which cuts off the coast from the vastness of the outback, these mountains were thought to be impenetrable by the early settlers, as the deep canyons were filled with millions of eucalyptus trees blocking the way. (Evaporating eucalyptus oil gives the mountains their characteristic colour.) Marvellous scenery, picturesque towns and cooler temperatures during the summer make this a worthwhile day trip from the big city. The foothills start just 65 km (40 miles) from Sydney.

In the Blue Mountains are Three Sisters turned to stone: Meehni, Wimlah and Gunnedoo.

Snowy Mountains

To experience the novelty of an Australian piste, head for the ski resorts at Thredbo, Charlotte Pass or Perisher Blue between June and October. The 5-km (3-mile) run at Thredbo is sure to get the adrenaline flowing. In summer, you can go hiking around Mount Kosciusko, at 2228 m (7309 ft) the highest peak in the country.

Broken Hill

In the far west of New South Wales, this historic mining town has some of the world's major deposits of silver, zinc and lead. Some of the old mines now have interesting tours. The amazing outback scenery has also made Broken Hill something of an artists' colony these days, and there are several galleries with plenty of interesting paintings on display.

CANBERRA

The City, Tidbinbilla

The idea of creating a capital city away from the rival giants of Sydney and Melbourne came about with Australian federation at the turn of the century. By 1908, a beautiful location had been chosen mid-way between the two cities in a river valley surrounded by mountains. A fitting name was found for the new city—Canberra is an Aboriginal word meaning "meeting place". A competition launched to find the right design was won by an American, Walter Burley Griffin. Building was delayed due to two World Wars and the Depression, and Burley Griffin died before his masterwork was completed.

The City

The design is bold and grandiose in scale—although like many planned cities, the enormous boulevards and vistas which appear visionary on the drawing board make it an exhausting town to visit on foot. Count three or four hours to walk around the major attractions in the central triangle with its apex on Capital Hill. Notwithstanding, Canberra, with some of the country's best museums and breathtaking modern architecture, is always an exciting city to experience.

Telstra Tower

For an initial overview of the city and surrounding countryside, the top of this 195-m (640-ft) tower on Black Mountain, west of the city centre, offers a spectacular 360-degree perspective. There are open platforms, a revolving restaurant and a coffee bar at the top, and an exhibition on telecommunications below.

National Botanic Gardens

Further down Black Mountain, these wonderful gardens contain an entirely Australian collection of flora. Among more than 6000 different species of native plant life, look out for the eucalypt lawn, with over 600 varieties of the koala's favourite tree. There are several educational walks, including an interesting Aboriginal plant trail.

Lake Burley Griffin

Named after Canberra's planner, the lake was created as recently as the 1960s by damming the Molonglo River. The city has maximized its use, with facilities for sailing, fishing, swimming and rowing, a popular cycle and walking path around its 35-km (22-mile) circumference, and several eyecatching features. The Captain Cook Memorial Water

Recover from the overwhelming treasures of Canberra's National Gallery in its fascinating Sculpture Garden.

Jet is the most striking. A spray of water is flung 140 m (460 ft) into the air and can give you a refreshing shower if the wind is blowing from the wrong direction.

On Aspen Island, east of the jet, the National Carillon consists of 53 bronze bells, a gift from the British government to mark the city's 50th birthday in 1963. Housed in a tall, white bell-tower made of three huge cement panels, they are played each day at lunchtime.

Civic Centre

Just north of the lake is the only area which might be called pedestrian-friendly. Here are the major banks, the main post office, cinemas, shopping malls, bus terminals and plenty of restaurants and cafes, all within easy walking distance of each other.

Australian War Memorial

At the foot of Mount Ainslie, this huge domed building is a powerful memorial to those 102,000 Australians who died in overseas conflicts from the Boer War to Vietnam. Beneath the dome is the Tomb of the Unknown Soldier, and along the colonnaded walls are inscribed the names of all the nation's war dead. The memorial also houses an excellent war museum, tracing Australia's military history and containing an aircraft hall, paintings, dioramas and the largest collection of Victoria Crosses in the world.

Blundell's Cottage

On the northern shore of the lake, near the bottom of Anzac Parade, this simple, mid-19th-century stone house is one of the few reminders of Canberra's life as a farming community before it was transformed by Burley Griffin's plans. Once inhabited by a farm worker's family, the house is now an enjoyable museum dedicated to the area's more modest history.

New Parliament House

The centrepiece of the public buildings which dominate the lake's southern shore, New Parliament House was opened in 1988, with perfect symbolic timing for Bicentennial year. Despite being one of the largest edifices in the southern hemisphere, the building has been brilliantly designed to follow the contours of Capital Hill and blends discreetly into its environment. The most visible part is the stainless steel flagmast, emerging from a grass-covered roof over which visitors are free to walk.

Outside the entrance, look out for *Meeting Place*, a mosaic by Aboriginal artist Michael Tjakamarra Nelson depicting a gathering of tribes.

The interior is truly magnificent. A huge foyer, with 48 grey-green marble columns representing a eucalyptus forest, gives way to the Great Hall, with a tapestry 20 m (66 ft) long based on a painting by Arthur Boyd, one of Australia's finest postwar artists. On the first floor you can visit the House of Representatives, where government and opposition slug it out, and the Senate.

The Parliament also has a collection of some 3000 works of art, selections of which are shown in rotation.

The whole package cost more than a billion dollars to create, over which many a hard-working Australian taxpayer has grumbled. But the magnitude and style of the building may make you think it was worth every cent.

Old Parliament House

On King George Terrace, towards the lake, the Old Parliament was in use from 1927 until the new one was inaugurated. For what was always intended as a provisional site, this elegant white neoclassical building is striking for its stateliness and grandeur. On the lawn in front of the building is the Aboriginal Tent Embassy, officially recognized as a site of cultural significance for it was here that the black, red and yellow Aboriginal flag was first flown in 1972.

Inside Old Parliament House you can view the debating chambers, cabinet rooms and the prime minister's office. The building is big enough to put on temporary exhibitions by the National Museum of Australia and also house the National Portrait Gallery.

National Gallery of Australia

Situated near the lake, the gallery possesses an outstanding collection of Australian and foreign art. Opened in 1982, it has acquired Australian works by early colonial artists, romantic-nationalists such as Tom Roberts, Frederick McCubbin and Arthur Streeton, and major postwar canvases—Sidney Nolan's ground-breaking *Ned Kelly* series from the 1940s, Russell Drysdale's stark *The Drover's Wife*, and the powerful expressionist paintings of Albert Tucker and Arthur Boyd. The gallery also has a formidable catalogue of works by artists such as Monet, Picasso, Jackson Pollock, Matisse, de Kooning and many other notables. Perhaps most interesting of all, though, is the collection of Aboriginal art near the entrance. The remarkable *Aboriginal Memorial 1988* consists of 200 decorated log coffins and offers a radically different perspective on the Bicentennial celebrations. There are also temporary displays of contemporary Aboriginal paintings.

High Court of Australia

Next door to the gallery, the highest court in the land is a modernist cube of concrete and glass, with a gigantic window for its façade and a large public entrance hall containing displays about how the court works. There is also a popular cafe overlooking the lake.

Questacon

The National Science and Technology Centre, immediately west of the High Court, has more than 200 hands-on exhibits demonstrating how science interacts with everyday life. A chance for budding scientists of all ages to be entertained and educated at the same time.

Tidbinbilla

For those who enjoy seeing stars, the Canberra Space Centre, about 40 km (25 miles) southwest of the city at Tidbinbilla, is one of only three NASA deep space tracking stations in the world. You can learn more about the history of space exploration in the centre's exhibition hall, and see the largest lump of moon rock outside America.

A little further out, koalas cling to eucalyptus trees, and kangaroos and wallabies abound at Tidbinbilla Nature Reserve. There are several nature trails, as well as convenient picnic grounds.

Victoria and Tasmania

Australia's smallest mainland state, Victoria is also its most densely populated, as well as its most industrialized. The first Europeans to arrive here were whalers, but a permanent settlement was established in 1835, when John Batman bought the land around the mouth of the Yarra River from local Aborigines and founded Melbourne. Just 16 years later, Victoria had broken away from New South Wales to form its own colony.

Floating off the south coast, Tasmania is the smallest of all the states, separated from the rest of the country by 240 km (150 miles) of sea. For the Aussies, it is ideal holiday country.

MELBOURNE

City Centre, Southbank, King's Domain

Known in the 19th century as "Marvellous Melbourne", the city has plenty to admire, although the abiding fascination for the locals seems to be the weather. As they are happy to point out: if you don't like what is on offer, just wait a minute and it will change.

Melbourne has a long-standing reputation for getting on with business, as its grand Victorian mansions and thrusting modern skyscrapers confirm. More than half of Australia's leading companies have established their headquarters here. In cricket and fashion as much as in finance and politics, the country's second-largest city maintains a serious rivalry with Sydney. But with many of the best restaurants in Australia, the superb Victorian Arts Centre, and a picturesque old tram system to trundle you about the vibrant city centre, it is a place to be enjoyed entirely on its own terms.

Melbourne is a curious mix of stateliness and avant-garde.

City Centre

The Golden Mile, as it has been dubbed, consists of 18 principal streets forming an organized grid north of the Yarra River. Tree-lined Collins Street and Bourke Street have exclusive department stores, shopping malls and individual speciality shops. Upper Bourke Street is the cinema and theatre district of Melbourne and always popular with locals in the evening. But keep your eyes wide open—although parts of Bourke Street are pedestrianized, those ancient trams still thunder along.

North of here, on Little Bourke Street, Melbourne's bustling Chinatown is the home of Australia's oldest Chinese community, dating back to the 1850s gold rush. If exploring on foot gets too tiring, hop onto the City Circle tram, which will rattle you around the Golden Mile's perimeter free of charge.

LEGENDARY OUTLAW

The most famous of Australia's 19th-century bushrangers was local boy Ned Kelly. Clad in a crude suit of armour, Ned was the leader of a gang which terrorized farmers and travellers, but managed to acquire a folklore reputation as Robin Hood-style helpers of the poor. Kelly was captured after a shoot-out with police, and was quickly tried and hanged in Melbourne gaol in 1880. It was hoped that this would put an end to the legend, but it was only the start—a feature film has been made about his life, and there is a famous series of Kelly paintings by Australia's outstanding postwar artist, Sidney Nolan.

Town Hall

Dominating City Square on the corner of Collins and Swanston Street, the Town Hall is a grand 1867 building with neoclassical façade, clocktower and a cavernous hall into which 3000 people can cram for public meetings.

St Paul's Cathedral

Not far away, Anglican St Paul's dates from 1880 and is an impressive example of Victorian Gothic Revival. Despite it being his undisputed masterpiece, the architect, William Butterfield, refused to come to Australia and never saw the building.

Rialto Towers

At the western end of Collins Street, the twin reflecting towers of this dramatic skyscraper stand high above the Melbourne skyline. The observation deck on the 55th floor has fantastic views across the city out to the Dandenong Ranges.

Around Flagstaff Gardens

Carry on north up King Street to pleasant Flagstaff Gardens. The foundation stone for St James' Old Cathedral, next to the park, was laid by Governor La Trobe in 1839, making it the city's oldest building. On the other side of the park, Queen Victoria Market from the 1870s is a vast, rumbustious place, where everything from fruit and vegetables to second-hand clothes is on sale.

Melbourne Central

A few blocks east along La Trobe Street, this stylish, modern shopping complex opened in 1991. Its distinctive glass pyramid completely encloses a 50-m (165-ft) high shot tower, built in the late 19th century. Shot for guns was made here, by dropping globules of lead from the top of the tower into water tanks, so forming perfectly round pellets.

State Library and National Gallery

An important Melbourne landmark, the domed State Library has undergone a massive redevelopment programme and now fills the entire building.

During the lavish refurbishment of its normal home near the Victorian Arts Centre on the south bank, the National Gallery of Victoria has taken up temporary residence on Russell Street behind the State Library. The excellent collection of Australian art covers the period from colonial times to the present day. There is also a strong section of Aboriginal art, including a few of Albert Namatjira's intense landscapes, and some especially fine British works by Gainsborough, Turner, Constable and the Pre-Raphaelites.

Old Melbourne Gaol

Ghoulish and fascinating at the same time, the gaol is one of the best museums in Melbourne. Only one cell block remains of the grim, squat 1840s prison building on Russell Street, and this now houses an imaginative and informative exhibition on the Victorian penal system and the extraordinary collection of inmates whose lives ended here.

Carlton Gardens

On Victoria Street, the gardens are home to the magnificent Exhibition Building, relic of the 1880 Great Exhibition. It looks like one of Louis XIV's palaces and was used as the state parliament in the first half of the 20th century.

Melbourne Museum

Planned to open in the year 2000, the new Melbourne Museum is located to the north of the Exhibition Building. Special features of the $263 million project are Bunjilaka (an Aboriginal Centre), a Children's Museum, the Gallery of Life (a forest environment) and a study centre.

Spring Street

Leading south from Carlton Gardens, Spring Street boasts some of Melbourne's finest Victorian buildings. The imposing State Parliament is a product of the gold rush days. Built in stages from 1856 onwards, it was the seat of Australia's federal government until 1927, when the parliament building in Canberra was completed. Opposite stand two examples of Victorian civic architecture, the neo-Gothic Windsor Hotel of 1887 and the opulent Princess Theatre. Further along, the Old Treasury Building from the 1850s now contains an exhibition documenting the history of Melbourne.

St Patrick's Cathedral

Located behind the State Parliament, St Patrick's was begun in 1850, although the three spires were added in the 1930s. Its sombre bluestone only heightens the gloomy Gothic ambience. There are attractive stained-glass windows inside, and the great church bells were cast in Dublin in 1851.

Fitzroy Gardens

The gardens lie 200 m east of the church, and were originally laid out in the pattern of the Union Jack. They boast beautiful flower displays, lakes, a conservatory and a model Tudor village. But most intriguing of all is the presence of Captain Cook's Cottage. The house was in fact owned by Cook's father in the 1750s, and moved here brick by brick from North Yorkshire in England in 1934. That made it instantly the oldest building in Australia. It now contains a small museum on Captain Cook's life.

Southbank

Here reigns an atmosphere very different from the business hubbub across the river. With three levels of upmarket restaurants and shopping at the Southgate Complex on the banks of the Yarra, and the marvellous art to be seen at the National Gallery, it is an area devoted to recreation, refreshment and culture.

Victorian Arts Centre

On St Kilda's Road, the ultra-modern building with a miniature Eiffel Tower on top is one of the largest visual and performing arts centres in the world. Here you will find the Melbourne Concert Hall, three different theatres, and a performing arts museum, which has exhibitions on subjects ranging from opera to television and pop music.

King's Domain

The main park of Melbourne is reached from the other side of St Kilda's road, and slopes down to the Yarra River. It is a delightfully shady spot, containing several points of interest.

Government House
Secluded in the middle of the park, Government House was built by the British in 1876 to establish a regal residency in the city. Indeed, it is the most grandiose of all Melbourne's early mansions. The ballroom is larger than that at Buckingham Palace, a fact which did not amuse Queen Victoria, who refused permission for it to be built. However, 19th-century communications were so slow that the reply took more than three months to arrive—so the job was completed before the royal rejection could prevent it.

Governor La Trobe's Cottage
Victoria's first lieutenant-governor brought this simple prefabricated house with him when he sailed from England in 1839. Moved to this location near Government House from its original site in Jolimont, it has been restored as closely as possible to its original state. The excellent little museum is a fitting memorial to the governor's life and his energetic role in developing the young colony.

Shrine of Remembrance
Across from the cottage, the massive World War I memorial sits at the end of a rising avenue of Bhutan cypress trees. Conceived as a classical Greek temple, its central hall has 16 black marble Ionic pillars and a stone of remembrance. There is a small war museum in the crypt, and you can also climb up to the roof for a fine view of the city.

Royal Botanic Gardens
Occupying 35 ha (86 acres) of the Domain, the gardens rank among the world's finest. They were established in 1846 and have an astonishing range of plants, an interesting Australian rainforest section, and a fern gully inhabited by flying foxes. The area around the lake is a lovely spot for picnicking on a Sunday afternoon.

2

THE TWO MOST INTERESTING PRISON MUSEUMS The first European settlements in Australia were penal colonies. The haunting ruins at **Port Arthur** were once the most feared gaol in the country. **Melbourne Gaol** has on display the armour used by notorious Ned Kelly, as well as the gallows where he met his end.

AROUND VICTORIA

Mount Dandenong, Phillip Island,
Wilson's Promontory, Ballarat, Great Ocean Road

Mount Dandenong

The range provides a beautiful backdrop to Melbourne, and a favourite recreation spot for its people. The hills are not high—Mount Dandenong tops them at 625 m (2050 ft)—but the view from the summit is panoramic. Take a ride on Puffing Billy, a picturesque old steam train that runs between Belgrave and Emerald Lake.

Phillip Island

Tourists flock to this island, 130 km (81 miles) south of Melbourne, for one thing—the penguin parade. At dusk, thousands of diminutive fairy penguins waddle back from the sea to their sand dune burrows. The island also has a wildlife park and a koala centre, as well as a colony of fur seals off the southwestern headland. There are excellent surf beaches, but beware of fierce currents and undertows.

Wilson's Promontory

"The Prom" is one of Australia's most popular national parks. Around 300 km (186 miles) to the southeast of Melbourne, this is as far south as you can get on mainland Australia—only Tasmania and a few smaller islands lie between you and the Antarctic. More than 80 km (50 miles) of hiking trails meander through varied terrain that ranges from marshes and mountain forests to secluded beaches. Wildlife abounds here, including emus, kangaroos and wombats.

Ballarat

This is the place where gold was first panned in 1851, setting off the great Victorian Gold Rush. The opulent architecture is testament to the wealth created by the rush. Find out more at the Gold Museum. Opposite, Sovereign Hill is a unique recreation of a 19th-century mining town, with suitably attired inhabitants and a chance to pan for gold yourself.

Great Ocean Road

One of the world's most spectacular coastal drives, the road winds through 300 km (186 miles) of rugged scenery past the Twelve Apostles, an imposing row of rock columns rising up from the sea. Inland, the Otway ranges offer rainforests and eucalypts, streams, waterfalls and walking trails. From June to October, spot southern right whales in the waters off the small seaside towns of Port Fairy and Warrnambool.

TASMANIA

Hobart, Around the Island

There is something special about arriving in Tasmania, the last landfall before the frozen wastes of Antarctica. You will get the feeling that you have come to another country. The mainlanders seem to agree, and love to stay here—so much so that "Tassie" prides itself on being the Holiday Isle. There are historic towns and the ruins of Port Arthur gaol to visit.

Hobart

Laid-back, spacious and with Mount Wellington as a majestic backdrop, Hobart sprawls along the picturesque bays and inlets of the Derwent estuary. Founded in 1804, only 16 years after Sydney, it is one of Australia's oldest settlements, and fortunately has preserved the Georgian houses, wharves and inns that recall its early days as a penal colony and whaling port.

The first British settlers developed farms and apple orchards (earning Tasmania the name of Apple Island), timber and paper industries, sheep rearing and mining in and around Hobart. But it is the smell and sparkle of the sea which dominate. Ships of all sizes, from merchant vessels to sailing dinghies, crowd the sheltered deepwater harbour, while each New Year spectators jostle on Constitution Dock to watch the end of the famous Sydney to Hobart Yacht Race.

The Harbour

This is the heart of the city and filled with the atmosphere of the early days. A few yards from the water stands the former customs house, a major Hobart landmark built by convicts during the 1830s and now serving as the Tasmanian parliament building. Continue down to pretty Salamanca Place, lined by a row of Georgian sandstone warehouses. These have recently been given a facelift and turned into craft shops and fashionable restaurants. A popular open-air Saturday market is held here, where you can buy anything from fresh fruit to furniture. For good but basic fare, try a takeaway from one of the floating fish-and-chip shops which bob up and down on Constitution Dock.

Battery Point

Reached from an alley between the warehouses on Salamanca Place, Kelly's Steps lead you up to the city's oldest quarter, named for the cluster of guns which pointed out over the estuary to protect the early settlers from seaborne invasion. It is the most complete colonial area in Australia, with houses and inns dating back 150 years or more.

A good place to start is at the Maritime Museum, which occupies Secheron House built in 1831. Filled with harpoons, model ships, paintings and naval bric-a-brac, it has a particularly interesting exhibition on Hobart's whaling past, and a nice view of the estuary from its veranda.

A few hundred metres inland, St George's Anglican Church dates from 1838. There is a delightful interior with box cedar pews and metal pillars, and the distinctive tiered spire is visible from all over Hobart.

Around the corner on Hampden Road, the Van Diemen's Land Folk Museum is situated in a fine Georgian-style mansion built in 1836 and surrounded by beautiful grounds. The museum has an interesting display of furniture, porcelain, silver and paintings from the colonial era.

Anglesea Barracks

At the end of Hampden Road turn left into Davey Street. The original barracks were built by convicts in 1811 and the area is still in use by the Australian Army. There is an interesting military museum inside the old military gaol, focusing on the role of the colonial army in Tasmania and on the history of the barracks.

City Centre

Head back towards town along Davey Street or Macquarie Street—both feature plenty of graceful Georgian architecture. On Davey Street, the pleasant St David's Park was Hobart's first cemetery and still contains many graves of the early settlers, including that of Lieutenant-Governor David Collins, the man who chose the site of Hobart in 1804.

North of here, Franklin Square is the focus of the city centre, filled with handsome oak and elm trees. On the northern side, the Town Hall on Macquarie Street stands on the spot where the city was founded. Further along, take a left turn into Campbell Street. The Theatre Royal, established in 1834, is the oldest existing theatre in Australia, elegantly decorated in Regency style. A tour around the historic Penitentiary Chapel and Criminal Courts, a couple of blocks up from here, will tell you more about the early penal system in Tasmania.

Tasmanian Museum and Art Gallery

An excellent double bill. The museum has some interesting exhibits on Tasmanian wildlife, including photos of the last Tasmanian Tiger—in fact a stripy, wolfish marsupial. There are moving and informative displays on the fated Tasmanian Aboriginals, the early whalers who co-existed with them, and the convicts.

The art gallery has a good collection of colonial art, including Tasmanian landscapes and portraits of local worthies by John Glover, Houghton Forrest and the Norwegian convict Knut Bull. The gallery also has many of Benjamin Duterrau's portraits of the last Tasmanian Aboriginals.

The Queen's Domain

North of the city centre, this large public park stretches along the banks of the Derwent and includes the extensive Royal Tasmanian Botanical Gardens.

Mount Wellington

There are hiking trails to the top of the mountain, but you can also drive up. At 1,271 m (4,170 ft), the summit is high enough to be dusted with snow in winter, and can be chilly even in summer. The views of the city and estuary are worth shivering for.

Around the Island

With its mountains, lakes and fjord-like coastline, Australia's only island state seems very different from the vast desert continent 240 km (150 miles) to the north. Surf beaches, rocky mountain trails and pristine forests combine with a temperate climate to make this a perfect outdoor destination. You can go horse riding, sailing, fishing and golfing, while Tasmania's 14 national parks offer some of Australia's best bushwalking. This unique landscape comprises one of the last great temperate wildernesses on our planet, and some 20 per cent of the island's area is on UNESCO's World Heritage List.

Richmond

Richmond, 26 km (16 miles) northeast of Hobart, is one of the best-preserved historic towns in Australia. There is a gaol built in 1825, now an interesting museum, the convict-built Richmond Bridge (1823), and a group of 50 early public buildings.

New Norfolk

A delightful colonial town set in the Derwent Valley, and known as a hop-growing area from the early days. Oast houses and tall poplars mark the countryside here, the latter having been planted to protect precious crops from the biting Tasmanian wind. The old Colony Inn now houses an excellent museum of colonial-period antiques and relics.

Port Arthur

A day in Port Arthur, on the south side of the Tasman Peninsula, provides a fascinating insight into the life of Australia's most notorious gaol, the dreaded "prison within a prison". In the decades after it was established in 1830, the gaol took in 10,000 of the most recalcitrant convicts transported from England. To make it even more secure, a line of ferocious dogs barred the only overland escape route at Eaglehawk Neck, the thin strip of land at the entrance to the peninsula. It is chilling to think that such hardship was suffered in pleasing Georgian sandstone buildings grouped around an idyllic harbour. You can walk among the remains of the penitentiary, the commandant's 1833 weatherboard house and the square-towered church, built by convicts and now desolate. On the Isle of the Dead in Port Arthur Bay lie the unmarked graves of nearly 2000 prisoners.

Launceston

Tasmania's second-largest city, 200 km (124 miles) north of Hobart, has a number of historic buildings. Macquarie House, on Civic Square, dates from 1830 and was originally a warehouse. It is now part of the excellent Queen Victoria Museum and Art Gallery, whose main building is on Wellington Street. To the west of town, near scenic Cataract Gorge, the Penny Royal World recreates 19th-century Tasmania.

A DEVIL OF A PLACE

The island has had two European names, both deriving from its Dutch discoverer. Abel Tasman arrived here in 1642 and called it Van Diemen's Land after the governor-general of the Dutch East Indies. This demonic-sounding name became grimly appropriate after the British took control. By 1831, all the Aboriginal inhabitants had been either killed or exiled to Flinders Island. Meanwhile, during the first half of the 19th century, 70,000 convicts were transported to Tasmania's penal colony from England. Many were assigned to farmers and tradesmen, while the worst offenders were detained in the "prison within a prison" at Port Arthur. At the same time, bushrangers—escaped convicts living as outlaws—preyed on settlers along the Derwent and Huon valleys. A change of direction came in 1856. Transportation had ended a few years earlier, colonial self-government was established, and the island voted to replace its uninviting name with that of its Dutch discoverer, Tasman. Tasmania's rebranding did not improve conditions overnight, but the path was set for a new and prosperous future based on the island's abundant natural resources, rather than on forced labour.

WESTCO
WESTCO

South Australia

Adelaide is a pleasant, civilized city sitting on the banks of the Torrens River, and home to 75 per cent of the state's entire population. However, the vast majority of South Australia's one million sq km (386,000 sq miles) lies beyond the lush southeast and is an awesome, empty expanse of baking desert. This is the driest state in the country, and the outback its dominant feature. The state's emblem is that hardy, burrowing marsupial, the hairy-nosed wombat.

ADELAIDE

City Centre, Light's Vision

In 1836 Colonel William Light landed on the coast and proclaimed the area a British colony. He chose a site a few miles inland for the capital, and designed it in neat rectangular blocks with elegant boulevards, interspersed with squares and surrounded by greenery. The city was named after the wife of William IV, Britain's monarch at the time. This colony was populated by skilled British artisans and labourers instead of convicts, while German Lutheran refugees cultivated orchards and vineyards to the northeast.

Encircled by parks and drenched in flowers, Adelaide cultivates the art of good living.

City Centre

Adelaide's original uncluttered design still holds. The twin segments of the business and northern residential quarters are cushioned by a green belt of parkland where you can picnic, cook a barbecue, see the zoo or botanic gardens, and watch cricket and horse racing—all within a few minutes' walk of the shops, restaurants and museums of the city centre.

Festival Centre

Attractively located by the Torrens River, Adelaide's riposte to Sydney's Opera House has become the focal point of the city. It is an extensive, 20-million-dollar performing arts complex, including the huge Festival Theatre, which seats up to 2000 for concerts, opera and ballet. The biennial Adelaide Arts Festival is known for the impressive range of national and international artists it attracts.

Holy Trinity Church

Near the western end of North Terrace, Adelaide's main cultural and sightseeing street, stands South Australia's oldest church, begun in 1838. The attractive, two-storey, colonial-style parsonage next door dates from the 1840s.

Adelaide Casino

Further along North Terrace, the massive former railway station, built from sandstone in 1928, has been converted into a ritzy casino. It is open until late during the week and non-stop at the weekend, and has all the usual means of relieving its patrons of their money, including roulette, blackjack and baccarat.

Parliament House

The marble-colonnaded parliament building was begun in the 1880s but took 50 years to finish. It replaced the small Old Parliament House next door, where South Australia's first self-governing parliament met in 1857.

Migration Museum

The museum district begins once you cross King William Street. Located behind the 1855 Government House on Kintore Avenue, this was the first museum in the country to be dedicated to the struggles of the immigrant communities who have given modern Australia its cosmopolitan character.

South Australian Museum

Large whale skeletons mark the entrance to this fine museum on North Terrace, founded in the Victorian era. It has an interesting mixture of exhibits on Australian flora and fauna, fossils, meteorites and minerals (especially opals), as well as an excellent collection of artefacts from Polynesia. On level 5, there is a gallery devoted to Aboriginal culture, with a particularly good Dreamtime display looking at the traditions of the Ngarrindjeri, who lived in this part of Australia before the Europeans arrived.

Art Gallery of South Australia

This solid collection of colonial art includes works by the intriguing Thomas Bock, who arrived in Tasmania as a convict and became one of Australia's most successful portrait painters. There are canvases by all the main romantic-nationalist artists such as Roberts and McCubbin, postwar works by Sidney Nolan and Douglas Roberts, and a large collection of Aboriginal art. The

European section has 20 bronze sculptures by Auguste Rodin, and some interesting paintings by artists such as Francis Bacon, Lucian Freud and members of the Bloomsbury Group. There's also a collection of Asian ceramics.

Ayers House

Located a couple of blocks east at 288 North Terrace, this 45-room bluestone mansion furnished in 19th-century style is one of Adelaide's grandest. It was home to South Australian premier Sir Henry Ayers—after whom Ayers Rock (Uluru) was named—from 1855 to the end of the century.

Botanic Gardens

Almost opposite, these delightful gardens were opened in 1857 and contain Australian and exotic plants, a Victorian Palm House, and the gigantic Bicentennial Conservatory, which recreates the conditions of the rainforest.

Adelaide Zoo

Just behind the Botanic Gardens, Adelaide's zoo has a good collection of Australian animals and birds, some of which you will probably never see in the wild, such as the Tasmanian devil, the koala and the hairy-nosed wombat. There are several species of kangaroo and wallaby as well, plus exotic creatures from other continents.

Rundle Mall

One street south of North Terrace is Adelaide's favourite shopping area. It is a brick-paved, traffic-free precinct of department stores, restaurants and arcades brightened by flower stalls and the music of street entertainers.

Victoria Square

Head south from the end of the mall along King William Street. In and around the square is a cluster of impressive Victorian public buildings. The Renaissance-style Town Hall dates from 1866. Next to it, the Old Treasury Building is one of the oldest structures in the city and now houses a museum on the exploration and settlement of South Australia. On the eastern side, the glowering Catholic Cathedral of St Francis Xavier was built in the 1850s. From the centre of the square, a vintage 1920s tram heads out to Glenelg on the coast.

Light's Vision

A statue of William Light stands on Montefiore Hill north of the Torrens River, pointing eternally at the city he founded. The view is excellent, although somewhat marred by the new floodlights of the Adelaide Oval just below. Nearby Pennington Terrace, with some fine colonial-style houses, leads to the neo-Gothic St Peter's Cathedral of 1869.

AROUND SOUTH AUSTRALIA

Glenelg, Adelaide Hills, Kangaroo Island, Barossa Valley, Coober Pedy

If your only experience of South Australia were Adelaide and surroundings, you might think that it resembled southern Europe: a place blessed by benevolent sunshine, green valleys, rich farmland and world-class vineyards. But the miners in the Stuart Ranges, where half the world's opals are extracted, live underground to escape the heat.

Glenelg

This pleasant seaside town lies 10 km (6 miles) southwest of Adelaide, with white beaches, a long jetty out into the ocean and an attractive main square. This was where the first colonists landed in 1836, and the colony of South Australia was proclaimed from the historic Old Gum Tree on McFarlane Avenue. A replica of their ship, *HMS Buffalo*, is moored in the boat harbour; it contains a museum and an excellent seafood restaurant.

Adelaide Hills

The Adelaide Hills, in the Mount Lofty Ranges, encircle the city on the east and south. A 20-minute drive through acacia and eucalyptus takes you up to the Cleland Conservation Park, where kangaroos and emus roam freely in the Wildlife Zone, and you can even cuddle a koala. A lookout at Mount Lofty, 770 m (2530 ft) high, provides a magnificent view of Adelaide.

Kangaroo Island

This nature lover's paradise is a mere 113 km (70 miles) from the

THE THREE BEST FILM LOCATIONS Australian cinema has made the most of the country's spectacular scenery. The spooky *Picnic at Hanging Rock* was filmed at **Hanging Rock** in Victoria, a popular destination for Melbourne's daytrippers. *Crocodile Dundee* encountered his deadly croc in **Kakadu National Park** in the Northern Territory. Meanwhile, *Mad Max* burned rubber in the apocalyptic landscape of **Coober Pedy** in South Australia, where the population lives underground to avoid the heat.

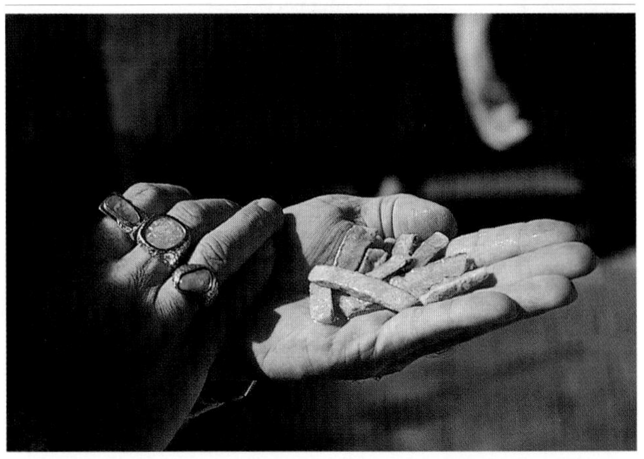

Learn everything you ever wanted to know about opals in Coober Pedy.

big city. Fur seals and hair seals bask on the rugged southern coast. Seal Bay belongs to the sea lions, who are completely unafraid of humans, while at the western end of the island, Flinders Chase National Park shelters emus, echidnas, sooty kangaroos, wallabies and the duck-billed platypus.

Barossa Valley

In the 19th century, German immigrants transformed this broad valley 55 km (34 miles) northeast of Adelaide into a landscape of neat vineyards. South Australia is the largest premium wine producer in the country, and the vineyards here are the best of the lot. A vintage festival is held every second year in March or April when the grapes are harvested, with wine auctions and traditional dancing.

Coober Pedy

Some 800 km (500 miles) to the northwest of Adelaide along the Stuart Highway, Coober Pedy is the quintessential outback mining town—it gets so hot in summer that almost half the population lives underground in dugouts. Most of the world's opals have come from here. You can visit the Umoona Opal Mine and Museum, and the Old Timers Mine.

Western Australia

If you love wide-open spaces and hate crowds, this is the place for you—a state the size of India with a population of less than two million people. Much of Western Australia is pure outback, the archetypal arid back-of-beyond. The British first colonized it in the 1820s. Things took off with the gold-rush era at the end of the century, while a postwar mining boom, the influx of new pioneers seeking their fortune, and thousands of kilometres of desert mean that the state retains the atmosphere of life at the frontier.

PERTH AND SURROUNDINGS

Perth, Fremantle, Excursions

The capital is one of the liveliest cities in the country, bustling with business by day and with a thriving nightlife. Away from the city, the magnitude of the geography means there are many exceptional natural features to enjoy.

Perth

Perth was founded in 1829 by Captain James Stirling, who became the first governor. With few colonists willing to settle so far from civilization, convicts were brought here in the mid-19th century to build civic Perth, and the result now forms the core of the old city. Despite the busy modernity of today's mainly high-rise cityscape, Perth retains an easy-going atmosphere, and is small enough to get around comfortably on foot. Straddling the Swan River, the city enjoys a Mediterranean climate, and has gleaming new museums, delightful parks and gardens and a riverfront beloved by walkers, joggers and cyclists alike. With the restaurants, nightclubs and late-night pubs of its lively Northbridge district, Perth will certainly tempt you to join the locals in a little West Coast revelry of your own.

King's Park

Start off with a perspective on Perth favoured by all the postcard photographers. Situated on a hill with spectacular views over the city and the Swan River, this is a

406 ha (1000 acre) area of natural bushland and wild flowers right on the edge of the city centre. The cultivated section in the Botanic Gardens is particularly delightful and contains thousands of different Western Australian plants.

Old Perth

Head downhill to St George's Terrace. The Barracks Archway is all that is left of the 1863 building, which housed army veterans sent here to guard the convicts. In Stirling Gardens, a few blocks further on, the city's oldest building, the Old Court House, was constructed in simple Georgian style in 1836. Nearby Government House, set in a nicely landscaped garden, dates from 1859–64 and was completed using convict labour. The Town Hall, on the corner of Barrack Street and Hay Street, was also built by convicts, and has eyecatching neo-Jacobean brickwork. Some way down Hay Street, the Perth Mint began operations in 1899 and is now an enjoyable museum, with a display of molten gold-pouring and the opportunity to mint your own gold coin.

City Centre

Central Perth is formed by several shopping precincts, focusing on Murray Street and Hay Street. Between St George's Terrace and Hay Street, a mock-Tudor gateway leads into London Court, a hive of souvenir shops built in 1937 in a wonderfully out-of-place 16th-century style, with wooden beams, leaded windows and hanging lanterns.

Art Gallery of Western Australia

Across the railway track in Northbridge, the gallery is part of a revamped area which has become a trendy arts complex. The gallery puts on many exhibitions from abroad as well as from within its own extensive collection of Australian and foreign works. There is a marvellous collection of Aboriginal art, as well as such colonial-era classics as John Longstaff's *Breaking the News* and Frederick McCubbin's *Down on his Luck*, with its archetypal swagman a-waltzing Matilda in the outback.

Western Australian Museum

Partly situated in Perth's original gaol of 1856 not far from the gallery, the museum has some interesting and eclectic exhibits on Western Australian wildlife, as well as giant meteorites, the skeleton of a blue whale and an exhibition on the history of European settlement in Western Australia. There is also a whole floor devoted to Aboriginal culture and the complexities of the Dreamtime.

Resolutely modern, Perth claims to be the sunniest of Australia's state capitals.

Perth Zoo

South of the Swan River, the zoo opened in 1898. There is a good Australian bushwalk section, where you can observe a host of indigenous animals in relatively open land. The zoo also has a fine collection of exotic birds, and a superb nocturnal house, with the possums, bushbabies and tree frogs you would never otherwise see.

Beaches

The Swan River offers safe swimming beaches in the suburbs of Crawley, Nedlands and Peppermint Grove. City, Grove and Swanbourne are popular, golden Indian Ocean beaches only 11 km (7 miles) away. Cottesloe Beach is a romantic spot for watching the sun sink into the ocean.

Fremantle

"Freo", as the locals call it, lies 19 km (12 miles) from Perth, and is best reached by a cruise along the Swan River. The town acts as Perth's seaport and attained sailing glory by hosting the 1987 America's Cup yacht race, for which it was thoroughly spruced up. Fremantle has plenty of charm and character, with rows of old houses and big gold-rush pubs on lively South Terrace. But one of the greatest pleasures in town is the simplest—eating delicious fish and chips outdoors on the wooden jetty overlooking Fishing Boat Harbour.

Round House

Overlooking the sea, and with good views of Fremantle, Western Australia's oldest building dates from 1831 and lodged the settlement's first prisoners, in the days before transported convicts began arriving.

Maritime Museum

On Cliff Street, the state museum shows in detail Western Australia's close relationship with the sea since the first Dutch ships arrived here in the early 17th century. Its most important display centres on the wreck of the *Batavia*, which went down off the coast in 1629.

Fremantle Markets

You can buy fresh fruits and exotic spices, handicrafts, jewellery and antiques at this atmospheric covered market on South Terrace, first established in 1897. It is open from Friday to Sunday.

Fremantle Prison

Just east of the markets, Fremantle Prison was built by convict labour from rock quarried on site, and served as a high-security gaol from 1855 till 1991. The excellent one-and-a-half-hour guided tour, given by knowledgeable ex-warders, explores the grimmer side of the prison's—and Western Australia's—history.

WHALE WATCHING

There are two main types of whale around the Australian coast, the humpback and the southern right whale, and both can easily be seen during the migration season, roughly between June and October. Some of the best whale-watching spots are Hervey Bay in Queensland (great for humpbacks), Victor Harbor and the Head of Bight in South Australia, Albany and Fremantle in Western Australia.

Excursions

The area around Perth and Fremantle is filled with exciting possibilities. You can see some of the country's most spectacular landscape, walk around ghost towns, or relax on a sunny island.

Rottnest Island

From Fremantle, you can see the island's outline on the horizon. It is famous for its colony of quokkas, cute marsupials which resemble midget wallabies and inadvertently gave the island its name: when the Dutch reached here in the 17th century, they thought that the quokkas were rats. Today, Rottnest is a favourite away-from-it-all resort, served by ocean ferries from Perth and Fremantle.

Swan Valley

The relaxed way to see the countryside is by sailing upriver through pleasant Swan Valley, to where the river cuts through the Darling Range around the Walyunga National Park. En route, you can visit the Swan Valley vineyards, some of which are open for tastings.

Yanchep National Park

A trip along the surf beaches north of Perth will take you to this park, with its colony of koala bears, natural bushland and magnificent springtime display of wild flowers.

The Pinnacles

In Nambung National Park, 200 km (125 miles) north of Yanchep, these strange, mysterious limestone pillars, some of them 5 m (16 ft) high, rise out of a bleak, sandy desert.

Wave Rock

At 350 km (220 miles) southeast of Perth, it seems a long journey just to see a rock. But this particular rock is exceptional—15 m (50 ft) high, 100 m (330 ft) long and petrified into the shape of a giant wave about to break.

Kalgoorlie

This old mining town, 600 km (370 miles) east of Perth, was the centre of a massive gold rush in the 1890s, and there is life in the old seam yet. To get a view from underground, you can go into a gold mine specially operated for tourists. On Hannan Street, with its impressive gold-boom architecture, the Museum of the Goldfields is a good introduction to the remarkable history of the area.

Around Kalgoorlie there are several ghost towns, which once swam in gold. Now, Coolgardie, Broad Arrow and Ora Banda are but shades of their former selves.

PADDY HANNAN

In 1893, an Irish prospector named Paddy Hannan spotted a gold nugget lying on the sandy soil. With two friends, he scooped up a fortune in a few days—and so began the great West Australian Gold Rush. Within 15 years, 200,000 people were living in the goldfields. Kalgoorlie flourished with several dozen hotels, a stock exchange, impressive public buildings and streets wide enough to turn a camel train in. In Kalgoorlie, Paddy is remembered in a street name, a statue and a tree which marks the spot where he found his first gold.

THE KIMBERLEY

Broome, Lake Argyle, Bungle Bungles

More than 2000 km (1240 miles) north of Perth, this vast, remote region is Western Australia's final frontier. Here the scenery changes dramatically, as the red wastes of the Great Sandy Desert give way to open grasslands, well watered from December to March by the spectacular monsoon rains of the Wet. The Kimberley has fewer than one inhabitant per square kilometre, and more than half the land is taken up by cattle stations the size of principalities. It is known best, perhaps, for its huge diamond industry, with the Argyle mine processing more than 30 million carats a year. But there are other natural jewels to be seen, most notably the Bungle Bungles, a fabulous mountain range in the far east of the region.

Broome

The English adventurer William Dampier discovered Roebuck Bay in 1699, but disliked the place and never returned. It was not until oyster beds were found off the coast at the end of the 19th century that a town sprang up. Before long, it was supplying 80 per cent of the world's mother-of-pearl, in demand for everything from buttons to furniture inlays. The pearl industry's heyday, when 3000 men were employed on up to 400 ketch-rigged luggers, is long gone. But Broome has blossomed in recent years to make a name for itself as a cosmopolitan travellers' centre and the gateway to the Kimberley.

City Centre

Many people still come to buy cultured pearls, sold in the old Chinatown centred on Carnarvon Street and Dampier Terrace. A nine-day pearl festival, Shinju Matsuri, is held every August. This has a strong Japanese flavour, reflecting the origins of many of the pearl divers who came to Broome. You can discover the history of pearling at the Broome Historical Society Museum, in the old customs house on Saville Street. You may even see a few old pearl luggers in the harbour, still collecting shells for the culture farms. Low tide reveals the wrecks of Allied flying boats, destroyed in a Japanese air raid in 1942.

Cable Beach

This 30-km (19-mile) stretch of white sand and crystal clear water offers many activities apart from swimming and sunbathing. You can try surfing, parasailing and windsurfing, or climb on a camel for a lope along the beach, a special treat at sunset. At the southern tip is Gantheaume Point, with striking red sandstone rocks. Low tide reveals the footprints of a dinosaur who walked this way some 120 million years ago.

Lake Argyle

Construction of a dam on the Ord River created Lake Argyle, Australia's largest reservoir. A tourist village has been built on the shore as a centre for swimming, boating, fishing and hiking.

Bungle Bungles

The newest of the Kimberley's national parks, located in the far east of the region, the Bungle Bungle Hills were discovered by white Australians only in 1983, although the local Aboriginal people have long been acquainted with them and know them as Purnululu. The beautiful beehive-shaped sandstone formations are striped with black lichen and orange-red silica, which form a fragile shell protecting the rock from erosion. The Bungle Bungles are difficult to reach: spectacular helicopter and light aircraft flights can be arranged at Halls Creek or Kununurra, while on the ground, only four-wheel-drive vehicles can negotiate the 80-km (50-mile) track from the main highway (impassable from January to March). For the intrepid, though, nothing can beat the 18-km (11-mile) hike to Piccaninny Creek, which gives an unrivalled view of ground-level plant life as well as the hills.

4

THE FOUR MOST ENTERTAINING FESTIVALS

There are exciting events happening around Australia throughout the year, but some are especially appealing. In July, the **Darwin Beer Can Regatta** has races where the boats are made from empty "tinnies". The August **Shinju Matsuri** in Broome celebrates the town's origins as a pearling port, and the predominantly Japanese divers who worked there. In the same month, the **Mount Isa Rodeo** has bucking broncos and belligerent bulls in Australia's largest event of its kind. The surreal **Henley-on-Todd Regatta** in October has the crews of bottomless boats running along the waterless Todd River in Alice Springs.

Northern Territory

It is in the Northern Territory that you finally confront Australia's Red Centre. Virtually all of this enormous area is a vivid red desert, where the sun burns all day and the famous outback squint is a natural response to its powerful glare. The Territory is one of the emptiest places on earth. Only 170,000 people live in its 1.3 million sq km (500,000 sq miles), and on the long and lonely Stuart Highway connecting Darwin with Alice Springs, rare sightings of other drivers are always acknowledged with a friendly wave. Not quite a fully-fledged state—it was run by Canberra until 1978, when it received self-government—the Territory nonetheless has a strong identity, and some argue that this is the "real" Australia.

DARWIN

Around Town, Kakadu National Park

The area was discovered by the surveyor aboard *HMS Beagle* in 1839 and named in honour of an old shipmate, the naturalist Charles Darwin. Australia's northernmost port is a true survivor. Bombed more than 60 times by the Japanese during World War II, it was rebuilt, only to be flattened by Cyclone Tracy in 1974. The planners went back to the drawing board to devise a bigger, better, and cyclone-proof city. Perhaps it is the isolation which breeds such resilience: Darwin is closer to Bali than it is to Sydney.

Darwin is a useful base for exploring the Top End, the tropical tip of Australia. The undoubted highlight of this area is the Kakadu National Park, rich in flora and birdlife and not to be missed.

Clumps of prickly spinifex dot Australia's red heart.

Around Town

There are still some handsome old buildings in Darwin, although they took a severe battering from Cyclone Tracy.

Indo-Pacific Marine

Begin your city tour at the Wharf Precinct, the modernized port area. Housed in the former Port Authority garage is an aquarium with a difference, the Indo-Pacific Marine, which concentrates on reef ecosystems, with living coral transplanted from the sea. In the same building is the Australian Pearling Exhibition.

Government House

Overlooking the harbour, Government House, with its distinctive verandas and gables, is an elegant example of colonial-style architecture. It dates from 1883 and replaced an earlier building devoured by white ants.

Smith Street

Smith Street Mall is a pedestrianized shopping area in the heart of the restored city. Lined with restaurants and shaded by palm trees and bougainvillaea, it is the perfect place for relaxed people-watching.

Brown's Mart, built in 1885, was originally a mining exchange and, with much restoration, now houses a theatre. Nearby, Christ Church Cathedral and the Old Town Hall were both virtually destroyed by Cyclone Tracy.

Further along, the Victoria Hotel is a classic example of Australian Victoriana and just about survived the devastation.

Darwin Entertainment Centre

On Mitchell Street, running parallel to Smith Street, the Darwin Entertainment Centre is an intriguing postmodernist building designed for the tropics, housing a theatre, shops, cafes and a hotel under one roof.

Aquascene

At Doctor's Gully, on the Esplanade, Darwin's most unusual sight is at Aquascene. Here, tourists wade into the sea at high tide to hand-feed metre-long milkfish, catfish, mullet and thousands of other heavyweight harbour inhabitants on stale bread.

Botanic Gardens

The gardens, 2 km (1.2 miles) north of the centre, have a brilliant display of tropical flowers and plants, spread across 40 ha (84 acres) of what used to be a vegetable patch. Pride of place goes to the frangipani, bougainvillaea and orchids.

Museum and Art Gallery of the Northern Territory

Over towards Fannie Bay, this excellent combination of museum and gallery has, as one might expect at the Top End, a marvellous collection of Aboriginal art, including bark paintings from Arnhem Land and works by the Tiwi people of Melville and Bathurst islands just off the coast.

The museum focuses on the Northern Territory's people, history and environment, with a Cyclone Tracy Gallery giving a graphic account of the traumatic events of Christmas 1974.

Fannie Bay Gaol

Further north, the gaol first opened for business in 1883 and was in operation until 1979. It now houses a museum looking at the early history of the Territory's penal system.

Aviation Heritage Centre

Situated on the Stuart Highway, 10 km (6 miles) out of town, this museum includes among its collection of aeroplanes a Japanese Zero fighter, shot down over Darwin in 1942, and most impressive of all, a gigantic American B 52 bomber.

Kakadu National Park

About 150 km (93 miles) east of Darwin, Australia's largest national park has something for birdwatchers, botanists, and even crocodile admirers—the rivers are full of the wide-jawed beasts, and you need to travel around in special croc-proof boats to avoid becoming lunch. The scenery is spectacular, a profusion of waterfalls, rivers, mangrove swamps and open grasslands, all of which can change dramatically between the July–September dry season and the Wet from November to March. The dry season is the best time of year to explore the park: it is slightly cooler, there are fewer mosquitoes, and more animals are visible as they congregate around shrinking waterholes.

Kakadu contains an unparalleled collection of ancient Aboriginal art; some of the paintings on its rock ledges have been there since Europe's Paleolithic cave paintings were created 20,000 years ago. Aboriginal people still live here and now own the land, but they have leased it to the National Parks Department. However, they take an active part in the management of the park and its heritage.

MONOTREME MONOPOLY

The bizarre duck-billed platypus has plenty of excellent features, none of which seem to match: a short body, a beaver-like tail, webbed feet with poisonous spurs on the end, and a rubbery bill. Even more strange, the platypus is a monotreme—a mammal which lays eggs, encased in a leathery skin. This strange creature is only found in Australia, and when the first naturalists went back to Europe and described what they had seen, people thought they were being hoaxed. No wonder!

RED CENTRE

Alice Springs, Uluru, Kata Tjuta, Yulara Resort

An enjoyable and interesting destination in itself, "The Alice" is also a base from which to visit magnificent Uluru (Ayers Rock) and the amazing formations of the Olgas, around 450 km (280 miles) away.

Alice Springs

A 1500-km (930-mile) drive south along the Stuart Highway brings you to this small town which symbolizes the pioneering attempt to settle Australia's centre. It grew up around the springs used by the workers who in 1871 strung the north–south Overland Telegraph linking Adelaide to Darwin and the Top End. The scheme was the brainchild of Sir Charles Todd, the Superintendent of Telegraphs in Adelaide, and the springs were named after his wife, Alice. The tiny outpost has grown into a vibrant, modern town, with an immaculate new airport, high-quality hotels and motels and a plush casino.

Town Centre

Central Alice is just five streets wide. The main shopping area is the Todd Street mall. Here you will find a very visible Aboriginal population, and you can visit the Aboriginal Centre for Art and Culture, which displays and sells Dreamtime paintings on bark or canvas, carvings, boomerangs and dijeridus.

Most of the historic buildings are in this area. On Todd Street, Adelaide House opened in 1926, the first hospital in Central Australia and designed with a unique convection-cooling system. It was the idea of John Flynn, founder of the Royal Flying Doctor Service, and the house is now a museum named in his honour. Opposite, he is also commemorated by the John Flynn Memorial Church.

Museum of Central Australia

On the first floor of the Alice Plaza on Todd Street, this museum has an eclectic collection that includes dinosaur skeletons, flora and fauna, meteorites, information on the Aboriginal population and fascinating pictures of Alice Springs showing how it has changed over the years.

Todd River

Just to the east of Todd Street, the name Todd River conjures up images of refreshing blue water flowing through the dusty terrain. However, this is a river for the non-swimmer, as it is usually bone dry. Each October the less-than-serious Henley-on-Todd regatta is held, where leg-propelled boats of all shapes and sizes are raced on the sandy riverbed.

Old Telegraph Station

Situated next to the springs which earned the town its name, this relic of Alice's origins as a mid-continental telegraph link has been restored as a museum. Just north of the town, it provides insight into 19th-century communications technology and the lives of the telegraph pioneers.

GHAN—BUT NOT FORGOTTEN

The pioneers used to travel across the outback by ship—the "ship of the desert", that is. Camels were introduced to Australia in the 19th century from Afghanistan. When they had outlived their usefulness, many of them were released into the wilds and left to fend for themselves. As a result, it is estimated that there may now be 12,000 camels living in the outback. They were eventually replaced by the Alice Springs to Adelaide train, which was named the Ghan (from Af*ghan*istan) in their honour. On the Ross Highway south of Alice, the Frontier Camel Farm is stocked with their descendants. A small museum relates their history, and every July, Camel Cup races are held at Blatherskite Park.

Royal Flying Doctor Service

You can tour the base of this pioneering service, close to the town centre on Stuart Terrace. Guided tours and films explain how the airborne medical service, begun in 1927, brought healthcare to the remotest corners of the outback.

Alice Springs Desert Park

West on Larapinta Drive, the park concentrates on the local environment and the special conditions of desert ecology, with hundreds of rare species of birds and animals and displays of native plants.

Anzac Hill

At the northern end of town, this hill gives wonderful views over Alice Springs across to the MacDonnell Range and the distinctive Heavitree Gap, through which the Stuart Highway heads south.

Uluru (Ayers Rock)

Rising out of the flat desert, this gigantic sandstone monolith is a geological work of art. From a distance it appears as an enormous, slumbering animal. Up close, its scaly surface is oddly lizard-like. Riddled with caves, rivulets, strange wounds and gashes, it has been revered by

Aboriginal people for thousands of years and is adorned with many ancient rock paintings.

The rock famously changes colour with the position of the sun, losing its red resonance altogether after sunset to turn dark purple then grey. The best times to see Uluru are dawn and dusk, when the desert heat is not too intense. It is worth getting up before the sun, so you can watch the first rays of light setting the rock ablaze. Only then does the desert world come to life as the first flies begin to buzz.

Completing the 9-km (5½-mile) circuit of the rock is no mean feat, and a four-hour walking tour with one of the park rangers is an invigorating way to work up a sweat. If you are fit enough, you can climb to the top. A trail is staked out at the western end and a chain will help you up the steep incline. It will be an arduous couple of hours and you will need to take drinking water.

Uluru means "meeting place", a reminder that for its original inhabitants the outback has never been an empty back-of-beyond. The excellent Uluru-Kata Tjuta Cultural Centre, near the rock's base, explains the spiritual and cultural significance of the area.

It's believed that two-thirds of Uluru lies below ground level.

Kata Tjuta (The Olgas)

The Uluru-Kata Tjuta National Park offers not just one remarkable sight, but two. From Uluru, these hills appear as huge, knobbly silhouettes on the western horizon. Kata Tjuta, their Aboriginal name, is accurately descriptive and means "Place of Many Heads". The ancient, scarred faces of the 36 sandstone domes are full of deeply vegetated gullies and valleys inhabited by rock wallabies. A walk around these incredible formations can be a far cooler experience than Uluru, as the rocks provide some shade from the scorching sun.

Yulara Resort

Just outside the park boundary, 20 km (12 miles) from Uluru, this miniature, purpose-built town caters to many of the visitors who flock to Uluru. Only one storey high, the resort is practically invisible from any great distance, so that it does not detract from the wild beauty and mystical significance of the surrounding area. The facilities on offer cover everything from top-class hotels to camping grounds, as well as a range of restaurants, a bank, a post office and shops. The Visitor's Centre provides information and audiovisual displays about the desert, its flora and fauna, and the Aboriginal myths concerning this unique landscape.

Queensland

Australia's "Sunshine State" is like the whole continent packed into one state. You can go from sun-baked outback to tropical rainforest, high-rise modern city to old pioneer town, cool mountain glades to stunning beaches and scenic offshore islands. The incredible Great Barrier Reef stretches for 2000 km (1240 miles) along its coast.

BRISBANE AND SURROUNDINGS

Brisbane, Gold Coast, Sunshine Coast, Fraser Island, Rockhampton

Queensland is the second-largest state in the country and has the fastest population growth. Descendants of pioneers, cattle drovers, gold prospectors and refugees from war-torn Europe, Queenslanders are famously egalitarian, no-nonsense people, individualistic and suspicious of the remote bureaucracy of federal government. Beneath the tough exterior you will find the ready warmth and hospitality of those who know they live in paradise.

Brisbane

The state capital has come a long way since 1823, when John Oxley, the Surveyor General, chose it as the site of a penal settlement to get "the worst class of offenders" away from Sydney. It was out of bounds to free settlers for 20 years, but the richness of the area meant that pioneers could not keep away. By 1859, they had created the separate colony of Queensland, with Brisbane as its chief city. Most of the early settlement was destroyed by fire in 1864, only to rise again from the ashes with the influx of people and money from subsequent gold rushes. However, the city, like the state, always seemed something of a backwater to Australia's southern sophisticates. But things have changed radically in recent times. Today, with its pleasant location on the meandering Brisbane River, Brisbane

If you want to cuddle a koala, best go to Lone Pine Sanctuary.

is an increasingly important commercial and industrial centre for a booming region, while many of those southern sceptics have found its relaxed sub-tropical lifestyle too attractive to resist.

Old Observatory

Next to Wickham Park, the city's oldest structure is one of the few survivors of Brisbane's past life as a penal settlement. Built by convicts as a windmill in 1828, its mechanism soon failed, so instead 25 convicts laboured 14 hours a day on a treadmill to grind corn, earning it the name of Brisbane's Tower of Torture.

St John's Anglican Cathedral

East of the observatory, on Ann Street, this beautiful neo-Gothic cathedral, with an impressive stone-vaulted ceiling and superb stained glass, was begun in 1901 and is still under construction. The Deanery is another rare pre-fire building, and was once used as government house.

Historic Centre

Towards the centre on lively George Square, the City Hall boasts a 92-m (300-ft) campanile, with the largest clock in Australia. You can take a lift up for panoramic views of the city.

The area around George Street, from the Queen Street Mall to the loop of the river, has many of Brisbane's most interesting buildings. Taking up a whole block near Victoria Bridge, the former treasury is now a casino, so the Queenslanders' hard-earned cash still ends up in its coffers. Not far away on William Street, the sandstone Commissariat Stores were completed in 1829 with convict labour; they now house the Royal Historical Society museum.

French Renaissance-style Parliament House in George Street dates from immediately after the fire of 1864. Around here are some impressive structures, including the large, colonial-style Queensland Club across the road from the parliament. At the end of George Street, Old Government House was the state governor's official residence from 1862 to 1910.

Botanic Gardens

On the other side of George Street, the gardens extend along to the loop of the river. They were originally fringed with rainforest, which was cleared in 1828 to make way for vegetable allotments to feed the new colony. The Botanic Gardens were established in 1855 and cover a 20-ha (50-acre) site, open 24 hours a day. Sub-tropical plants, colourful jacaranda trees and plenty of welcome shade make this a delightful escape from the noise and heat of the city.

Queensland Cultural Centre

Across the Victoria Bridge, this vast, modern complex, comprising art gallery, museum, performing arts theatre and library, has put Brisbane on the cultural map. The museum encompasses an intriguing mixture of natural history, technology, state history and ethnography, with good exhibits on Melanesian culture, pioneer women in Queensland and aviation. The art gallery next door houses a collection of works by Nolan, Drysdale, Namatjira and other Australian and Aboriginal notables, as well as paintings by artists from Picasso and de Kooning to Gilbert and George.

South Bank Parklands

The site of Brisbane's Expo 88 has been turned into a very pleasant riverside walk, with restaurants, a butterfly house, picnic areas and the Gondwana Rainforest Sanctuary, where you can explore a rainforest environment which includes over 700 native birds, animals and reptiles as well as tropical plants.

Castlemaine Brewery

East of the city on Milton Road lies the source of one of Queensland's most famous exports. The free tour (at 1 p.m. and 3.30 p.m. Mon–Wed) explains the brewing process and allows visitors to sample the product.

Mount Coot-tha Forest Park

Only 8 km (5 miles) from the city centre, this enclosed expanse of natural bushland is renowned for its eucalyptus trees and fabulous exotic plants. Here you can see the Tropical Display Dome, with more than 2000 hothouse plants, and the Sir Thomas Brisbane Planetarium, largest of its kind in Australia.

Gold Coast

South of Brisbane, the glitziest, most commercialized resort area in the country is a kind of Costa del Queensland with surfing. The liveliest resort of the lot is Surfer's Paradise, where you can flex

EUCALYPTUS EULOGY

The koala is Queensland's state emblem. With its round face, black, leathery nose and large, fluffy ears, it seems to be every child's ideal bear, but in fact it is yet another amazing marsupial. Unlike kangaroos and wallabies, though, the koala's pouch is on its back, allowing the mother to keep her paws free for what koalas like doing best—clinging on to trees and either sleeping or munching eucalyptus leaves. One of the best places to see them is the Lone Pine Koala Sanctuary, 11 km (7 miles) southwest of Brisbane.

your sun-tanned muscles on the beach by day and throw yourself into a hectic nightlife after dark. The coast offers the visitor some fine nature reserves, including the excellent Currumbin Sanctuary with its thousands of brightly coloured birds, and Seaworld, an aquatic amusement park always popular with children.

Sunshine Coast

For an altogether more relaxed atmosphere, head for the beaches north of Brisbane, with the chance for some good surfing and scuba diving. At Mooloolaba, Underwater World is a tropical oceanarium where you can swim with the seals. At Nambour, famous for pineapple growing, the big attraction is a 15-m (50-ft) fibreglass pineapple which you can climb up inside. The spectacular Noosa headland forms a delightful national park, with scenic walking trails.

Fraser Island

Reached by ferry from Hervey Bay, this is the world's largest sand island, with an area of around 1,840 sq km (710 sq miles). To the Aboriginal people it was N'gaki—Paradise—and there is something otherworldly about its infinity of sand, piled up into dunes and huge, multi-coloured sand cliffs known as the Cathedrals.

The island supports a unique rainforest, eucalypts, ravines and "perched" lakes, such as Lake McKenzie and Lake Boomanjin, whose incredibly pure water comes direct from the water table below. There are no roads on the island, and four-wheel-drive cars and buses traverse narrow, sandy paths between the comfortable resorts and viewing spots.

While you are out and about, be sure to keep an eye open for some of the interesting island wildlife. There are brumbies (wild horses), dingoes, goanna and more than 200 species of bird. Dolphins can often be spotted off the coast, as can migrating whales between August and October. The seas are populated by a fantastic variety of fish, but swimmers and scuba divers should be aware that these include sharks.

Rockhampton

Known as "Rocky", Australia's beef-producing capital is an attractive town with some handsome Victorian architecture, particularly along Quay Street next to the Fitzroy River. The Dreamtime Cultural Centre, to the north of Rockhampton, claims to be the largest centre devoted to Aboriginal culture in Australia. Just south of the city is the Tropical Marker, marking the exact latitude of the Tropic of Capricorn.

NORTH QUEENSLAND

Mackay, Whitsunday Islands,
Townsville, Cairns, Great Barrier Reef

After Rockhampton, things get noticeably steamier as you enter the tropics. With countless miles of sugarcane fields and rainforest-clad mountains just a short distance from the coast, you could think yourself in the Caribbean. This part of the state is justly renowned for its beaches, offshore islands and tropical scenery and is, of course, the gateway to the Great Barrier Reef.

Mackay

Life is sweet in Mackay: the town processes a third of the nation's sugar crop. If you are interested in the process, you can tour a sugar mill: Pleystowe Mill, Farleigh Sugar Mill and Polstone Cane Farm all offer guided tours. Eungella National Park, 80 km (50 miles) west of town via mountainous terrain and the Finch Hatton Gorge, is the largest in Queensland.

Whitsunday Islands

Lying just off the coast at Airlie Beach, the Whitsundays are as pleasant as their name. They are mainly continental islands—the peaks of submerged mountains—and offer everything from pristine national parks to luxury resorts, while many are fringed by their own reef systems.

Hayman Island

On the most northerly of the Whitsundays, a hugely expensive

FRANKENSTEIN'S TOAD

The story of the cane toad demonstrates perfectly the dangers of experimenting with nature. The cane toad was introduced into Queensland in the 1930s from South America, to curb a plague of sugarcane beetles which were devouring the state's precious crop. But these giants of the toad world, as large as a dinner plate and reaching almost 2 kg (4.5 lb), ate local toads, lizards, birds—in fact, everything but the cane beetle. The population has multiplied dramatically and is spreading beyond Queensland's borders. But in a development typical of non-conformist Queensland, cane toads have acquired cult status. Films have been made about them and some people have turned them into pets, while others suggest that the cane toad should become the new state emblem.

WHITSUNDAY ISLAN
Picnic Bay
Arcadia
Townsville
Stuart
Cleveland Bay
Cape Cleveland
Cape Cleveland National Park
Aust. Institute of Marine Sciences
Nome
Alligator Ck.
Mt. Elliot 1234 m
Cromarty
Bowling Green Bay
Giru
Barratta
Lochinvar
Pioneer
Haughton R.
Brandon
Ayr
Home Hill
Inkerman
Clare
Burdekin River
Bobawaba
Millaroo
Bogie River
Gumlu
Guthalungra
Dalbeg
Wheeler Reef
Davis Reef
Broadhurst Reef
Cape Bowling Green
Viper Reef
Shrimp Reef
Bowden Reef
Prawn Reef
Coral S
Stanley Reef
Darley Reef
Old Reef
Leopa Reef
Cape Upstart
Cape Upstart Nat. Park
Abbot Bay
Wallaby Reef
Abbot Point
Holbourne Island
Gou
Wilmington
Mt. Abbot 1056 m
Highlander´s Bonnet National Park
Mt. Aberdeen Nat. Park
Merinda
Bowen
Net Ree
Armuna
Mookarra
Port of Bowen
Edgecumbe Bay
Gloucester Island
Strathmore
Binbee
Briaba
Bait Reef
George Point
Heidelberg
Longford Ck.
Collinsville
Bowen River
Airlie Beach
Shute Harbour
Daydream I.
Passage
Hayman I.
Hoo
Cannonvale
Hook I.
WHITS I. GR
Havilah
Proserpine
Sth. Molle I.
Border I.
Whitsunday
Whitsunday Island
Gunyarra
Long I.
Haslewood I.
Dent Island
Hamilton Island
CONWAY RANGE NAT. PARK
Broken River
Repulse Bay
Lindeman Island
Bloomsbury
Repulse Island
LINDEMAN G
Byerwen
Shaw I.
Yalboroo
Blenheim
Eungella Nat. Park
MOUNT BEATRICE NATIONAL PARK
Calen
Goldsmith I.
Rabbit I.
Linne Island
Mt. Dalrymple 1277 m
Newry Island
Glendon
Eungella
Mt. Ossa
Glenden
Exevale
Netherdale
Seaforth
Carlisle I.
Finch Hatton
Brampton I.
Cockermouth I.
CAPE HILLSBOROUGH Nat. Park
Kuttabul
Wigton Isla
Gargett
Mt. Blackwood 639 m
Keswick Island
CUMBER ISLAN
Mirani
Bucasia
St. Bees Island
Marian
Farleigh
Homevale
Scawfell
Red Hill
Mackay

revamp back in 1987 created a luxury island resort, where visitors can still expect to be treated royally. Scuba divers may well be rewarded with a sight of loggerhead turtles.

Hamilton Island

So extensive is the resort, with an airstrip for jets, a 400-boat marina and a 14-storey apartment tower, that the island is virtually a town. But the bonus is that you can indulge in all manner of sports, go big-game fishing, parasail and enjoy a colourful fauna reserve.

The island's best walk goes up to rocky Passage Peak, from where you can enjoy the fantastic panorama over the surrounding islands.

Lindeman Island

Some of the advantages of Lindeman are that as well as the usual water-based activities, you can also go horse riding or play a round of golf. The course is set high on a plateau, offering a good view over the Whitsunday Passage. The island has 20 km (12 km) of trails, from which you can head down to any of the seven beaches, one for every day of the week.

South Molle Island

Near to the mainland, and with a large resort, South Molle has some good, long beaches and a whole network of walking trails. Climb to the summit of 198-m (650-ft) Mount Jeffreys, the island's highest point, for a panorama of the nearby islands.

Daydream Island

Daydream is just a stone's throw from South Molle and the smallest resort island in the group. Whether it lives up to its name depends on whether you take advantage of the many sports facilities or simply lounge on the sun-bleached beaches and dream the day away.

Hook Island

This is the best place in the Whitsundays for diving. There is an underwater observatory, where you can survey the scene at 10 m (33 ft) depth without getting wet. Two large inlets bite into the southern half of the island. In one of them, the lovely Nara Inlet, you can see some Aboriginal cave paintings.

Whitsunday Island

Still unspoiled, the largest island of the group has no resort, but there are camping grounds. Whitehaven Beach offers 6 km (3.7 miles) of gloriously uninterrupted sand and is generally reckoned to be the best in the area. The best diving and snorkelling are to be found off the southeastern coast of the island.

Townsville

Townsville is dominated by Castle Hill, a 300-m (984-ft) granite outcrop. Much of the city's old colonial elegance is still in evidence, particularly along Flinders Street.

At the bottom of the street, towards the harbour, the Great Barrier Reef Wonderland is not to be missed. Apart from the world's largest coral reef aquarium, with a glass tunnel beneath waters populated by sharks, reef fish and rays, there is the Omnimax Theatre, with 3-D films about the reef, and the Museum of Tropical Queensland. This has displays on local Aboriginal culture and north Queensland's wildlife, and an "Age of Reptiles" section. Ferries depart from outside here to Magnetic Island.

Magnetic Island

The island is so close to Townsville that it is an easy trip by catamaran ferry for islanders who work on the mainland, and for day-trippers who want to enjoy the flora and fauna of the island's national park along with good beaches, a koala sanctuary and an aquarium. Magnetic Island was given its name by Captain Cook, who thought the island was exerting a strange pull on his compass —scientists now know that it was a magnetic irregularity in the seabed which caused the trouble.

Cairns

Founded in 1876 as a port for the inland goldfields, Cairns is sandwiched between two World Heritage Sites. Inland is a tropical rainforest, while just offshore lies the Great Barrier Reef. With an average 225 hours of sunshine per month, the town is the perfect base from which to explore the astounding natural beauty of these unique environments.

Waterfront

A walk along the Esplanade gives wonderful views across to the rainforest-covered mountains and the estuary. There are mudflats rather than beaches here, attracting an array of migrating water birds. At the eastern end, the Pier is an up-market shopping plaza with a lively Sunday craft market. Most of the boats go out to the reef from here. There is also a good aquarium, and a new glass-domed casino opposite. The Trinity Wharf area, on the other side of the Pier, is the oldest part of the city, with some imposing neo-classical buildings.

Cairns Museum

Situated on Spring Street in the centre of town, the museum is housed in the two-storey School of Arts building, dating from 1907. On the upper floor you will find a slightly tatty, but nonetheless enjoyable collection of displays on local Aboriginal culture, the nearby goldfields and the construction of the Brisbane-Cairns railway, an event which transformed Cairns from a settlement into a city.

Botanic Gardens

At the northern edge of town, the gardens offer a taste of the rainforest. There are 200 varieties of palm and a profusion of orchids, including the mauve Cooktown orchid, Queensland's state flower. From here, trails lead up through the Mount Whitfield Environmental Park, giving the visitor the chance to experience some genuine rainforest and good views over Cairns.

Kuranda

The mysterious, green stillness of the tropical rainforest can be experienced from the Kuranda Scenic Railway, which runs to the tiny turn-of-the-century market town of Kuranda. From 1888, hundreds of men spent four years hacking through the virgin rainforest of the Atherton Tablelands, which rise up to 900 m (2950 ft) above Cairns, to build this engineering marvel. Each twist of the 34-km (21-mile) track opens new vistas, from a fantastic panorama of Cairns' Trinity Bay to the Barron Gorge, thundering Barron Falls and finally Kuranda Station with its hanging baskets of ferns and orchids and profusion of potted plants. An alternative mode of ascent is the Skyrail Cableway, an amazing 7.5-km (4.7 mile) cable car ride which glides above the rainforest canopy, offering breathtaking views of the coastal plain.

5

THE FIVE MOST INTERESTING ISLANDS

The Australian coastline is dotted with beautiful and unusual islands. **Rottnest**, near Perth, is known for its relaxed atmosphere and its quokkas—strange-looking little marsupials. **Kangaroo Island**, Australia's third largest, is a wildlife haven close to Adelaide. Off the Victoria coast, **Phillip Island** is famous for its "penguin parade" every day at sunset. In Queensland, the amazing **Fraser Island** is the biggest sand island in the world. Further north, **Whitsunday Island** is near the Barrier Reef and, in Whitehaven, has one of the best beaches in the country.

Great Barrier Reef

From the air, you see the deep blue of the Pacific broken by jagged white lines, delineating iridescent patches of emerald and turquoise. Close up, whether you are scuba diving, snorkelling, or sitting in the comfort of a glass-bottomed boat, semi-submersible or underwater observatory, the reef looks like an enactment of the beginning of the universe, with some gardens of coral as intricate as petrified lace, others in large convoluted masses.

The Reef

In colours ranging from lettuce green to flaming red, the coral has developed into hundreds of outlandish forms, such as staghorn, brain and spaghetti coral. It is indeed a miracle of evolution. Millions of tiny marine organisms known as coral polyps build the reef on the skeletons of their ancestors. It has taken some 25 million years to create the thousands of reefs and 600 islands which comprise this 207,000 sq-km (80,000 sq-mile) barrier stretching from the northern tip of Australia to near Brisbane. It is still under construction, as each dead polyp adds its minute skeleton to an underwater architecture of Gothic complexity and striking beauty.

The mysterious coral world lies just beneath the surface.

It is amazing to think that this underwater world is a living organism. It lives by feeding on microscopic algae, and is the centre of a whole ecosystem, including at least 1500 species of specialized reef fish, with names almost as extraordinary as their shapes and brilliant colours—pullers, humbugs, footballers, yellow-tailed fusiliers, damselfish, Moorish idols and unicorns.

The Islands

True coral islands (as opposed to continental islands like the Whitsundays, which have fringe reefs) are called cays and, as they are formed by the accumulation of sand around a coral platform, they sit right on the reef itself. Cays are generally found on the Outer Reef, on the edge of the Australian continental shelf. Because of this, they are often hard to get to. However, the reef sweeps inland off the coast of Cairns, so you can visit a cay such as Green Island, a mere 24 km (15 miles) offshore, in one-and-a-half hours. Other accessible cays along the Queensland coast are the Low Isles, near Port Douglas, Heron Island, reached from Gladstone or Airlie Beach, and Lady Elliot and Lady Musgrave Islands, 80 km (50 miles) out from Bundaberg.

CULTURAL NOTES

Aboriginal Art. The most prominent type of Aboriginal art you will see in galleries and salesrooms, and even on T-shirts, is the distinctive dot-and-circle style. Originating as a ceremonial art form among the tribes of the Central Desert, these deceptively simple-looking paintings of animals and geographical features are on closer inspection revealed to be complex, minutely detailed works. In a sense they can be seen as landscape paintings, responses to a natural world known intimately for 40,000 years. Each painting represents a closely mapped-out Dreamtime journey undertaken by ancestral beings as they created particular features of the Australian continent, including the rocks, rivers, animals and plants. For those used to the European-style landscape art through which colonial artists represented Australia from the early 19th century onwards, Aboriginal art demands a radical shift in perspective. Comparing the two traditions at any of the major Australian art galleries, which contain excellent collections of works by both Aboriginal and colonial artists, provides an important insight into how two very different Australian cultures view the land.

Anzacs. Wherever you are in Australia, you will notice memorials to the Anzacs—the Australia and New Zealand Army Corps. During World War I, on April 25, 1915, they attacked the Turkish positions near Gallipoli in the Dardanelles, with the intention of forcing an entrance to the Black Sea and thereby weakening Turkey's Russian front. Two thousand Australians died that night, and over the next eight months another 9000 were killed before the Anzacs were withdrawn. Gallipoli became a major defining event in 20th-century Australian society. Only 14 years after the country had come into existence through federation, the Anzacs had demonstrated the courage and maturity of a people determined to fight under their own steam. But the nation's memorials, and the solemnity of Anzac Day, a national holiday on April 25, also remind younger Australians that their country's rite of passage had a terrible price.

Architecture. For a continent that had not a single permanent structure prior to 1788, Australia can boast an impressive range of public architecture. In the years following British settlement, the contemporary Georgian style brought an incongruous European classicism to the remote penal colony. Hobart and Richmond in Tasmania are probably the best-preserved Georgian towns in the country, while the convict-architect

Francis Greenway's Hyde Park Barracks and St James' Church in Sydney are notable examples. With vast amounts of gold-rush money available in the second half of the 19th century, opulent Victorian churches, mansions and town halls appeared in most of the state capitals: Melbourne is one of the finest Victorian-era cities anywhere in the world. The beginning of the 20th century saw the more restrained, low-level Federation style come into fashion, but in the postwar boom some amazing structures appeared on city skylines, making Australia one of the most exciting architectural hotspots in the world. There can be no more distinctive modern building than Sydney Opera House, which became an immediate symbol of the modern Australian nation, while the audacious New Parliament House in Canberra demonstrates a triumphant return to the grand gesture in political architecture, not seen for almost a century.

Beach Life. It has been suggested that the beach is Australia's true democracy. Certainly, this is a country where private property stops at the promenade steps. Given that the vast majority of Australians live next door to the sea, it is no surprise that the beach should assume such a major role in the Australian identity. It is the place where everyone—wealthy or working class, old-school or immigrant—has the right to swim, strut, lounge or surf the day away. And who, shivering in northern climes, has not dreamt of a Christmas Day spent by the Pacific Ocean, as dinner sizzles on the barbie and the sun beats down on surfers riding the waves? The American Dream may include becoming the boss and having a large house. But the Australian equivalent is far more accessible—"why toil to get rich to do exactly the same thing that you are doing now, not rich?", a beach-loving Sydneysider asked back in the 1920s. She had a point.

Patrick White (1912–90). Australia's only winner of the Nobel Prize for Literature was born in England, when his parents, owners of a New South Wales sheep station, were on a two-year visit. He was sent to an expensive English school, where he felt excluded because of his Australianness: "I hardly dared open my mouth for fear of the toads which might tumble out", he later wrote. It was only in the 1950s that he settled permanently in Australia. But his novels ooze with the power and passion of the sun-baked continent, and convey the vastness and mystery of the Outback and its psychological effects upon the Europeans who try to master it. Among his classic novels are *Voss*, based on the real story of Ludwig Leichhardt's doomed exploration of the outback in 1848, *A Fringe of Leaves* and *The Twyborn Affair*.

Shopping

Australia offers the visitor a range of distinctive goods to take home. Items which play with stereotypical images of Australia —known collectively as "Australiana" and including Digger hats with one brim up, fluffy koalas and T-shirts emblazoned with Aussie flags—contrast with the sublime complexities of Aboriginal art, and stylish jewellery made from the nation's vast reserves of precious and semi-precious stones.

Where to Shop

The major cities offer shopping as fashionable and sophisticated as the best in London or New York. A good mix of department stores, smart boutiques and other specialized shops makes them enticing places for the dedicated shopper. Most Australians head for the pedestrianized shopping malls, found in almost all towns and cities, where you will probably be able to get everything you need. In more out-of-the-way towns, such as Alice Springs and Hobart, old-fashioned high-street shops are good places to buy local products and artefacts.

Aboriginal Art

In most of the large Australian cities, as well as towns such as Alice Springs where there is a substantial Aboriginal population, you will be able to buy classic dot-and-circle paintings depicting animals and locations from the Dreamtime. The technique has been handed down to specially initiated artists for thousands of years. Traditionally, tree bark was used, but modern artists also paint on canvas. Aboriginal artefacts, such as boomerangs, dijeridus and wooden sculptures of animals and birds, make excellent gifts and mementoes and are often decorated in the same style.

Clothing

In a country where sheep vastly outnumber people, there is no shortage of good sheepskin coats and boots, woollen sweaters and scarves. If you are looking for a more unusual material, you might consider kangaroo skin. Unsurprisingly, Australia is also the place for fashionable swimwear and casual resort clothes. For a classic Australian souvenir, take home the stylish, wide-brimmed hat worn by Australia's stockmen.

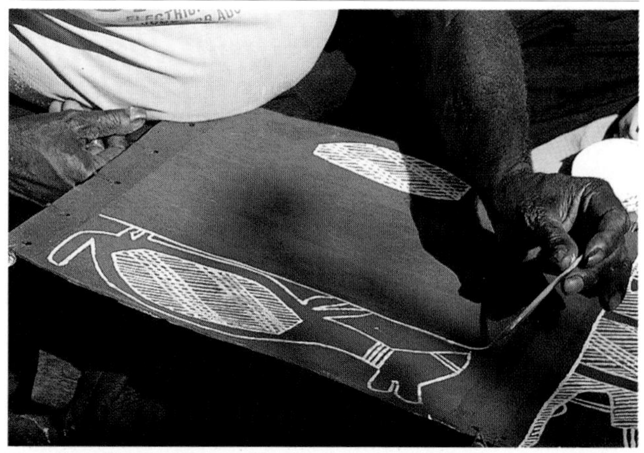

Cross-hatching is a feature of bark paintings in Arnhem Land, mainly done in natural, earthy pigments.

Food and Drink

Succulent macadamia nuts are indigenous to Queensland and come coated in everything from chilli to chocolate, while high-quality honey from the blossoms of the Tasmanian leatherwood tree is made nowhere else in the world. Both red and white Australian wines are excellent. Famous vineyards to look out for include those of the Swan Valley in Western Australia, the Barossa Valley in South Australia, and the Hunter Valley in New South Wales. For something stronger, Queensland, with all those sugar molasses to dispose of, is the place for rum.

Jewellery

Diamonds from the Kimberley region in Western Australia supply the jewellery stores of Perth, Sydney and Melbourne. Look out especially for rings and brooches set with the famous pink diamonds.

Australia's best-known gem is the opal. These beautiful, iridescent stones are sold both unset and in the form of elaborate jewellery. The best are expensive; top-quality opals are solid, translucent stones. Lower-priced opals are made by stacking layers of inferior opal under part of a good one: the resulting stones are called doublets or triplets.

Sports

If any one thing unites Australians, it is their love of sport, both as spectators and as participants. The country almost stops when a big event is staged, such as the Melbourne Cup, the Ashes or the Aussie Rules Final, and the nation's sporting mania has been further increased by the excitement surrounding the Sydney 2000 Olympics.

In the Sea

To Australians the beach is like a second home. The water is wonderful for swimming, although in certain areas around the northern tropical coast in summer you should take notice of warnings about box jellyfish. You will find facilities around the coastline for windsurfing, parasailing, water skiing, scuba diving and most famously, surfing.

There are many opportunities for big-game fishing, with the huge, half-ton black marlin providing as thrilling a challenge as you will get anywhere. (Good freshwater fishing can be had in the lakes and rivers of New South Wales, Victoria and Tasmania.)

By the Beach

You can find just as much to do at the beach without getting wet. Cycle hire is easy, and there are several excellent beachfront cycle tracks. Or else just follow the joggers, rollerbladers and walkers.

Bushwalking

The national parks have trails, although you will still need a map, as well as essentials such as a hat, food and water. Famous places for bushwalking include the Flinders Range in South Australia, the spectacular 80-km (50-mile) Cradle Mountain to Lake Clair trail in Tasmania, and Victoria's rugged Grampians.

Horse Riding

Horses can be hired in many national parks and tourist spots around Australia, and there is no better way of exploring the terrain than on horseback.

Skiing

Australia's ski resorts are surprisingly well developed—the snowfields at Mount Kosciusko alone are bigger than all those in Switzerland put together—and there are fine pistes in the Snowy Mountains in New South Wales and the Victorian Alps.

Take to a canoe to explore the intricacies of Katherine Gorge.

Spectator Sports

Always played with verve and a buccaneering spirit, cricket is the sport at which the Australians most enjoy beating the Poms. The international test series between Australia and England has been called The Ashes since an Australian touring side beat the English in 1882. *The Sporting Times* newspaper in London published an obituary for the great English game and carried out a mock cremation, reducing a set of bails to ashes. Since then, great Australian cricketers, from Donald Bradman in the 1930s to Shane Warne in the 1990s, have mercilessly tormented their old rivals. Test matches can be seen in all of the state capitals. A day spent on "The Hill" at Sydney Cricket Ground, sipping a cold beer and watching the green-capped national team in full flow, is a quintessential Australian experience.

Other favourite national sports are Australian Rules football—a fast and furious 18-a-side game which is similar to Gaelic football and can get pretty wild on the pitch—rugby, swimming, tennis and hockey. Horse racing appeals to the national love of gambling. Top racing driving comes with the Australian Formula One Grand Prix held in Melbourne every March.

Dining Out

With the country's vast open spaces, variety of climates, endless sunshine and wide range of waters to fish in, the Australians have an abundance of fresh produce available at all times. In the past, Australian culinary skill was thought to extend no further than slapping a steak on the barbie and providing plenty of cold beer to wash it down. Modern Australian restaurants give the lie to this stereotype, although there is really no such thing as an Australian national cuisine. As a result of postwar immigration you will find good Chinese, Italian, Greek, Malay and Vietnamese food in any sizeable town or city.

Breakfast

Like the country itself, Australian breakfasts are traditionally outsize, and involve large quantities of eggs, bacon, toast, juice and tea or coffee. Some places even serve steak for breakfast.

Meat

Australia is certainly a good place for the carnivore. The gargantuan cattle and sheep stations across the outback put top-quality beef and lamb on the nation's dinner plates. Lamb chops and stews, roast rib of beef and *filet mignon* can all be outstanding. You may have to insist on steak being grilled "blue" if you like it rare, however, as there is a tendency to overcook. Duck, chicken and other poultry appear on menus around the country. But why stop there? Australia's remarkable fauna offers the chance to sample some unusual cuts of meat. So look out for succulent kangaroo kebabs, buffalo steaks, crocodile vol-au-vents, camel curry and medallion of emu.

Fish and Seafood

Australian food is perhaps at its most enticing when it comes to seafood, and it pays to experiment with what is a truly exotic range. Mainstream fish meals will feature whiting, John Dory, red snapper and the ever popular barramundi, found in both fresh and salt water. A "barra" grows up to 15 kg (33 lb) in weight and is a firm, meaty fish.

Queensland has a great selection of reef fish, the most prized being coral trout (try it served around a grilled banana), red emperor (one of the best reef fish and delicious stuffed with macadamia nuts), bream, mangrove jack and sweetlips.

The Queensland coast also offers some interesting shellfish. The Moreton Bay bug, a cross between a mini-lobster and a giant prawn, is a lot tastier than it sounds; the Queensland mud crab weighs in at several pounds. In Adelaide, you can sample the local delicacy, a small freshwater lobster caught in the Murray River and known as a "yabby".

Ethnic Food

The Chinese first arrived in Australia at the time of the 19th-century gold rushes, and the long-established Chinatowns in Sydney and Melbourne guarantee good *dim sum*. More recent immigrants from southeast Asia, such as the Vietnamese and Malays, have brought their distinctive cooking to the big cities, as well as to the Northern Territory capital, Darwin, the first port of call for many of them.

Australians have almost made Italian cuisine their own, and you will find good pasta and pizza across the country. Melbourne, on the other hand, is the place to go for *souvlaki*—amazingly, it is the third largest Greek city in the world after Athens and Thessaloniki.

Fast Food

Given the long-standing cultural links with England, it is no surprise that Australia has some excellent fish-and-chip shops. In areas such as South Australia, pie floaters—substantial meat pies, marooned bottom-up in a sea of mushy green peas—are served from roadside pie carts. Pub food is usually good value for money.

Bush Tucker

If you get the chance, be sure to try the original Australian cuisine. Genuine bush tucker kept the Aboriginal people healthily fed for 40,000 years. It would be wise to take advice from an experienced guide before you tuck in, but it is a unique culinary experience to sample juicy, protein-rich witchetty grubs, roast wallaby, stewed lizard, leaves, seeds and grasses, followed by berries, fruit and, for those with a sweet tooth, succulent golden honey ants.

Desserts

Australians are responsible for the invention of the pavlova, created for the Russian ballerina when she visited their shores. It consists of an airy meringue base topped with cream and exotic fruit, generally kiwi.

A country which is partly tropical and partly temperate, Australia has fantastic fruit all the year round. Mangoes and watermelons, paw paws and pineapples compete with the more southerly pleasures of strawberries, raspberries and Tasmanian apples.

Soft Drinks

Colas, fruit drinks and mineral water are readily available. Tea is still the most popular late-afternoon drink, and in places like the Adelaide Hills it is served genteelly with traditional English scones and clotted cream as well. Coffee tends to be weak, although the profusion of Italian cafes mean that a cappuccino or pick-me-up espresso is always a possibility.

Beer

Australians are renowned for their fondness for beer, which is usually lager and always served ice cold. Some of the top breweries, such as Foster's, Castlemaine and Swan have been successful in spreading their name around the world. But there are many other local brews of note, including VB (the darker Victoria Bitter), and Cascade, a Tasmanian beer. If you would prefer a pint of Guinness, you will find it on draught in the many Irish pubs in the larger cities and towns.

Wine

Australian wines have moved into the big league in recent times. The quality is reliably good, and the product sunny, fruity and very enjoyable year after year.

As with any wine-producing country, different regions are better for different grapes. Chardonnays from the Hunter Valley, in New South Wales, were among the first to make the Europeans take notice of Australian wine. The Yarra Valley in Victoria is strong on Chardonnay and Pinot Noir. In South Australia, the most important region in terms of the sheer quantity produced, Coonawarra is known for its Cabernet Sauvignon and Clare Valley for Riesling, while the famous Barossa Valley turns out fine Shiraz. The delightful Swan Valley in Western Australia and the Margaret River vineyards in the southwest of the state produce excellent Semillon and Sauvignon wines.

Spirits

A side-product of the wine industry is the manufacture of port and brandy. But the spirit which was consumed most widely in the early years of Australia, and even used as a currency, was rum. Made from the molasses left over from sugar refining, it is little wonder that the bulk of it comes today from Queensland. The connoisseurs favour Bundaberg rum, and you can do a tour of the distillery to see it being made.

The Hard Facts

To plan your trip, here are some of the practical details you should know about Australia:

Airports

The main international gateways to the continent are Sydney, Melbourne, Brisbane, Cairns, Darwin and Perth. Surprisingly, there are no direct international flights to the capital, Canberra. Smaller international airports exist at Hobart, Adelaide and Townsville.

Taxis are available at all airports, and many large hotels are served by special Airporter bus services.

Climate

Australia lies wholly in the southern hemisphere, so summer is from December to February and winter from June to August. High season is around Christmas, when schools have their summer break. Despite its vast size, Australia has a relatively uniform climate, and variations are mainly dependent on whether you are north or south, in the desert or by the coast. In spring and summer, most of the country is warm or hot, the north being more tropical, and the south having milder nights. Autumn and winter leave northern and central Australia with clear, warm days and cool nights, while the south experiences cool days with occasional rain. Snow is only common in mountainous regions.

Communications

Post offices are open 9 a.m.–5 p.m., Monday to Friday. The Sydney and Melbourne general post offices also open on Saturday mornings. Stamps can be bought at Australian Post agencies, often located in general stores, newsagents and hotels.

International direct-dialling and reverse-charge phone calls can be made from practically all public phone boxes. Following deregulation, there are now two telephone companies, Telstra (formerly Telecom Australia) and Optus. If you are making regular calls overseas, it might be worth finding out which has the better prices at the time. To telephone abroad from Australia, dial 0011 + country code (UK 44, USA and Canada 1) + area code (minus the initial 0) + number.

Phone cards are available from newsagents, chemists and supermarkets for $5, $10, $20 and $50. Credit-card phones are to be found in most airports and city centres and in many hotels. Larger hotels also offer fax services. In the major cities you will find plenty of internet service providers.

Customs

Visitors over 18 may import the following goods duty free: 250 cigarettes or 250 g of tobacco or cigars, 1 litre of any alcoholic liquor, and dutiable goods intended as gifts up to the value of $400 ($200 for visitors under 18). There are very strict regulations against potential sources of disease and pestilence, which apply to many foodstuffs. All plants and animal products will be confiscated at customs. If you are unsure about any goods you are carrying, be sure to notify a customs officer.

Disabled Travellers

The needs of disabled travellers are increasingly provided for, but the best way to ensure a hassle-free time at hotels, restaurants, cinemas, etc. is to call in advance and let them know what your requirements are. For more information once you are in Australia, contact NICAN, PO Box 407, Curtin, ACT, 2605. Tel. (06) 285 3713; fax (06) 285 3714; e-mail nican@spirit.com.au.

Driving

Australia is a huge country, with vast distances separating cities and little public transport. The car is therefore accepted as the main way to get around. Roads outside the cities are uncrowded, although there are very few multi-lane highways. Often highways are simply two-way roads, and the only other vehicle you will come across may be the occasional road-train, an enormous 50-m-long lorry. Always make sure you have plenty of room ahead before attempting to overtake one of these juggernauts. Speed limits are 60 kmh (37 mph) in cities and towns and 100 kmh (62 mph) on motorways and highways unless otherwise indicated, and are strictly enforced. Australians, like the British, drive on the left.

Brisk competition among car rental companies often leads to good deals like unlimited mileage or weekend discounts. Please note that you have to be over 21 to hire a car from most companies, and some impose a minimum age limit of 25, especially on four-wheel-drive vehicles. If you intend to drive in the outback, make sure your insurance covers you for all eventualities, including hitting kangaroos (a very common hazard). Many remote, and often not so remote, roads are still unsealed, and only recommended for four-wheel-drive vehicles. You will find that several tour operators offer trips into the outback, and it may be a more comfortable and safer experience to travel in the wilderness with drivers who know the terrain, rather than attempt to drive yourself.

Even if you are only motoring between cities, distances are so great that it is wise to take some precautions before setting off. Always ensure that you have enough petrol to get you to your next service station (it may be 300 km away). Carry important spare parts in case they are not available in smaller towns. Take plenty of water, and if going somewhere really remote, check whether you need to report to the police before you start out (so they can send a search party if you fail to check in at the other end).

Electric Current

Electrical supply is 240/250-volt, 50-cycle AC. Sockets are for plugs with three flat pins, and an adapter will probably be necessary for electrical equipment brought from overseas. Many hotels have outlets for small 110-volt appliances such as razors.

Emergencies

In case of a serious emergency, dial 000, free from any phone. The operator will put you through to police, ambulance or fire brigade.

Essentials

You can get most things in Australia which are available at home, so if on the flight over you suddenly remember that you forgot to pack something important, don't panic. What you should take is largely governed by the Australian climate. Essential clothing includes lightweight cottons year round in the central/ northern states, with a sweater or light jacket for cooler winter evenings and early mornings. Warmer clothes are necessary for winter months in the south. The style of clothes, even in the cities, tends to be casual. Australians would undoubtedly say that the most essential item of all is a bathing costume.

Sunglasses, sunhats and sunblock lotion are recommended year round in the north and during the summer months in the south.

Formalities

Everyone wishing to enter Australia requires a visa (except Australian and New Zealand passport holders). They are issued at Australian embassies and consulates and can usually be obtained on the same day. There is no fee for tourist visas of less than three months. Citizens of the UK, Germany, USA, Holland and many other Western European countries can benefit from the Electronic Travel Authority system (ETA); it can usually be obtained from travel agents when arranging flights, and is valid for multiple entry.

Health

No vaccinations are required for entry unless you have visited a yellow fever area in the six days preceding your arrival.

There is a reciprocal healthcare agreement with the UK, New Zealand, the Netherlands, Italy, Sweden, Finland and Malta. This is only for emergency treatment, though, and it is wise to take out personal insurance to cover other eventualities (such as ambulance services, for example).

The greatest health hazard will probably be too much exposure to the powerful Australian sun. Visitors from cooler climates need to take great care to protect themselves, and can be burnt to a crisp even on overcast days. Always follow the Australian government's euphonious "slip, slop, slap" policy: slip on a shirt, slop on the sunblock and slap on a hat.

Other health problems may come from Australia's exotic wildlife. When swimming, always check that the beaches are clear of jellyfish—the sting from some can be fatal. These are a particular danger in tropical regions during the summer period—just when you will be in the mood for a carefree plunge in the ocean. You should also take heed of shark warnings and, of course, beware of crocodiles. Poisonous spiders may be lurking in the most innocent of places, so be careful where you put your hands and feet. The often overwhelming numbers of black flies in Central Australia are a nuisance, but they do not bite. More serious are the mosquitoes near waterways—never go without insect repellent.

If you go diving, follow your instructor's advice about the underwater fauna: coral is beautiful but can also burn on touch or cause nasty cuts.

Holidays and Festivals

Australia's national public holidays are:

January 1	New Year's Day
January 26	Australia Day (held on nearest Monday)
March/April (movable)	Good Friday and Easter Monday
April 25	Anzac Day
June (except W.A.)	Queen's Birthday (held on second Monday)
October (in W.A.)	Queen's Birthday (held on first Monday)

December 25 Christmas Day
December 26 Boxing Day
(except S.A.)

Each state also has separate public holidays (such as the Northern Territory's Picnic Day on the first Monday in August), as well as ones which apply only to certain regions within the state (Melbourne's Cup Day on the first Tuesday in November, for example).

Language

English is the official language of Australia. There are also about 30 different Aboriginal languages spoken around the country.

Australian English, or "Strine", is a rich vernacular made up from old convict slang, Aboriginal loan words, and a peculiarly antipodean delight in shortening words and adding a vowel (so that afternoon becomes "arvo" and barbecue is "barbie"). It can be a little difficult at first for an English-speaking visitor, but before long you will be talking dinkum Strine with the best of them. A few examples are given on the front inside cover of this guide.

Media

There is only one national daily paper in Australia, the *Australian,* owned by Rupert Murdoch. Most newspapers tend to be associated with particular cities, two of the most notable being the *Sydney Morning Herald* and the Melbourne *Age*. There are several local papers, which are useful for checking out events. In the major cities, some newspapers and monthly magazines from the UK, France and the US are available.

Radio and television are often regional as well. Sydney and Melbourne have three commercial TV stations, while Alice Springs can boast Imparja, an Aboriginal TV channel. There are two government-funded broadcasters, which are advertisement-free and go out nationwide: the Special Broadcasting Service (SBS), with subtitled multicultural programmes, and the Australian Broadcasting Corporation (ABC), which has both TV and radio channels, including a popular, youth-oriented radio station called Triple J.

Money

The unit of currency is the Australian dollar (abbreviated either to $ or $A), which is divided into 100 cents (c). Coins are issued in denominations of 5c, 10c, 20c, 50c, $1 and $2; banknotes have values of $5, $10, $20, $50 and $100.

International credit cards are widely accepted at hotels, restaurants and shops in the big cities and popular tourist areas. If you are carrying traveller's cheques, buy them in Australian dollars to avoid commissions and fluctuating exchange rates. Alternatively, if you have an international cashpoint card you will be able to take out local currency from ATMs which have the Cirrus-Maestro sign. Check with your bank before leaving.

Opening Hours

The following times are a general guide, and some of them may be subject to local variations.

Banks open Monday to Thursday 9.30 a.m. to 4.30 p.m. and until 5 p.m. on Fridays. Exchange facilities at some major banks in the big cities may open earlier and close later.

City *shops* open Monday to Saturday 9 a.m. to 5 p.m. Each state has its own late-night shopping once a week, when stores stay open until 9 p.m.

Museums are usually open every day from 10 a.m. to 5 p.m., although they often open at midday on Sunday.

Bars are usually open from 11 a.m. to 11 p.m., although in metropolitan areas they often close later.

Photography

All the well-known brands of photographic and video film are readily available. Camera shops are abundant and offer the usual range of services, including one-hour developing. Film processing is much the same price and quality as in other Western countries.

When taking photographs, bear in mind that Australia's light is intense and exposure needs to be adjusted accordingly. Be sure to store film in a cool place and, especially in the outback, beware of dust and sand getting into the lens.

Many Aboriginal people do not like having their photograph taken, so please ask for their permission first and respect their wishes.

Religion

With Australia's population largely descended from British colonists, the predominant religion is Protestant. There are two main churches, the Uniting Church (an amalgam of smaller Protestant churches) and the Church of England. The Catholic Church also has a large presence, due mainly to the great number of Irish immigrants and, more recently, those from the Mediterranean. All the major non-Christian religions are to be found, especially in Australia's big cities. It is always worth remembering that some of the country's greatest natural features, such as Uluru (Ayers Rock), have profound spiritual significance for the Aboriginal peoples.

Security
Compared to North America and Western Europe, Australia is a fairly safe part of the world, and its big cities are refreshingly relaxed places to stroll around. Nevertheless, the usual precautions should be taken. Leave your passport and valuables in the hotel safe where possible, keep car doors locked, beware of pickpockets in crowded places, and always keep your money well concealed.

Time zones
Australia is divided into three time zones. Western Standard Time (in Perth, for example) is GMT+8. Central Standard Time (in Darwin, Alice Springs, Adelaide) is GMT+9½. Eastern Standard Time (Sydney, Melbourne, Tasmania) is GMT+10. Confusion sets in during the summer, when some states, mainly in eastern Australia, put their clocks forward by one hour between October and March. This does not happen in Western Australia, Queensland or the Northern Territory. The Tasmanians, however, keep up their island independence and alter their clocks a month earlier than the mainlanders.

Tipping
Being innately democratic and eternally suspicious of patronage, the Australians do not have a tipping culture. This even extends to taxi drivers. Restaurants rarely include a service charge (although some might at weekends). In upmarket hotels and restaurants, however, waiters and porters might expect tips. As always, the choice is yours.

Toilets
The civilized Australian authorities know that one of the most important requirements for the visitor is an abundance of clean, accessible public toilets. You will find them in airports, railway and bus stations, department stores and shopping arcades.

Tourist Offices
Each state has its own tourist office, based in state capitals and important tourist centres. They provide brochures and excellent maps. Check addresses and telephone numbers in local directories or on website www.aussie.net.au. The Australian Tourist Commission is an external government agency, which can assist with tourists' enquiries before they leave for Australia. Within the UK call (0891) 070 707; fax (0171) 940 5221. For the US call (805) 775 2000; fax (805) 775 4448.

Transport
Air. The distances between regions in Australia are vast, so un-

less you have plenty of time you will need to take an internal flight to reach some of the more remote sights. Luckily, the two main airline companies, Qantas and Ansett Australia, provide an extensive domestic network. Fares are high, but there are frequent special offers and discounts available, especially out of season, so be sure to check with the airline or travel agent. If you know your exact itinerary before you leave, buying an airpass might be the most economical option. It is always wise to make advance reservations during the busy school holiday periods, as the whole of the country seems to be on the move at these times.

Intercity Buses. Express coaches operate between all the major cities, and are good value when compared to airline prices. Although considerably slower, they are a much better way to see the countryside and get a real sense of the epic dimensions of the land. The dominant national companies, Greyhound Pioneer and McCafferty's, have a variety of special discount passes on offer. Their buses are comfortable, with air-conditioning, on-board toilets and strict no-smoking regulations.

Local Transport. Bus services in the cities are normally efficient but often stop running fairly early at night, after which time you will need to hail a taxi. Taxi ranks can usually be found at big hotels, shopping centres and railway stations. Sydney and Melbourne have small subway train services, while most big cities have an extensive commuter train network serving the suburbs. The Melbourne tram system is justly famous, and is an effective as well as picturesque way of getting around the city. In Sydney, where many suburbs cluster around the huge harbour, ferries are an integral part of city life.

Trains. The train might be the slowest way to get around, but it is certainly the most fun. Some of the world's great rail journeys are to be had in Australia. Modern air-conditioned trains, complete with sleeping compartments, showers, restaurant cars and lounges, take you across desert and rainforest in considerable style. The most popular journeys may need to be booked anything up to a year in advance. This particularly applies to the mighty Indian-Pacific train, operating between Sydney and Perth and taking 65 hours to traverse the continent; the Ghan, the legendary route between Alice Springs and Adelaide; and the Queenslander, the tropical train from Brisbane to Cairns.

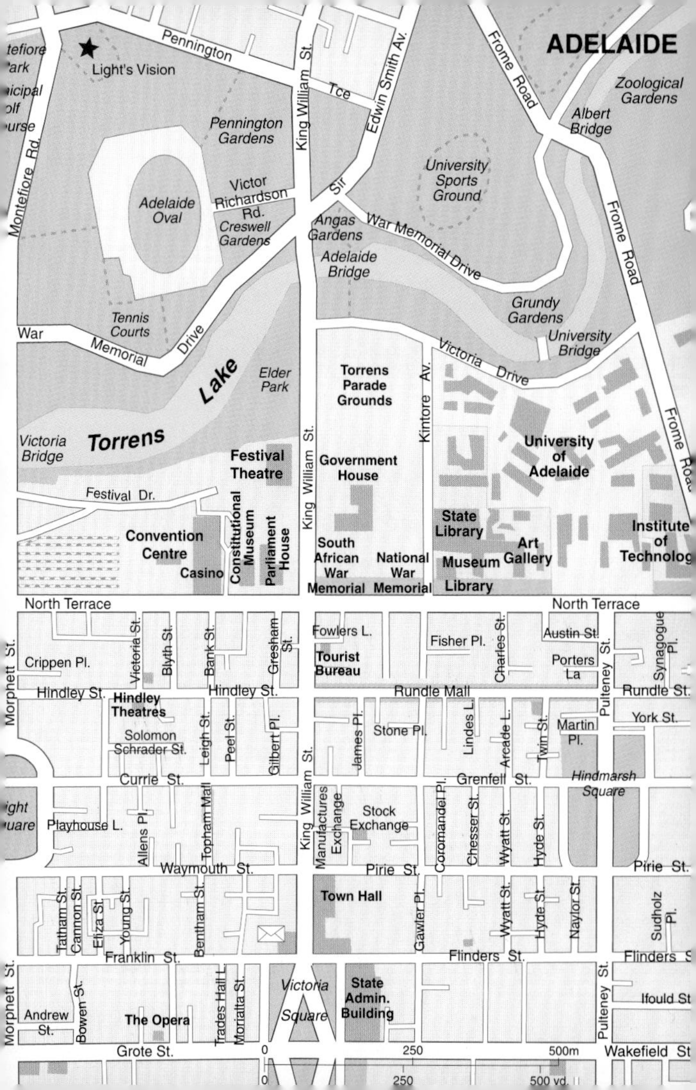

ADELAIDE
Light's Vision
Pennington
Pennington Gardens
King William St.
Tce
Edwin Smith Av.
Sir
Frome Road
Zoological Gardens
Albert Bridge
Montefiore Rd.
Adelaide Oval
Victor Richardson Rd.
Creswell Gardens
University Sports Ground
Angas Gardens
War Memorial Drive
Adelaide Bridge
Grundy Gardens
University Bridge
Tennis Courts
War Memorial Drive
Lake Torrens
Elder Park
Torrens Parade Grounds
Kintore Av.
Victoria Drive
Victoria Bridge
Festival Theatre
Government House
University of Adelaide
Festival Dr.
Convention Centre
Casino
Constitutional Museum
Parliament House
South African War Memorial
National War Memorial
State Library
Museum
Library
Art Gallery
North Terrace
Morphett St.
Crippen Pl.
Victoria St.
Blyth St.
Bank St.
Gresham St.
Fowlers L.
Tourist Bureau
Fisher Pl.
Charles St.
Austin St.
Porters La
Pulteney St.
Synagogue Pl.
Hindley St.
Hindley Theatres
Rundle Mall
Rundle St.
York St.
Solomon
Schrader St.
Leigh St.
Peel St.
Gilbert Pl.
James Pl.
Stone Pl.
Lindes L.
Arcade L.
Twin St.
Martin Pl.
Currie St.
Grenfell St.
Hindmarsh Square
Playhouse L.
Allens Pl.
Topham Mall
Manufactures Exchange
Stock Exchange
Coromandel Pl.
Chesser St.
Wyatt St.
Hyde St.
Waymouth St.
Pirie St.
Town Hall
Tatham St.
Cannon St.
Eliza St.
Young St.
Bentham St.
Gawler Pl.
Naylor St.
Sudholz Pl.
Franklin St.
Flinders St.
Andrew St.
Bowen St.
The Opera
Trades Hall L.
Moriatta St.
Victoria Square
State Admin. Building
Ifould St
Grote St.
Wakefield St
0
250
500m
500 yd.

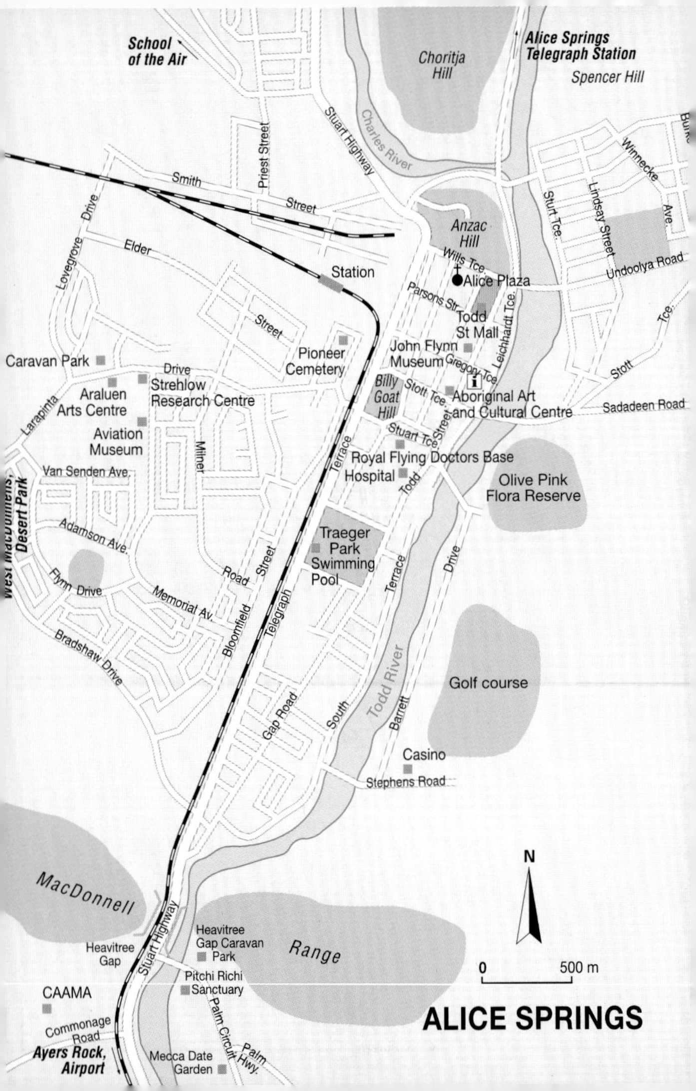

School of the Air
Alice Springs Telegraph Station
Choritja Hill
Spencer Hill
Stuart Highway
Charles River
Priest Street
Smith Street
Winnecke Ave.
Sturt Tce.
Lindsay Street
Anzac Hill
Wills Tce.
Alice Plaza
Undoolya Road
Lovegrove Drive
Elder Street
Station
Parsons Str.
Todd St Mall
Leichhardt Tce.
Tce.
John Flynn Museum
Gregory Tce.
Stott Tce.
Stott
Caravan Park
Pioneer Cemetery
Drive
Araluen Arts Centre
Strehlow Research Centre
Billy Goat Hill
Aboriginal Art and Cultural Centre
Sadadeen Road
Larapinta
Aviation Museum
Stuart Tce.
Milner
Terrace
Royal Flying Doctors Base
Hospital
Todd Street
Olive Pink Flora Reserve
Van Senden Ave.
West MacDonnells Desert Park
Adamson Ave.
Traeger Park Swimming Pool
Road
Street
Terrace
Drive
Flynn Drive
Memorial Av.
Bloomfield
Telegraph
Bradshaw Drive
Todd River
Golf course
Gap Road
South
Barrett
Casino
Stephens Road
N
MacDonnell
Range
Stuart Highway
Heavitree Gap Caravan Park
Heavitree Gap
0
500 m
Pitchi Richi Sanctuary
CAAMA
ALICE SPRINGS
Commonage Road
Palm Circuit
Palm Hwy.
Ayers Rock, Airport
Mecca Date Garden

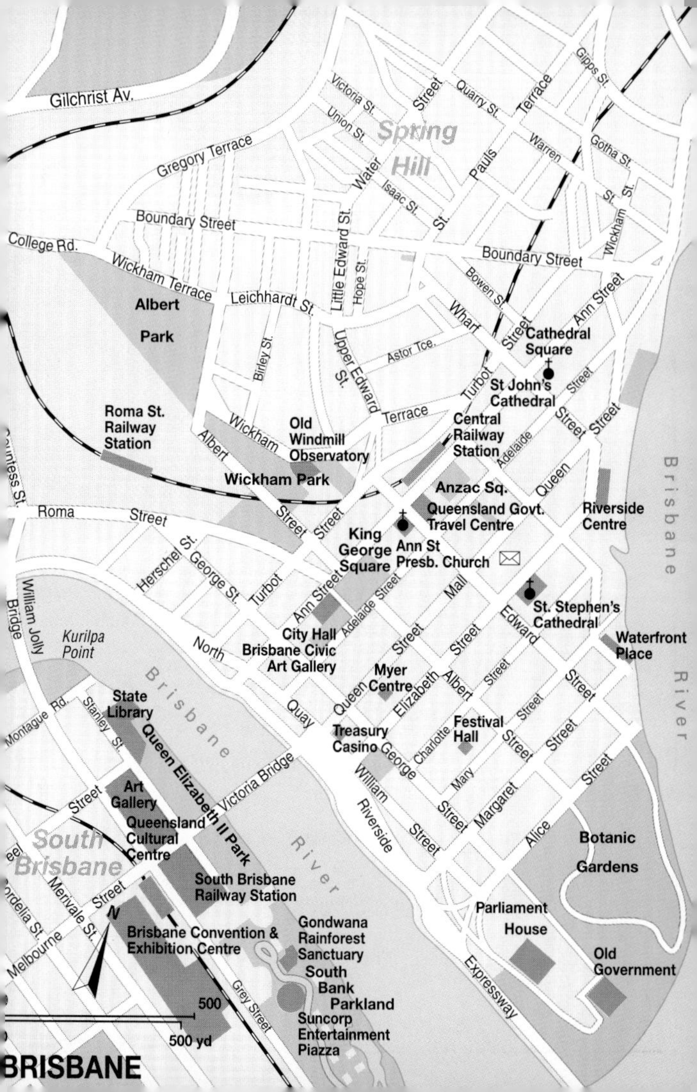
Gilchrist Av.
Gregory Terrace
Victoria St.
Union St.
Street
Quarry St.
Terrace
Gipps St.
Spring Hill
Warren
Gotha St.
Water
Isaac St.
Pauls
St.
St.
Wickham
Boundary Street
College Rd.
Little Edward St.
Hope St.
Boundary Street
Wickham Terrace
Leichhardt St.
Bowen St.
Ann Street
Albert Park
Wharf
Street
Cathedral Square
Birley St.
Upper Edward St.
Astor Tce.
Turbot
St John's Cathedral
Street
Roma St. Railway Station
Wickham
Old Windmill Observatory
Terrace
Central Railway Station
Adelaide
Street
Street
Albert
Wickham Park
Anzac Sq.
Queen
Roma
Street
Street
Street
Queensland Govt. Travel Centre
Riverside Centre
King George Square
Ann St Presb. Church
Herschel St.
George St.
Turbot
Ann Street
Adelaide Street
Mall
St. Stephen's Cathedral
William Jolly Bridge
Kurilpa Point
North
City Hall
Brisbane Civic Art Gallery
Street
Street
Edward
Waterfront Place
Brisbane
Myer Centre
Queen
Elizabeth
Albert
Street
Street
River
State Library
Stanley St.
Montague Rd.
Quay
Treasury Casino
George
Charlotte
Festival Hall
Street
Street
Queen Elizabeth II Park
Victoria Bridge
William
Mary
Street
Art Gallery
Street
Queensland Cultural Centre
South Brisbane
River
Riverside
Street
Margaret
Street
Alice
Botanic Gardens
South Brisbane Railway Station
Merivale St.
Street
Parliament House
Gondwana Rainforest Sanctuary
Brisbane Convention & Exhibition Centre
Melbourne
South Bank Parkland
Old Government
Expressway
Grey Street
500
500 yd
Suncorp Entertainment Piazza
N
BRISBANE

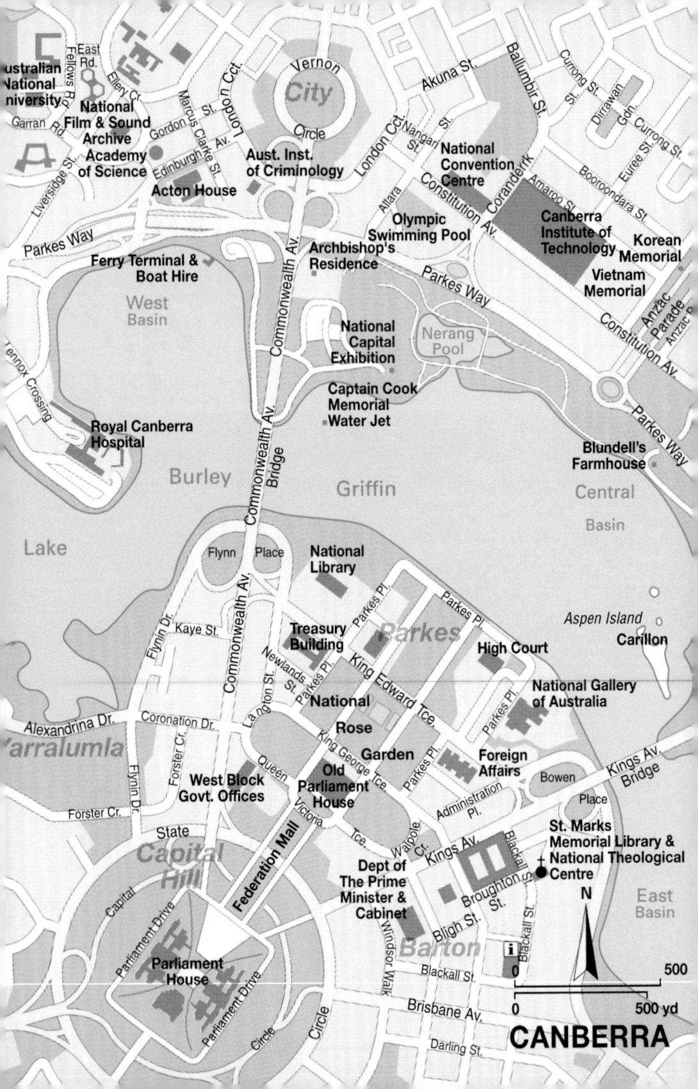
CANBERRA
Australian National University
National Film & Sound Archive
Academy of Science
Acton House
Aust. Inst. of Criminology
City
Vernon Circle
National Convention Centre
Olympic Swimming Pool
Canberra Institute of Technology
Korean Memorial
Vietnam Memorial
Archbishop's Residence
Ferry Terminal & Boat Hire
West Basin
National Capital Exhibition
Nerang Pool
Captain Cook Memorial Water Jet
Royal Canberra Hospital
Blundell's Farmhouse
Burley
Griffin
Lake
Central Basin
National Library
Treasury Building
Parkes
High Court
Aspen Island
Carillon
National Gallery of Australia
National Rose Garden
Foreign Affairs
West Block Govt. Offices
Old Parliament House
Yarralumla
Capital Hill
Federation Mall
Dept of The Prime Minister & Cabinet
St. Marks Memorial Library & National Theological Centre
East Basin
Barton
Parliament House
Parkes Way
Commonwealth Av.
Commonwealth Av. Bridge
Constitution Av.
Anzac Parade
Kings Av.
Kings Av. Bridge
Flynn Place
Bowen Place
Coronation Dr.
Alexandrina Dr.
State Circle
Capital Circle
Parliament Drive
Brisbane Av.
Blackall St.
Darling St.
N
0 500
0 500 yd

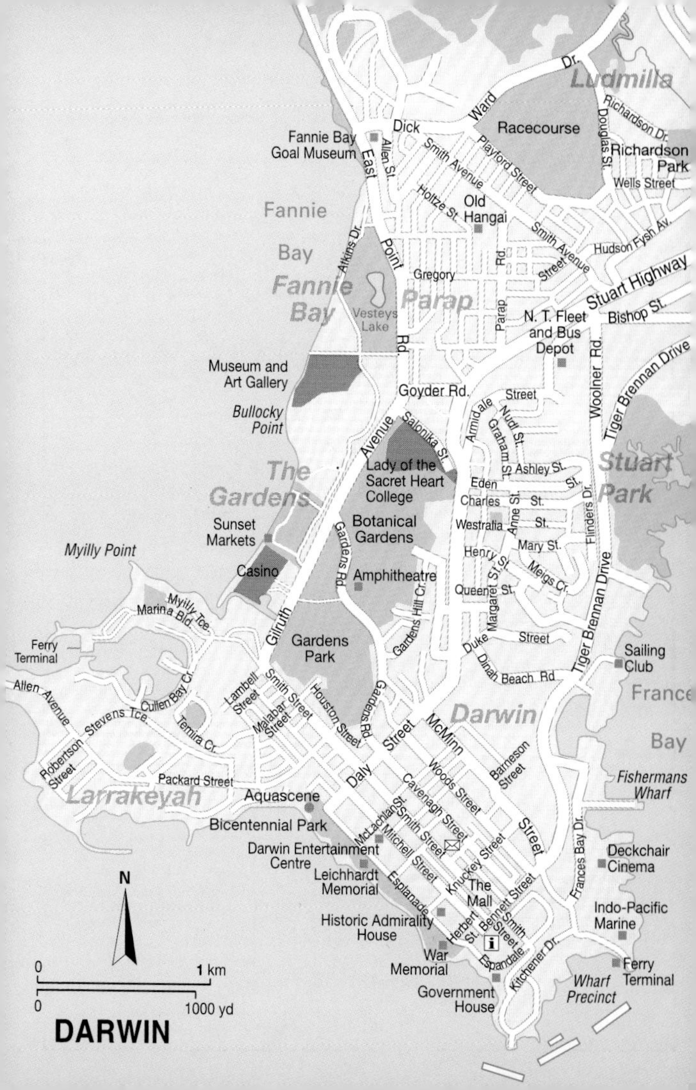
Ludmilla
Racecourse
Richardson Park
Richardson Dr.
Douglas St.
Wells Street
Ward Dr.
Dick
Fannie Bay Goal Museum
East Point Rd.
Allen St.
Smith Avenue
Playford Street
Holtze St.
Old Hangai
Fannie Bay
Atkins Dr.
Hudson Fysh Av.
Street
Gregory
Rd.
Parap
Vesteys Lake
Stuart Highway
Bishop St.
N. T. Fleet and Bus Depot
Woolner Rd.
Tiger Brennan Drive
Museum and Art Gallery
Goyder Rd.
Bullocky Point
Salonika St.
Avenue
Armidale
Street
Nudl St.
Graham St.
The Gardens
Lady of the Sacret Heart College
Ashley St.
Eden St.
Stuart Park
Charles St.
Anne St.
Flinders Dr.
Botanical Gardens
Westralia St.
Sunset Markets
Gardens Rd.
Mary St.
Myilly Point
Henry St.
Meigs Cr.
Casino
Amphitheatre
Queen St.
Margaret St.
Myilly Tce.
Marina Bld.
Gardens Hill Cr.
Gilruth
Gardens Park
Duke Street
Sailing Club
Ferry Terminal
Dinah Beach Rd
Allen Avenue
Cullen Bay Cr.
Lambell Street
Smith Street
Houston Street
Gardens Rd.
Street
McMinn
Darwin
Frances Bay
Stevens Tce.
Temira Cr.
Malabar Street
Barneson Street
Robertson Street
Daly
Woods Street
Fishermans Wharf
Packard Street
Cavenagh Street
Larrakeyah
Aquascene
McLachlan St.
Bicentennial Park
Smith Street
Street
Darwin Entertainment Centre
Mitchell Street
Knuckey Street
Frances Bay Dr.
Deckchair Cinema
Leichhardt Memorial
Esplanade
The Mall
Bennett Street
Historic Admirality House
Herbert St.
Smith Street
Indo-Pacific Marine
War Memorial
Espandale
Kitchener Dr.
Ferry Terminal
Wharf Precinct
Government House
N
0
1 km
0
1000 yd
DARWIN

INDEX

GENERAL EDITOR:
Barbara Ender-Jones
EDITOR:
Steve Williams
LAYOUT:
Luc Malherbe
PHOTO CREDITS:
Rachel Cavassini: front cover, pp. 6, 22, 35, 46, 54;
Hémisphères/Gardel: back cover, pp. 12, 40, 49, 79;
Claude Huber: pp. 2, 16, 25, 45, 62, 72
Martine Gaillard: pp.1, 28, 60;
Hémisphères/Reynard: pp. 5, 77
MAPS:
Elsner & Schichor
Huber Kartographie
JPM Publications

12, avenue William-Fraisse,
1006 Lausanne, Switzerland
E-mail:
information@jpmguides.com
Web site:
http://www.jpmguides.com/

Every care has been taken to verify the information in the guide, but the publisher cannot accept responsibility for any errors that may have occurred. If you spot an inaccuracy or a serious omission, please let us know.

Printed in Switzerland
Gessler/Sion (CTF)

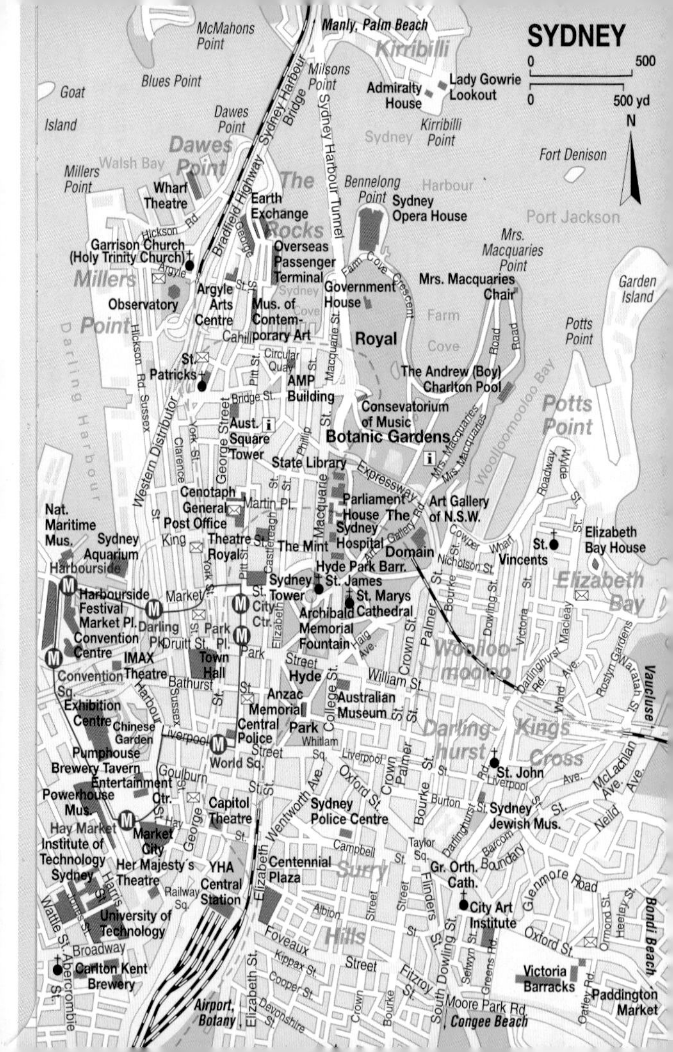
SYDNEY
0 500
0 500 yd
N
Manly, Palm Beach
McMahons Point
Blues Point
Goat Island
Dawes Point
Millers Point
Walsh Bay
Kirribilli
Milsons Point
Sydney Harbour Bridge
Sydney Harbour Tunnel
Admiralty House
Lady Gowrie Lookout
Kirribilli Point
Sydney Harbour
Fort Denison
Port Jackson
Bennelong Point
Sydney Opera House
Wharf Theatre
Earth Exchange
The Rocks
Bradfield Highway
Hickson Rd.
Garrison Church (Holy Trinity Church)
Overseas Passenger Terminal
Sydney Cove
Government House
Mrs. Macquaries Point
Mrs. Macquaries Chair
Garden Island
Potts Point
Observatory
Argyle Arts Centre
Mus. of Contemporary Art
Royal Botanic Gardens
Farm Cove
Cahill Expressway
Circular Quay
AMP Building
St. Patricks
The Andrew (Boy) Charlton Pool
Consevatorium of Music
Woolloomooloo Bay
Darling Harbour
Western Distributor
Aust. Square Tower
State Library
Cenotaph
General Post Office
Martin Pl.
Parliament House
The Sydney Hospital
Art Gallery of N.S.W.
The Domain
Nat. Maritime Mus.
Sydney Aquarium
Harbourside
Theatre Royal
The Mint
Hyde Park Barr.
St. James
Sydney Tower
St. Marys Cathedral
Archibald Memorial Fountain
Harbourside Festival Market Pl.
Darling Pk
City Ctr.
Park Pl.
Convention Centre
IMAX Theatre
Town Hall
Hyde Park
Convention Sq.
Exhibition Centre
Chinese Garden
Anzac Memorial
Australian Museum
Central Police
World Sq.
Pumphouse Brewery Tavern
Entertainment Ctr.
Powerhouse Mus.
Capitol Theatre
Sydney Police Centre
Hay Market
Market City
Institute of Technology Sydney
Her Majesty's Theatre
YHA
Central Station
Centennial Plaza
Surry Hills
University of Technology
Carlton Kent Brewery
Railway Sq.
Broadway
Airport, Botany
Elizabeth Bay House
St. Vincents
Elizabeth Bay
Woolloomooloo
Darlinghurst
Kings Cross
St. John
Sydney Jewish Mus.
Gr. Orth. Cath.
City Art Institute
Taylor Sq.
Victoria Barracks
Paddington Market
Moore Park Rd.
Congee Beach
Bondi Beach
Vauclause
Glenmore Road
Oxford St.
William St.
Liverpool St.
Whitlam Sq.
Goulburn St.
Campbell St.
Albion St.
Foveaux Street
Kippax St.
Cooper St.
Devonshire St.
Elizabeth St.
Abercrombie St.
Wattle St.
Jones St.
Harris St.
George St.
Sussex St.
Kent St.
York St.
Clarence St.
Pitt St.
Castlereagh St.
Phillip St.
Macquarie St.
College St.
Crown St.
Palmer St.
Bourke St.
Dowling St.
Victoria St.
Macleay St.
Darlinghurst Rd.
Ward Ave.
Roslyn Gardens
Waratah St.
McLachlan Ave.
Neild Ave.
Barcom Ave.
Boundary St.
Flinders St.
South Dowling St.
Selwyn St.
Greens Rd.
Oatley Rd.
Ormond St.
Heeley St.
Fitzroy St.
Burton St.
Cowper Wharf Rd.
Nicholson St.
Art Gallery Rd.
Mrs. Macquaries Road
Wylde St.
Roadway
Farm Cove Crescent
Bridge St.
Market St.
Park Street
King St.
Bathurst St.
Druitt St.
Hay St.
Argyle St.
Haig Ave.
Harbour St.
Liverpool

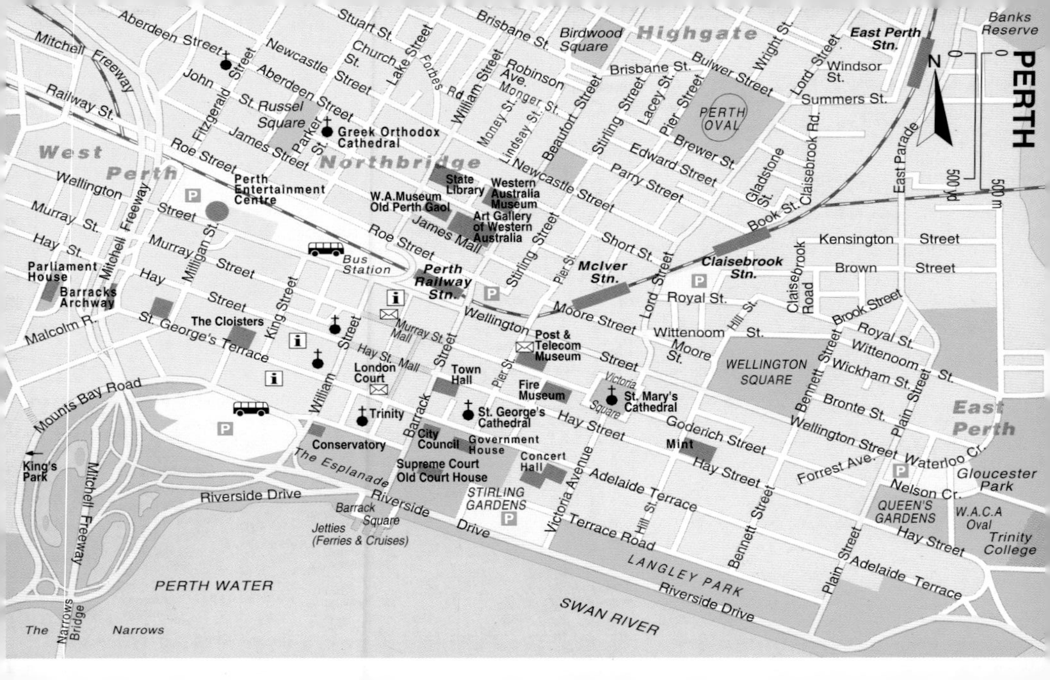
PERTH
0
500 m
0
500 yd
N
Banks Reserve
East Perth Stn.
Highgate
Birdwood Square
Northbridge
West Perth
East Perth
Gloucester Park
W.A.C.A Oval
Trinity College
QUEEN'S GARDENS
WELLINGTON SQUARE
PERTH OVAL
St. Russel Square
STIRLING GARDENS
Victoria Square
LANGLEY PARK
SWAN RIVER
PERTH WATER
The Narrows
Narrows Bridge
King's Park
Claisebrook Stn.
McIver Stn.
Perth Railway Stn.
Bus Station
St. Mary's Cathedral
Mint
Post & Telecom Museum
Fire Museum
St. George's Cathedral
Concert Hall
Government House
Town Hall
City Council
Supreme Court
Old Court House
Trinity
Conservatory
London Court
Western Australia Museum
Art Gallery of Western Australia
State Library
W.A.Museum Old Perth Gaol
Greek Orthodox Cathedral
Perth Entertainment Centre
The Cloisters
Barracks Archway
Parliament House
Jetties (Ferries & Cruises)
Barrack Square
The Esplanade
Riverside Drive
Mitchell Freeway
Mounts Bay Road
East Parade
Claisebrook Rd.
Claisebrook Road
Kensington Street
Brown Street
Brook Street
Royal St.
Wittenoom St.
Wickham St.
Bronte St.
Plain Street
Wellington Street
Waterloo Cr.
Nelson Cr.
Hay Street
Adelaide Terrace
Forrest Ave.
Bennett Street
Goderich Street
Hill St.
Terrace Road
Victoria Avenue
Moore Street
Moore St.
Lord Street
Pier Street
Pier St.
Stirling Street
Beaufort Street
Newcastle Street
Lindsay St.
Money St.
William Street
Forbes Rd
Lake Street
Church St.
Stuart St.
Aberdeen Street
Fitzgerald Street
John Street
James Street
Roe Street
Milligan St.
Murray Street
Murray St.
Hay St.
St. George's Terrace
King Street
Barrack Street
Murray St. Mall
Hay St. Mall
James Mall
Short St.
Parry Street
Edward Street
Brewer St.
Lacey St.
Bulwer Street
Wright St.
Summers St.
Windsor St.
Gladstone St.
Book St.
Brisbane St.
Robinson Ave.
Monger St.
Parker St.
Malcolm R.
Railway St.
Wellington Street